Governance and Limited Statehood

Series Editor
Thomas Risse
Freie Universität Berlin
Berlin, Germany

This ground-breaking monograph series showcases cutting edge research on the transformation of governance in countries with weak state institutions. Combing theoretically informed and empirically grounded scholarship, it challenges the conventional governance discourse which is biased towards modern developed nation states. Instead, the series focuses on governance in Africa, Asia and Latin America including transnational and trans-regional dimensions. Located at the intersection of global governance and international relations, on the one hand, and comparative politics, area studies, international law, history, and development studies, on the other, this innovative series helps to challenge fundamental assumptions about governance in the social sciences.

More information about this series at
http://www.palgrave.com/gp/series/15020

Christine Hackenesch

The EU and China in African Authoritarian Regimes

Domestic Politics and Governance Reforms

Christine Hackenesch
German Development Institute / Deutsches Institut
für Entwicklungspolitik (DIE)
Bonn, Germany

Governance and Limited Statehood
ISBN 978-3-030-09698-4   ISBN 978-3-319-63591-0   (eBook)
https://doi.org/10.1007/978-3-319-63591-0

© The Editor(s) (if applicable) and The Author(s) 2018. This book is an open access publication.
Softcover re-print of the Hardcover 1st edition 2018
Open Access This book is licensed under the terms of the Creative Commons Attribution 4.0 International License (http://creativecommons.org/licenses/by/4.0/), which permits use, sharing, adaptation, distribution and reproduction in any medium or format, as long as you give appropriate credit to the original author(s) and the source, provide a link to the Creative Commons license and indicate if changes were made.
The images or other third party material in this book are included in the book's Creative Commons license, unless indicated otherwise in a credit line to the material. If material is not included in the book's Creative Commons license and your intended use is not permitted by statutory regulation or exceeds the permitted use, you will need to obtain permission directly from the copyright holder.
The use of general descriptive names, registered names, trademarks, service marks, etc. in this publication does not imply, even in the absence of a specific statement, that such names are exempt from the relevant protective laws and regulations and therefore free for general use.
The publisher, the authors and the editors are safe to assume that the advice and information in this book are believed to be true and accurate at the date of publication. Neither the publisher nor the authors or the editors give a warranty, express or implied, with respect to the material contained herein or for any errors or omissions that may have been made. The publisher remains neutral with regard to jurisdictional claims in published maps and institutional affiliations.

Cover illustration: Bill Frymire

Printed on acid-free paper

This Palgrave Macmillan imprint is published by the registered company Springer International Publishing AG part of Springer Nature.
The registered company address is: Gewerbestrasse 11, 6330 Cham, Switzerland

Acknowledgements

The idea for this project has been on my mind since the very beginning when I started researching the European Union's (EU's) and China's relations with Africa back in 2008. China's relations with African countries had attracted great attention after the Forum for China-Africa Cooperation (FOCAC) summit in Beijing in 2006, and scholarly interest in the drivers and effects of this relationship was burgeoning. The most controversial debates during public events, academic conferences and in the media always evolved around the impact of China's rise on political reforms in Africa and implications for the EU's and other actors' good governance policies. Interestingly, despite heated debates there has been and still is little academic evidence on this issue. This made me curious to develop an analytical framework to address this question and to delve into the empirics—a challenge in itself, in view of the rapidly evolving relations between China and Africa.

This work would not have been possible without the great support from colleagues and friends. Special thanks go first and foremost to Tanja Börzel and Dirk Messner. Their intellectual guidance and encouragement has been vital to the success of this project. I am also very grateful to my colleagues and friends from the German Development Institute who gave moral support and discussed portions of this book, including Mark Furness, Jörn Grävingholt, Niels Keijzer, Stephan Klingebiel, Erik Lundsgaarde, Timo Mahn, Mario Negre, Imme Scholz and Jörg Faust. Sven Grimm, Svea Koch, Julia Leininger and Silke Weinlich have been extremely valuable partners to discuss the EU's good governance strategies in Africa and implications of China's rise, on numerous occasions. Debates with Julia Bader have been tremendously helpful at various instances throughout the whole process. Her critical and constructive remarks have been crucial during the final stages of the preparation of this book.

In addition, I owe an enormous debt of gratitude to the more than 200 government officials, business representatives and civil society activists from China, Angola, Ethiopia, Rwanda, the European Union and EU member states for sharing their insights and taking the time to discuss with me. They will remain anonymous in this book, but their perspectives have greatly enriched my understanding of the dynamics between the EU's and China's engagement in Africa and domestic politics in African authoritarian, dominant party systems. I could not have realised this project without financial assistance from the German Federal Ministry for Economic Cooperation and Development. The editorial team at Palgrave has provided very professional assistance throughout the publication process. I would also like to thank Thomas Risse for considering this book for the 'governance and limited statehood' series and for his helpful remarks. Two anonymous reviewers should be acknowledged for insightful comments. A special thanks also goes to Eleonora Hoffmann, Anna Hornik, Dominik Pieper, Steffen Stürznickel and Dennis Weidner for their research assistance.

Finally, I would not have finished this book without the loving support, encouragement and patience of my family and friends. My deepest gratitude goes to my parents, Sabine and Hans Hackenesch. I dedicate this book to them.

Contents

1 **Introduction**   1
  1.1 *EU Good Governance Strategies Face Two Challenges: The Predominance of African Dominant Party Systems and China's Rise in Africa*   3
  1.2 *Different Parts of the Same Elephant? Researching EU Good Governance Strategies and China's Engagement in Africa*   10
  1.3 *Why Angola, Ethiopia and Rwanda?*   14
  1.4 *Structure of the Book*   17

2 **The Initial Puzzle: Why Governments in Dominant Party Systems Engage with the EU on Good Governance Reform, or Not**   21
  2.1 *The EU's Strategies to Promote Governance Reforms*   24
  2.2 *African Governments' Responsiveness*   29
  2.3 *Survival Strategies of Governments in Dominant party Regimes*   31
  2.4 *African Economic Dependence on the EU*   41
  2.5 *The Rise of China: What Effect?*   43
  2.6 *Map of the Puzzle: Explaining African Governments' Responsiveness*   47

3	**Rwanda**	49
	3.1 Structural Factors Shaping Rwanda's Survival Strategies	50
	3.2 Rwanda Reluctantly Engaged with the EU in the Early 2000s	51
	3.3 Rwanda Proactively Engaging with the EU in the Late 2000s Despite China Looming	63
	3.4 A U-turn in the EU's Strategies in 2012 But Little Change in Rwanda's Responsiveness	83
	3.5 Conclusions	87
4	**Ethiopia**	99
	4.1 Structural Factors Shaping Ethiopia's Survival Strategies	100
	4.2 Ethiopia Reluctantly Engaging with the EU in the Early 2000s	101
	4.3 The 2005 Election Crisis: A Turning Point in EU-Ethiopia relations	114
	4.4 Ethiopia Reluctantly Engaging with the EU in the Late 2000s Despite China's Strong Presence	118
	4.5 Brief Breeze of Change in EU–Ethiopia Cooperation Between 2011 and 2014	137
	4.6 Conclusions	138
5	**Angola**	149
	5.1 Structural Factors Shaping Angola's Survival Strategies	150
	5.2 Angola Reluctantly Engaging in Governance Reforms in the Early 2000s Despite China Emerging	151
	5.3 The Late 2000s: Angola Largely Indifferent Towards EU Demands to Engage on Governance Reforms Even Though the EU Narrows Its Strategies	163
	5.4 Conclusions	185

6	Conclusions	193
	6.1 EU Good Governance Strategies: Not Strategic Enough	194
	6.2 Quite Diverse: African Dominant Party Systems' Survival Strategies	198
	6.3 Economic Dependence: Less Important Than Thought	205
	6.4 Does China Matter? Yes, But Less Than Expected	209
	6.5 Some Avenues for Future Work	219
	6.6 Policy Implications: Facing a Fork in the Road?	222

References 227

Index 251

Acronyms

ACP countries	Africa, Caribbean and Pacific countries
AfDB	African Development Bank
AU	African Union
CADFund	China Africa Development Fund
CASA-CE	Broad Convergence for the Salvation of Angola-Electoral Coalition
CCP	Chinese Communist Party
CIF	China International Fund
CNDH	Rwanda's Human Rights Commission
CSO	Civil Society Organisations
DAC	Development Assistance Committee of the OECD
DRC	Democratic Republic of Congo
EC	European Commission
EDF	European Development Fund
EIDHR	European Instrument for Democracy and Human Rights
EPRDF	Ethiopian Peoples' Revolutionary Democratic Front
EU	European Union
EXIM Bank	Export Import Bank
FDI	Foreign Direct Investments
FDLR	Forces Démocratiques de Libération du Rwanda
FEAC	Federal Ethics and Anti-corruption Commission of Ethiopia
FNLA	Frente Nacional de Libertação de Angola
FOCAC	Forum for China-Africa Cooperation
GDP	Gross Domestic Product
GNI	Gross National Income
GRN	Gabinete de Reconstrução Nacional

IMF	International Monetary Fund
JGA	Joint Governance Assessment
JWF	Joint Way Forward
MDGs	Millennium Development Goals
MDR	Mouvement Démocratique Républicain
MOFCOM	Chinese Ministry of Commerce
MoU	Memorandum of Understanding
MPLA	Movimento Popular de Libertação de Angola
NGO	Non-governmental organisation
NURC	Rwanda's National Commission for Unity and Reconciliation
ODA	Official Development Assistance
OECD	Organisation for Economic Cooperation and Development
PBS	Provision of Basic Services Programme
PDR	Parti Démocratique pour le Renouveau
PEFA	Public Expenditures and Financial Accountability
PRSP	Poverty Reduction Strategy Paper
PSCAP	Public Service Capacity Administration Programme
RPF	Rwanda Patriotic Front
SME	Small and Medium-sized Enterprises
TPLF	Tigray People's Liberation Front
UK	United Kingdom
UN	United Nations
UNCTAD	United Nations Conference on Trade and Development
UNDP	United Nations Development Programme
UNITA	National Union for the Total Independence of Angola
USA	United States of America
USD	United States Dollar
WGI	Worldwide Governance Indicators
WTO	World Trade Organization

LIST OF FIGURES

Fig. 1.1	Political regimes in Africa in 2012	7
Fig. 1.2	African governments' responsiveness to EU good governance strategies	17
Fig. 2.1	Explaining African governments' response strategies	24
Fig. 2.2	The EU's good governance instruments: between confrontation and rewards	28
Fig. 2.3	African governments' survival strategies meet EU good governance strategies	32
Fig. 3.1	Net ODA as a share of GNI in Rwanda	60
Fig. 3.2	ODA flows to Rwanda (disbursements in USD million)	61
Fig. 3.3	Government effectiveness and control of corruption in Rwanda	72
Fig. 3.4	Rwanda's exports to selected countries (in USD thousands)	77
Fig. 3.5	Annual bilateral visits RPF–CCP	82
Fig. 4.1	Government effectiveness and control of corruption in Ethiopia	109
Fig. 4.2	Net ODA as a share of GNI in Ethiopia	111
Fig. 4.3	ODA to Ethiopia, selected donors (disbursements in USD million)	112
Fig. 4.4	Ethiopia's exports to selected partners (in thousands of USD)	113
Fig. 4.5	Annual bilateral visits EPRDF–CCP	114

Fig. 5.1	Net ODA as a share of GNI in Angola	159
Fig. 5.2	Government effectiveness and control of corruption in Angola	172
Fig. 5.3	Angolan oil exports to selected partners (in USD thousands)	178
Fig. 5.4	Annual bilateral visits MPLA–CCP	185
Fig. 6.1	EU instruments to support governance reforms 2000–2014	196
Fig. 6.2	Economic dependence of Angola, Ethiopia and Rwanda on the EU between 2000 and 2014	205
Fig. 6.3	Number of bilateral visits between the Chinese Communist Party and African ruling parties (2002–2014)	214

LIST OF TABLES

Table 2.1	Four approaches of external good governance support	26
Table 2.2	Interaction effects between EU good governance strategies and African governments' response	30
Table 2.3	The costs and benefits of cooperating on governance reforms	38
Table 2.4	How economic dependence on the EU affects African governments' willingness to cooperate on governance reforms	43
Table 2.5	Cooperation with China: what effect on African governments' willingness to cooperate on governance reforms?	44
Table 3.1	EU governance aid to Rwanda 2000–2014 (in USD million and in per cent)	52
Table 3.2	EU statements and *démarches* related to governance reforms 2000–2011	54
Table 3.3	Chinese aid projects 2000–2005	62
Table 3.4	EU aid to non-state actors through the EIDHR 2000–2011	64
Table 3.5	China's aid projects 2006–2012	79
Table 4.1	EU governance aid to Ethiopia 2000–2014 (in USD million and in per cent)	102
Table 4.2	EU statements and *démarches* related to governance reforms 2000–2012	103
Table 4.3	EIDHR projects in Ethiopia	123
Table 4.4	Chinese official flows to Ethiopia 2006–2012	131
Table 5.1	EU governance aid commitments to Angola (in USD million and in percent)	152
Table 5.2	EU statements and *démarches* related to governance reforms 2000–2012	153
Table 5.3	EU aid as a share of total DAC donors' aid (in USD million and in per cent)	159

Table 5.4	EIDHR projects in Angola 2000–2010	165
Table 5.5	Selected credit lines to Angola (in USD)	177
Table 5.6	Chinese loans to Angola 2002–2012 (excluding CIF funds)	180
Table 6.1	EU approaches to promote governance reforms between 2000 and 2014	195
Table 6.2	Engaging with China—effect on the three governments' willingness to cooperate on governance reforms	217

CHAPTER 1

Introduction

About 25 years after Francis Fukuyama proclaimed the 'end of history', ideological and strategic competition between democracies and autocracies has firmly reentered international relations. The rise of China has fuelled debates about the economic performance of authoritarian regimes compared with democratic ones (Zhao 2010; Acemoglu and Robinson 2012). Questions about the attractiveness of alternative development models have gained prominence, not least with the economic and financial crises that hit the European Union (EU) but left China largely unaffected. In addition, several observers have identified a pushback across the developing world against EU and USA good governance support, which is at least partly driven by the rise of China and other authoritarian powers (Puddington 2008; Carothers and Brechenmacher 2014).

One prominent aspect in these discussions is the question of whether and how China's engagement in Africa affects the EU's attempts to support governance reforms in African countries. Some argue that China's economic cooperation 'with no strings attached' undermines the EU and other Western actors' efforts to support human rights and democratic structures (Halper 2010). Others point out that for the EU and other Western actors security, economic or aid policy interests often trump efforts to support political reforms (Olsen 1998; Brown 2005; Brüne 2007; Jünemann and Knodt 2007). China's presence would thus have a minor effect, if any. More than 15 years after China began intensifying its

© The Author(s) 2018
C. Hackenesch, *The EU and China in African Authoritarian Regimes*, Governance and Limited Statehood,
https://doi.org/10.1007/978-3-319-63591-0_1

engagement with Africa, a comprehensive study on the interaction effects between China's presence in Africa and the EU's good governance strategies is still lacking. This book makes one of the first theoretically guided and empirically grounded contribution to this debate.

Empirical evidence suggests that governments in Africa have responded very differently to the EU's demands to engage in governance reforms. Autocratically governed countries, such as Angola, Ethiopia and Rwanda, started to reluctantly engage with the EU on governance reforms in the early 2000s. Yet, since the mid-2000s when China's presence started to reduce Africa's dependence on the EU, the openness of countries like Angola, Ethiopia and Rwanda to engage with the EU has varied widely. Since the mid-2000s, Rwanda has willingly cooperated with the EU on governance reforms; Ethiopia has remained very reluctant to engage; and Angola has largely ignored EU requests for cooperation. These different reactions cannot easily be explained. All three regimes can be classified as authoritarian, dominant party systems with similarly low levels of political liberalisation. Moreover, all three have seen a reduction in their dependence on the EU because of increased access to cooperation with China.

Two main questions are therefore at the core of this book. What explains the differences in African governments' willingness to engage with the EU on governance reforms? To what extent does China's presence affect African governments' openness to engage with the EU on governance reforms? The analysis thus focuses on African governments' strategies towards the EU and China. It analyses how and to what extent African governments engage with the EU on governance reforms, and it investigates whether access to cooperation with China influences African governments' cooperation strategies.

Linking research on good governance support and on authoritarian regimes, the book develops a theoretical framework to address these questions. It contributes to the academic debate on the influence of external actors on governance reform elsewhere. In particular, it explains how the domestic logic of political survival shapes authoritarian governments' incentives to engage with the EU and China.

Moreover, the analysis makes an empirical contribution by providing an in-depth analysis of the interaction of the EU's good governance strategies, the survival strategies of dominant party systems and the engagement of China with three African authoritarian regimes—Angola, Ethiopia and Rwanda—between 2000 and 2014. The empirical analysis is informed by more than 200 semistructured interviews conducted with government officials and non-state actors in the EU, China, Angola, Ethiopia and

Rwanda between 2009 and 2013. The analysis centres on the EU's engagement in African dominant party regimes and on China as a third external actor. However, the findings yield broader implications for authoritarian regimes beyond Africa and for the EU's and China's engagement in other regions.

The main argument of this book is that the survival strategies of governments in dominant party systems are the most important factor that influences African governments' willingness to engage in governance reforms. The survival strategies define the government's basic preferences for cooperating with the EU. Other variables, such as the specific good governance strategy the EU uses, African countries' dependence on the EU and access to cooperation with China, set additional incentives that make cooperation more beneficial or less costly. In contrast to widespread assumptions that the growing presence of China in Africa has made it more difficult for the EU to support good governance, this study finds little evidence that would support this claim. Instead, China's engagement with African countries is part of a broader set of factors that influences African governments' openness to engage with the EU. These findings have important implications for researchers as well as policy-makers.

1.1 EU GOOD GOVERNANCE STRATEGIES FACE TWO CHALLENGES: THE PREDOMINANCE OF AFRICAN DOMINANT PARTY SYSTEMS AND CHINA'S RISE IN AFRICA

While bringing good governance reforms more prominently onto the agenda in its relations with African countries, the EU has been confronted with two key challenges. First, dominant party systems have become the predominant type of political regime in Africa and political liberalisation has been on the decline, making it more difficult for the EU to promote reforms. Second, the growing presence of China in Africa has fundamentally changed the broader context in which the EU seeks to support reforms, raising questions about the implications of China's rise for the EU's good governance policies.

EU Good Governance Strategies in Sub-Saharan Africa

Support for democracy, human rights and the rule of law became an explicit objective in the EU's external relations with the signing of the Maastricht Treaty in 1992. During the 1990s, the EU could rely mainly on sanctions and small volumes of governance aid to support reforms in sub-Saharan Africa and beyond (Crawford 2001). The turn of the century then brought a qualitative and quantitative shift in the EU's policies. Since 2000, good governance support has become a more prominent issue in the EU's development policy and other areas of external relations. The EU has developed a positive approach to support governance reforms in sub-Saharan Africa that aims to establish an active cooperation with the target government. Particularly reforms in the international aid system have allowed the EU to expand its positive instruments since 2000.

Over time, the EU has broadened its understanding of good governance (see also Börzel and Risse 2009; Carbone 2010). In the 2005 European Consensus on Development, the EU presented good governance as a precondition for sustainable and equitable development as well as for providing effective development assistance (European Union 2005). At the same time, good governance was put forward as an important objective of EU development policy and EU external relations. In the 'Agenda for Change' (European Commission 2011), the EU's more recent development policy strategy, the EU has made assistance for democratic governance one of the two main areas on which development policy should concentrate. The Agenda for Change confirmed that the EU views 'good governance' as a comprehensive concept, stating that the EU aims at promoting 'human rights, democracy *and other key elements* of good governance' (European Commission 2011; emphasis author).

However, one has to bear in mind that even as support for governance reforms has become a more important concern in the EU's external relations, it is obviously only *one* of the EU's policy objectives and interests (for an overview on conflicting objectives in democracy promotion, see Grimm and Leininger 2012). In its relations with African countries and elsewhere, the EU often prioritises security, stability and cooperation on migration management over good governance (Kopstein 2005; Burnell and Calvert 2005; Jünemann and Knodt 2007, for Africa see Olsen 1998; Brüne 2007; Brown 2005). EU energy, trade and other economic interests mitigate the EU's willingness to push for governance reforms. Moreover, development policy interests and objectives may also conflict with the EU's good governance support. Similar to other aid bureaucracies that are under (public) pressure to show that development aid positively impacts poverty reduction and economic growth, the EU is less likely to push for political reforms and use negative conditionality in countries with good economic performance and progress in poverty reduction (Del Biondo 2011).

Between 2000 and 2014, the EU developed a range of instruments that allow it to not only *react* to imminent political crises, but to proactively support tendencies towards political openness and prevent degradations in political liberalisation. In its relations with sub-Saharan African countries, the EU seeks to promote good governance through political and aid policy dialogues, the provision of governance aid and (non-) material incentives. According to statistics from the Organisation for Economic Cooperation and Development's (OECD) Development Assistance Committee (DAC), EU good governance aid gradually increased between 2000 and 2014 in absolute and relative terms. The EU institutions provide almost as much governance aid to Africa as Germany and the UK combined (Hackenesch 2016). The EU also strengthened political dialogue as defined in Article 8 of the Cotonou Agreement. It introduced new instruments such as the Governance Incentive Tranche that aims at setting positive incentives to support reforms (Molenaers and Nijs 2009). While the EU could also rely on sanctions to respond to serious violations of human rights or a *coup d'état*, it has been more reluctant to apply sanctions in the 2000s than it was in the 1990s (Portela 2010; Zimelis 2011).

The EU's positive approach towards good governance reforms requires that African governments are, at least to some extent, willing and open to engage with the EU on the implementation of its good governance instruments (see also van Hüllen 2015). If African governments are not ready to engage in political and aid policy dialogues, to respond to positive incentives such as the Governance Incentive Tranche, and to cooperate on the implementation of governance aid, the EU has few means by which to engage with them on governance reforms. While the EU has enhanced its positive approach to support good governance, dominant party systems with very specific domestic incentive structures have become the most prominent regime type in Africa. Moreover, China has become an alternative cooperation partner, potentially affecting African governments' incentives to engage with the EU.

The 'New Authoritarianism' in Africa: Dominant Party Systems

The EU started developing its good governance instruments in the 1990s, when the third wave of democratisation triggered greater political openness and regime change in a number of sub-Saharan African countries. However, after a period of political liberalisation, it quickly became evident that many countries in sub-Saharan Africa remained authoritarian despite democratic institutional façades (Ottaway 2003; Kemmerzell 2010, 348; Levitsky and Way 2010).

The variation in authoritarian institutions and regime types is immense. Scholars commonly differentiate between monarchies, military, one-party and dominant (or multiparty) regimes (Hadenius and Teorell 2007; Magaloni and Kricheli 2010). These distinctions are based on the different modes of maintaining power: hereditary succession (monarchies), threat of the use of force (military) or elections (party regimes) (Hadenius and Teorell 2007, 147f). Dominant party regimes are characterised by a hegemonic party that dominates the political and economic life in a country. They hold regular elections and allow opposition candidates to participate in elections, but their elections are not free and fair, and possibilities for opposition candidates to participate are considerably restricted. On the other hand, dominant party regimes are distinct from one-party systems as one-party systems forbid all parties other than the one in power (Hadenius and Teorell 2007, 147f).

Globally speaking, the incidence of different types of authoritarian regimes changed markedly over time. Macroanalyses find that the number of dominant party systems has significantly increased since the early 1990s. Magaloni and Kricheli (2010) demonstrate that today dominant party regimes constitute by far the largest category of authoritarian regimes and about one-third of all political regimes. Hadenius and Teorell (2006, 2007) argue that since the early 1990s, more than 50 per cent of all authoritarian regimes are dominant party autocracies.

As these macro-quantitative studies do not focus on specific regions, they overlook the fact that the high number of dominant party systems that we observe today is driven to an important extent by regime changes in sub-Saharan Africa in the early 1990s. The large majority of African authoritarian regimes can be classified as dominant party systems (Fig. 1.1). Many African autocracies combine dominant party rule with a strong personalistic element (Bratton and Van de Walle 1997; Geddes 2003). Many countries have institutionalised regular elections. In fact, by 2017 only two countries in Africa had not held elections.[1] However, whether elections and other formally democratic institutions contribute to more democracy in Africa has been controversially discussed (Lindberg 2009; Lynch and Crawford 2011; Cheeseman 2015). Clearly, authoritarianism in Africa has not vanished. But compared to the postcolonial states in the 1960s, 1970s and 1980s that were dominated by military and one-party

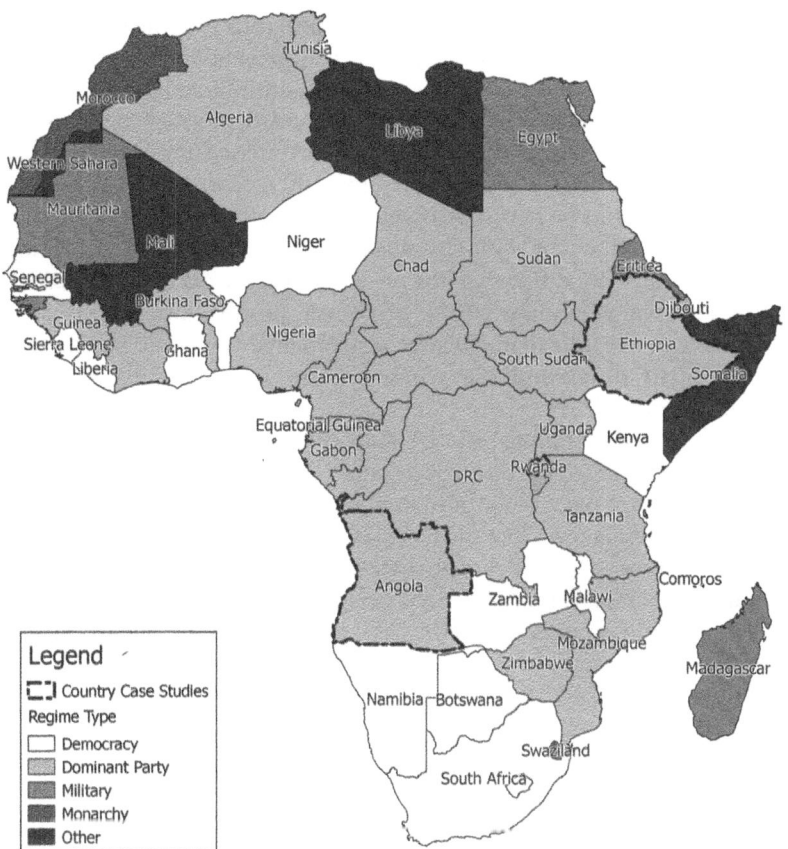

Fig. 1.1 Political regimes in Africa in 2012
Source: Author's compilation, building on Magaloni et al. (2013) but with several modifications

regimes (Bratton and Van de Walle 1997; Kemmerzell 2010, 337f), the political institutions of authoritarianism in Africa today are considerably different in nature.

Insights from studies on the domestic politics of authoritarian regimes give reason to be tentatively optimistic about the EU's and other external actors' chances of supporting democratisation in African dominant party systems. Quantitative research finds that development aid and democracy aid are more likely to support democratisation in party-based autocracies than in other types of authoritarian regime (Wright 2009; Cornell 2012).

The effect of aid and democracy aid is attributed to the role of the ruling party: in party-based regimes, the ruler can afford higher levels of political liberalisation and is more likely to remain in an influential position even after regime breakdown. Development aid and democracy aid thus produce lower costs for political leaders in party-based regimes compared with other authoritarian regimes (Wright 2009; Cornell 2012). Foreign aid has been found to have a stronger positive effect on democratisation since the end of the Cold War (Escribà-Folch and Wright 2015); a finding that is in line with earlier studies on the effect of development aid on democratisation (Dunning 2004). Moreover, positive instruments apparently have more effect than negative instruments: economic sanctions are less likely to destabilise party-based autocracies (Escribà-Folch and Wright 2015).

Based on these findings, the EU and other external actors should be more successful in supporting governance reforms in party-based autocracies than in other types of authoritarian regimes. However, empirical findings in this book suggest that the EU's success in encouraging governments in these regimes to address governance reforms varies widely across countries and over time. A more nuanced perspective regarding the factors that explain these differences within the large group of dominant party systems thus seems necessary.

China's Rise in Africa

Support for governance reforms became a priority in the EU's and other Western actors' policies towards Africa at a very specific period in time, and with regard to the international context. During the 1990s, the EU and other Western actors were the most important international political and economic partners for African countries. Moreover, the normative underpinnings of the good governance agenda were largely unchallenged. This international context has changed considerably since the early 2000s and notably as a result of the rise of China. China's emergence as a major actor in Africa is part of a broader international power shift; but China is by far the most substantive actor in terms of its economic size and global reach (Humphrey and Messner 2008). Moreover, it is the only one of the emerging powers that potentially represents an alternative economic and political model.

China's engagement in Africa intensified tremendously within a relatively short period of time. From 2000 onwards, activities including trade, investment, assistance and diplomacy have reached previously unknown heights. While political interests dominated China's relations with African countries until the mid-1990s, economic interests have been at the core of the relationships since. Intensification and diversification of economic relations between China and Africa are both a direct consequence of China's economic growth since the mid-1990s and of reforms in China's foreign economic policy.

Aid, trade, investments and loans often form comprehensive packages in Chinese relations with individual states (Alden 2007). In 2009, China became Africa's second-largest trading partner after the EU (in total), ahead of the USA and far ahead of other emerging economies, such as India or Brazil. With regard to aid volumes, the exact amount is hard to establish, due to a lack of comparable statistics (Grimm et al. 2011; Brautigam 2011). In recent years, the Chinese aid budget has increased by about 30 per cent annually. Chinese aid was estimated to have been at around USD7.1 billion in 2013 (Kitano and Harada 2015). About half of Chinese aid is provided to African countries (Information Office of the State Council 2011). This would have made China a donor comparable to Germany and much larger than India or Brazil—but considerably smaller than the EU institutions. Chinese loans to Africa appear to greatly exceed aid volumes: Brautigam and Hwang (2016) estimate that China provided about USD86.3 billion between 2000 and 2014. Chinese banks, such as the Export Import Bank and the China Development Bank, are giving preferential and commercial loans to African countries at low interest rates. These loans are often linked to resource revenues, and they are used for infrastructure projects that are implemented by Chinese state-owned companies (at either the central or provincial levels).

The implications of China's rise for Western governance and democracy promotion are still mostly discussed within the media and the policy community; academics have only recently started taking an interest in this topic. While African countries are in great need of more financial support to advance their economic development, many commentators in Europe suspect that China's growing engagement undermines Western actors' efforts to support governance reforms in African countries.

Three main lines of argument are put forward. First, some observers suggest that China reduces the leverage of the EU and other Western actors to set incentives for reform. EU diplomats in Uganda, for instance, openly complain that they are 'rapidly losing influence'.[2] Second, China is perceived to represent an alternative development model that competes with a European/Western model. The former German Minister for Development Cooperation, Dirk Niebel, observed: 'China perceives our value-based development cooperation as interference in the domestic affairs of developing countries. There is indeed a competition among donors. We are asked for issues related to good governance. China is approached for supporting large infrastructure projects'.[3] Third, some argue that China and other authoritarian regional powers bolster authoritarianism in third countries. Recent quantitative work demonstrates that China's economic cooperation with party-based autocracies tends to have a stabilising effect (Bader 2015b). This would make it more challenging for the EU and other Western actors to support governance reforms.

1.2 Different Parts of the Same Elephant? Researching EU Good Governance Strategies and China's Engagement in Africa

In order to investigate why African dominant party systems are willing to engage with the EU on governance reforms, this book brings together debates related to EU good governance support, authoritarian regimes and China's engagement in Africa. Each of these fields of research, if taken individually, gives limited insights to analyse why African governments engage with the EU in governance reforms, or not. Despite an impressive body of studies on (the EU's) good governance strategies and on authoritarian regimes, the interaction between international factors and the behaviour of political actors in the target country remains underresearched. This book therefore combines research on EU good governance support and on authoritarian regimes and develops a theoretical framework to analyse the interaction between the EU, African governments and China.

Debates on external good governance support have been particularly concerned with the EU's influence on its immediate neighbours. Studies on external Europeanisation and EU external governance have developed comprehensive frameworks on what works, what does not work and why in the EU's attempts to support political reforms beyond its borders (Schimmelfennig and Sedelmeier 2005; Vachudova 2005; Lavenex and Schimmelfennig 2009; Youngs 2009; Freyburg et al. 2011; Börzel and Risse 2012; van Hüllen 2012). Yet, the theoretical frameworks in these strands of research cannot be easily transferred to investigate the EU's support for governance reforms in Africa in light of the rise of China and to identify the factors that shape African governments' willingness to engage with the EU on governance reforms. The necessary conditions, causal mechanisms and scope conditions for effective rule and norm transfer—for instance, the level of statehood or interdependence with the EU—differ considerably between the EU's neighbours and countries in sub-Saharan Africa.

Beyond research on the EU's influence on political reforms in neighbouring countries, a vibrant discussion on the effectiveness of democracy aid and other instruments to promote democratic reforms has emerged since the late 1990s. This research is driven by an 'instrument-logic', focussing on the effect of specific (EU) instruments such as development aid (Goldsmith 2001; Dunning 2004), democracy aid (Kalyvitis and Vlachaki 2010; Dietrich and Wright 2012), sanctions (Portela 2010; Zimelis 2011; Del Biondo 2015) or budget-support suspensions (Hayman 2011; Molenaers 2012; Faust et al. 2012; Molenaers et al. 2015) on governance reforms (see also Warkotsch 2008; Kotzian et al. 2011). This work is generally interested in two main questions: why does the EU use a specific instrument or strategy in a given situation, and not others? How effective are the EU's instruments, measured in terms of their impact on governance reforms? Both questions are closely related. The coherence and consistency in the EU's usage of certain instruments (for example sanctions or budget-support suspensions) is one important factor that influences the success of these instruments. By doing so, however, the agency of domestic actors, which is crucial for political reforms, is often neglected.

In turn, studies on authoritarianism have traditionally been concerned with the *domestic* factors that explain regime durability or transition to democracy. Analyses on authoritarianism have thrived over the past decade (for example, Wintrobe 2001; Bueno de Mesquita et al. 2003; Burnell and Schlumberger 2010; Croissant and Wurster 2013; Köllner and Kailitz 2013; Gerschewski 2013). While most of this work is interested in the stability, durability, and social and economic performance of authoritarian regimes, some researchers have began using insights into the domestic logic of political survival to study the influence of aid, democracy aid and sanctions (Lektzian and Souva 2007; Wright 2009; Cornell 2012; Escribà-Folch 2012; Bader and Faust 2014) or to ascertain the effects of external linkage and leverage on political reforms (Levitsky and Way 2010). Research on the effects of external good governance support in authoritarian regimes provides first insights on the effect of aid, democracy aid and sanctions on political liberalisation and democratisation in different types of authoritarian regimes. Yet, this work gives little explanation for why aid, democracy aid and other instruments have differential effects on the same type of authoritarian regime, such as the large group of dominant party systems.

Literature on the influence of external actors on authoritarian regimes is dominated by studies analysing the effects of democracy promotion instruments on political reforms. In parallel, a new research agenda on the influence of authoritarian powers, such as China, Russia, Venezuela or Iran, on political reforms elsewhere has started to evolve (Bader et al. 2010; Burnell 2010; Melnykovska et al. 2012; Vanderhill 2012; Tolstrup 2013; Bader 2015a; von Soest 2015). These studies conduct macro-quantitative analyses or investigate the influence of authoritarian great powers on their immediate neighbourhood. Only very few authors explicitly address the implications of authoritarian powers for the EU's or other actors' attempts to support democratic reforms (e.g. Risse and Babayan 2015). These studies mostly focus on the interaction between the EU and Russia in Eastern Europe and the former Soviet republics (Dimitrova and Dragneva 2009; Tolstrup 2013).

Finally, China's engagement in Africa has been widely researched in recent years. Scholars interested in China–Africa relations have been investigating, for instance, the role of different actors involved in the decision-making process of China's Africa policy; how China's aid, trade and investment in Africa have developed; and what factors explain the intensification of bilateral relations (Alden 2007; Reilly and Na 2007; Alden et al. 2008; Brautigam 2009; Taylor 2010; Brautigam 2015). Some have also analysed interaction effects between China and the EU's engagement in Africa with regard to development, security or other policy fields (Men and Barton 2011; Wissenbach 2011; Carbone 2011; Grimm and Hackenesch 2017). These bodies of work have made great empirical contributions to deepen our understanding of the current power shift. To date, however, no structured analysis has been conducted to investigate the implications of China's rise for the EU's good governance policies in Africa.

Why Should We Focus on African Governments' Strategies?

In order to examine the effects of China's presence on the EU's good governance policies, this book centres on domestic politics and African governments' strategies to engage with the EU and China. Investigating whether and if so why African governments are willing to engage in the implementation of the EU's governance instruments is essential for understanding whether these instruments result in their intended outcomes. In this regard, the findings of this book matter for several reasons:

First, research on external democracy and governance support (Carothers 1999; Andrews 2013), EU political conditionality in the neighbourhood (Checkel 2000; Schimmelfennig and Sedelmeier 2005; van Hüllen 2012), economic conditionality (Killick 1997) or democratic sanctions (Portela 2010; Blanchard and Ripsman 2013) has argued time and again that the political will of the decision-makers in the target country to engage with external actors is a precondition for effective governance support. Similarly, literature on the effectiveness of development aid has demonstrated that 'ownership' of the recipient country, in other words the political will of the partner government to engage with external actors in the implementation of reforms, substantially shapes the impact of external support (Fraser and Whitfield 2009). Yet, research on good governance promotion and aid effectiveness has so far paid little attention to the factors that actually influence the willingness of African governments to engage with the EU.

Second, gaining a better understanding of why governments in dominant party systems are (not) willing to engage with the EU on governance reforms is of important empirical relevance. Dominant party regimes constitute by far the largest group among the authoritarian regimes today (Magaloni and Kricheli 2010). No consensus exists regarding the likelihood of dominant party regimes democratising or transitioning to another form of authoritarian rule. Some argue that dominant party regimes are more likely to transform into single party regimes (Magaloni and Kricheli 2010, 133), while others find that they are the 'typical stepping stones to democracy' (Hadenius and Teorell 2007, 152). Understanding why governments in these regimes are (not) willing to engage with the EU on governance reforms thus contributes to deepening our knowledge of whether the EU ultimately supports these regimes to democratise or to transition to another form of authoritarianism.

Third, insights into why governments in dominant party regimes are willing to engage or not in governance reforms may lead to a more nuanced perspective on the effects of China's rise on the EU's good governance instruments. Debates in the media and academia are often biased in two ways: they start by assuming that China has mainly negative implications for the prospects of democratic reforms in third countries and for external good governance support; and they rarely enquire about the negative effects and unintended side-effects of the EU's good governance strategies. In this regard, analysing the domestic incentives of African authoritarian governments to engage in governance reforms provides a starting point for assessing how attractive (or costly) not only the EU's but also China's support to African countries is.

Finally, this specific research perspective also holds relevance in judging the legitimacy of external good governance support. The rise of the good governance agenda has been characterised as a substantial shift in donor–recipient relations (Moore 1995; Herdegen 2007). The traditional understanding of sovereignty, in which a government could organise its domestic political processes without interference from the international community, gave way to a modified view on sovereignty according to which not every form of political system regardless of its organisation is seen as valuable and worth preserving (Moore 1995, 94; Dolzer 2004, 54; Herdegen 2007, 122f). Several observers have challenged the legitimacy of external good governance support and argued that it should become more demand driven (Tilly 2007). In development policy, this controversy centres on the question of how external good governance support relates to African countries' 'ownership' (i.e. Pender 2007). In authoritarian countries, where governments do not allow for meaningful political competition, normative considerations that external actors should not *impose* their priorities face a fundamental dilemma. A better understanding of the incentives for African governments when presented with the EU's demands to engage on governance reforms is therefore also paramount to advance debates about the legitimacy of the EU's policies.

1.3 Why Angola, Ethiopia and Rwanda?

The EU's success in making African authoritarian, dominant party regimes address governance issues has varied markedly since the turn of the century. Empirical evidence presented here illustrates that African dominant party regimes have responded very differently to the EU's demands to engage on governance reforms. We will investigate three dominant party regimes—Angola, Ethiopia and Rwanda—where the difference in the governments' openness towards EU good governance policies has been particularly pronounced. At the same time, the cases differ with regard to the four main explanatory factors identified in the theoretical framework—the EU's good governance strategies, African governments' survival strategies, their dependence on the EU, and their access to cooperation with China. This variance on the dependent variable and explanatory factors across countries and over time allows for assessing the explanatory power of each variable (Gerring 2007, 97f).

Three Dominant Party Regimes

Angola, Ethiopia and Rwanda can all be classified as dominant party regimes. In all three countries, political life is controlled by a ruling party that has strongly entrenched itself in power. The Ethiopian Peoples' Revolutionary Democratic Front (EPRDF) has dominated Ethiopian politics since it overthrew the militarist Marxist Derg regime in the early 1990s (Abbink 2006). In Rwanda, the Rwandan Patriotic Front (RPF) has controlled political and economic developments since the genocide in 1994 (Beswick 2010). In Angola, the People's Movement for the Liberation of Angola (MPLA) has dominated political life since independence and particularly since the end of the civil war in 2002 (Roque 2008; Soares de Oliveira 2015).

Research on authoritarian party regimes suggests that the way the ruling party comes to power considerably impacts its resilience and durability (Smith 2005; Brownlee 2007). All three ruling parties have their origins in well-organised guerrilla movements with strong internal discipline and a high level of indoctrination. All three parties came to power after a violent struggle. All three had a difficult relationship with the international community during their power struggle. All three parties have maintained relatively high levels of independence from international pressure, influence and financial support.

A close connection between the party, the military and the business sector has emerged in all three regimes, at least partly as a result of the liberation struggle. All three governments have strongly centralised access to rents. In Ethiopia (Vaughan and Gebremichael 2011) and Rwanda (Booth and Golooba-Mutebi 2012), party-run companies dominate the private sector. These companies not only allow for the creation of sources of income for regime supporters, they also make it possible for the ruling party to generate important revenues. In Angola, the state-owned oil company Sonangol gives the presidency centralised access to oil revenues and their distribution. Moreover, the policy of 'Angolanisation'[4] permits the party to use its access to rents from foreign investments to generate support for the regime.

At the same time, Angola, Ethiopia and Rwanda have set up formally democratic institutions: they hold regular elections, have established parliaments and some—at least formal—separation of powers. Yet, governments in all three countries do not allow for meaningful political competition or a change of government. All three countries score low on political rights and civil liberties according to international macroindices, such as the one published by Freedom House or the Worldwide Governance Indicators (WGI). Moreover, the institutionalisation of succession remains a fundamental challenge. In Rwanda, President Kagame initiated a referendum and changed the constitution to remain in power when his second term ended in 2017. In Ethiopia, the issue had to be addressed when Prime Minister Meles died suddenly in the summer of 2012. In Angola, discussions on the succession of President Dos Santos started ahead of the parliamentary elections in 2012. The president did not have to step down formally, but his age and health situation required him to leave office in 2017.

In a Nutshell: Angola's, Ethiopia's and Rwanda's Responsiveness

The case studies will investigate Angola, Ethiopia and Rwanda's responsiveness in more detail. In a nutshell, the analysis finds that in the early 2000s, the Rwandan, Ethiopian and Angolan governments all started to reluctantly engage in political dialogue with the EU. All three governments cooperated with the EU on the implementation of governance aid, albeit reluctantly. All three have been willing to engage on governance reforms related to improving the effectiveness and efficiency of government institutions, but have been hesitant to cooperate on democratic governance. Despite these strong similarities between the three countries in the early 2000s, some differences can also be observed. From the beginning, the Angolan government was more hesitant in responding to EU demands to cooperate compared with Ethiopia and Rwanda (Fig. 1.2).

From the mid-2000s onwards, in parallel to China's rise in Africa, the openness of these countries towards EU demands to cooperate has varied widely. Rwanda has willingly engaged in political and aid policy dialogues, has implemented governance aid and committed to a comprehensive strategy to promote governance reforms. Ethiopia has remained

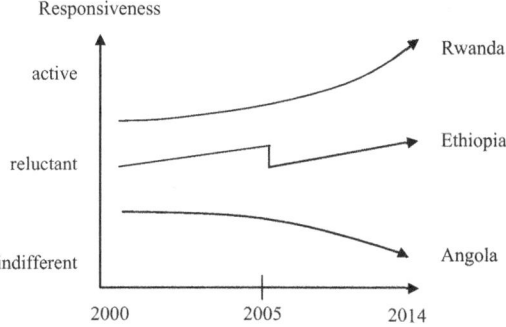

Fig. 1.2 African governments' responsiveness to EU good governance strategies
Source: Author's compilation

much more reluctant to institutionalise political and aid policy dialogues on governance reforms, to commit to governance reform objectives and to cooperate on the implementation of governance aid. Angola has largely ignored EU demands for cooperation and showed little interest in engaging in dialogue or the implementation of governance aid.

The clear variance with regard to Angola, Ethiopia and Rwanda's openness to engage with the EU makes these countries particularly pertinent cases. Angola, Ethiopia and Rwanda represent 'diverse cases' (Gerring 2007, 97f) that capture the full range of possible variation on the dependent variable. African government's strategies towards the EU are conceived as a continuous variable that can range from (pro)active cooperation to indifference. On this continuum, Angola and Rwanda represent 'extreme cases', where the government is particularly open to cooperation (Rwanda) or indifferent towards the EU (Angola). Selecting 'extreme cases' builds on the premise that the insights gained from these cases can be generalised to the cases located between the two extremes (Rolfing 2012, 70). Ethiopia is an interesting example for what could be called a 'mean' or 'median' case, where the government is reluctant to cooperate with the EU on governance reforms. The strategies of the three governments change over time, which gives additional variation for analysing the explanatory factors.[5]

1.4 Structure of the Book

Building on the domestic logic of political survival in authoritarian regimes, this book develops a theoretical framework to explain why African dominant party regimes are (not) willing to cooperate with the EU on governance reforms in light of the rise of China (Chap. 2). Building on research on the EU's good governance strategies and the politics of authoritarian regimes, Chap. 2 argues that differences in African governments' openness to engage with the EU on governance reforms can be explained by the interaction of four factors: the specific good governance strategies that the EU adopts in its relations with individual African countries; the domestic survival strategies of African authoritarian regimes; the economic dependence of African authoritarian regimes on the EU; and African countries' access to cooperation with China as an alternative cooperation partner.

Chapters 3, 4 and 5 delve into the cases of Rwanda, Ethiopia and Angola. For each country, two to four time periods are identified, depending on how the EU adapts its good governance strategies towards African dominant party regimes. For each period, the case studies investigate the interaction of the four main variables established in the theoretical framework to explain why African governments respond differently towards the EU's demands to engage in governance reforms. Chapter 6 summarises the main findings, highlights contributions to academic research, and discusses policy implications that emerge from the analysis.

Notes

1. The two countries are South Sudan and Eritrea.
2. See Süddeutsche Zeitung, 'Wettlauf gegen die Zeit und gegen andere. Noch können Deutsche und Europäer ihre Hilfe an Bedingungen knüpfen. Doch sowohl die Konkurrenz aus China als auch das Öl könnten das Gewicht westlicher Werte deutlich schmälern', 3 June 2013, page 6.
3. Niebel Interview for Die WELT on 4 February 2013; online: http://www.welt.de/politik/deutschland/article113349127/Meine-Soehne-haben-inder-Schule-den-Promi-Malus.html, last access 3 June 2014. Author's translation.
4. All international companies have to give their Angolan business partner a 30 per cent stake in their investments. The MPLA may influence which companies or individuals are nominated as potential partners for international businesses, which makes sizable opportunities for cooptation.
5. This study analyses three diverse cases with regard to African governments' openness to engaging with the EU in governance reforms. No conclusions can be drawn as to what extent these cases mirror the distribution of variation in the responsiveness of African governments across all African dominant party regimes. A cursory review of EU documents, interviews in

Brussels with EU officials who are well-versed in EU–Africa cooperation on governance reforms across all African countries and evaluations of the EU's good governance instruments suggest that many other African countries are probably situated somewhere in the middle of the spectrum, similar to the Ethiopian government that cooperates reluctantly.

Open Access This chapter is licensed under the terms of the Creative Commons Attribution 4.0 International License (http://creativecommons.org/licenses/by/4.0/), which permits use, sharing, adaptation, distribution and reproduction in any medium or format, as long as you give appropriate credit to the original author(s) and the source, provide a link to the Creative Commons license and indicate if changes were made.

The images or other third party material in this chapter are included in the chapter's Creative Commons license, unless indicated otherwise in a credit line to the material. If material is not included in the chapter's Creative Commons license and your intended use is not permitted by statutory regulation or exceeds the permitted use, you will need to obtain permission directly from the copyright holder.

CHAPTER 2

The Initial Puzzle: Why Governments in Dominant Party Systems Engage with the EU on Good Governance Reform, or Not

When choosing to cooperate on governance reforms, the EU and African governments have to assess their choices in light of domestic and international, short- and long-term costs and benefits that this cooperation entails. Sometimes the EU's and African governments' preferences converge and cooperation provides joint gains; sometimes, preferences diverge. The EU and African governments do not make their decisions about when, how and on what aspects of governance reforms they want to cooperate in isolation. Their decisions are deeply embedded in negotiations about development aid and interests in the wider network of bilateral economic, security and political cooperation. The costs that the EU and African governments might have to bear when deciding to cooperate on governance reforms may be outweighed by benefits reaped from other parts of the relationship.

Whereas the EU's motives for and interests in promoting governance reforms are comparatively well researched, much less is known about the factors that shape African governments' willingness to engage with the EU. This is the central concern of this book. This chapter develops an analytical grid to assess African governments' responsiveness towards EU demands to engage in governance reforms and identifies the factors that shape African governments' response strategies.

The analysis adopts a basic, rationalist framework for interaction. Actors are assumed to make decisions about cooperation consciously and to base

© The Author(s) 2018
C. Hackenesch, *The EU and China in African Authoritarian Regimes*, Governance and Limited Statehood,
https://doi.org/10.1007/978-3-319-63591-0_2

their decisions about engaging in cooperation on rational (im)material cost–benefit calculations shaped by the information available to them and by their underlying belief systems. The basic interest for both—the EU and African governments—is to remain in power, and their decisions to cooperate on governance reforms are also informed by this basic interest. EU–Africa cooperation on governance reforms can then be conceived of as a situation of strategic interaction in which both sides have a preference for a specific outcome of the cooperation and a certain amount of bargaining power to influence that outcome. This framing builds on recent research which has conceived donor–recipient relations in general (Whitfield and Fraser 2009) and the implementation of the EU's good governance instruments in particular (van Hüllen 2015) as a situation of international cooperation.

According to Keohane's (1984, 51) seminal definition, cooperation occurs 'when actors adjust their behavior to the actual or anticipated preferences of others, through a process of policy coordination'. This definition presumes that actors' behaviour is directed towards some goal(s) and that cooperation provides gains or rewards to the actors. These rewards do not have to be equally large for both actors. But cooperation emerges only if the interaction leaves both better off (or at least not worse off) than unilateral action and no agreement. Through cooperation, actors do not necessarily seek to help each other; the adjustment of policies is done in anticipation that it will bring gains for one's own situation (Milner 1992, 468).

Cooperating on governance reforms confronts the EU and African governments with three cost–benefit calculations. First, both sides assess the immediate benefits and costs that cooperation on governance reforms entails. Second, they analyse their interest in the bilateral relationship and weigh the benefits and costs of cooperating on governance reforms against those of engaging in other areas and policy fields within the context of their bilateral relations (e.g. trade, investment or security cooperation). Third, they weigh the costs and benefits of their bilateral cooperation against opportunities for cooperation offered by third actors, such as China. In this regard, cooperating on governance reforms can be described as a 'two-level game' (Putnam 1988), where the EU's and African governments' preferences for cooperation and their bargaining power are substantially shaped by the domestic costs and benefits that cooperation entails.

EU–Africa cooperation on governance reforms is highly asymmetric in several ways. The instruments and the institutional framework for cooperation are substantially shaped by the EU: the EU makes an offer for cooperation; it asks African governments to engage in political dialogue, aid policy dialogues, the implementation of governance aid or to comply with EU demands for political reforms. African governments then decide if they want to engage with the EU. Through its agenda-setting power, the EU can substantially influence the outcome of cooperation. By promoting a specific content of good governance and by using specific instruments to promote governance reforms, the EU pre-defines and structures possible sets of outcomes.

In addition, cooperation is asymmetric because the distributional consequences of cooperating on governance reforms vary widely for the EU and African governments. The EU and African governments both weigh their decisions to cooperate on governance reforms against the domestic costs and opportunities that this cooperation entails. For the EU, asking African governments to engage in governance reforms only indirectly affects domestic politics within the EU. By contrast, for African governments, cooperation on governance reforms has very direct (and potentially disruptive) consequences for their chances of staying in power. African governments' decision to engage in governance reforms may affect the stability and longevity of their rule. By cooperating with African governments on governance reforms, external actors become closely involved in domestic decision-making processes in African countries (Leininger 2010).

Moreover, EU–Africa cooperation on governance reforms is highly asymmetric, since it is closely linked to the provision of development aid. The EU has operationalised most of its instruments to support governance reforms in Africa within the context of its development policy. Asymmetric interdependence in donor–recipient relations thus allows the EU to inflict direct costs or set financial incentives to leverage in favour of cooperating on governance reforms.

Building on research on EU good governance support and authoritarian regimes, the following sections identify the factors that shape African governments' strategies to engage with the EU in governance reforms. This book argues that African governments' openness to cooperate is influenced by four main factors (Fig. 2.1): first, the EU's good governance strategies—the 'content' and the 'instruments' that the EU 'offers' for cooperation—shape African governments' willingness to engage. Second, African governments' openness to cooperate is influenced by their survival strategies. Third, African governments take into account their interests to engage with the EU 'beyond' governance reforms and notably their

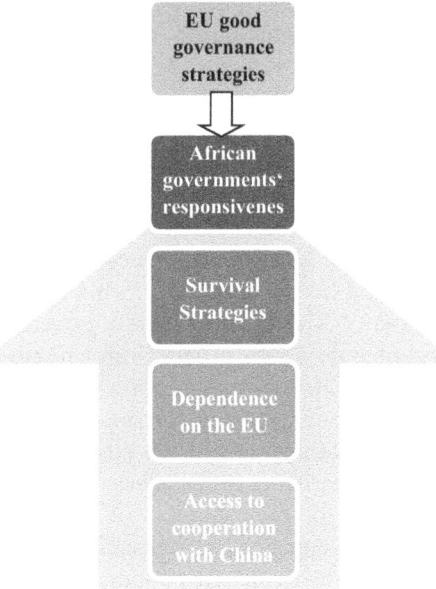

Fig. 2.1 Explaining African governments' response strategies
Source: Author's compilation

economic dependence on the EU. Fourth, African governments consider opportunities for cooperation offered by third actors, such as China. The following sections describe each of these factors and their interaction effects in more detail.

2.1 The EU's Strategies to Promote Governance Reforms

To assess the EU's strategies to promote governance reforms in African countries, this analysis builds on research that has analysed the EU's strategies for promoting governance reforms (Börzel and Risse 2009; Wetzel and Orbie 2011; Magen and McFaul 2009; Jünemann and Knodt 2007). I distinguish two dimensions of the EU's good governance strategies. First, the EU may emphasise a different content or substance of good governance and use a different channel to support governance reforms. This part of the framework draws particularly on Börzel et al. (2008a, b).

Second, I argue that the EU can choose different instruments and thereby promote reforms through either a more *conflictive* or *cooperative* strategy.

The EU's Approach: Content and Channels

The definition of 'good governance' has been intensely debated (Kohler-Koch and Rittberger 2006). One can distinguish between a broad and a narrow definition of good governance (Leftwich 1994; Börzel et al. 2008a; Robinson and Hout 2009). Some scholars and practitioners of democracy promotion have adopted the former; the development aid community and researchers working on development policy have initially advocated the latter.

Some scholars adopt a narrow understanding of good governance which is limited to the efficient and effective functioning of the state. They closely associate good governance with the management and performance of the administration and the regulatory framework of the state. Principles such as efficiency and effectiveness, predictability, transparency, accountability, the level of corruption or sound financial management constitute important elements of this understanding (Conzelmann 2003; Faust 2004; Andrews 2013). This narrow definition has been strongly influenced by development policy, and notably by the World Bank (Kaufmann et al. 1999; Fuster 1998). The EU could choose to promote the transparency of decision-making processes, the fight against corruption, the strengthening of public financial management, and civil service and administrative reforms, or it could support the capacities of government institutions to improve the functioning of the administration.

Other authors working in the field of democratisation and external democracy promotion adopt a broader definition with a stronger normative dimension relating to the input dimension of 'good' governance, such as the respect for human rights and democracy (Burnell 2000; Santiso 2003). In their understanding, good governance also entails political aspects, and democratic structures are perceived as key components of good governance. Following this broader understanding, the EU could seek to promote competitive democratic politics, including the strengthening of electoral regimes, political and civil rights, the separation of powers, and horizontal and vertical accountability.

The content of EU good governance policies can be differentiated according to two dimensions of legitimacy formulated by Scharpf (1999)—input and output legitimacy. Output legitimacy corresponds to the narrow (regulatory) understanding of governance, whereas input legitimacy is equated with the wider (political) concept of good governance predominant in the fields of democratisation and democracy promotion studies.

In addition to the content of EU good governance policies, the EU may use different channels of influence and target state or non-state actors to promote governance reforms. In using the intergovernmental channel, the EU could seek to alter the preferences of the target government to introduce reform processes by manipulating their cost–benefit calculation, or it could aim at changing the target government's preferences for achieving outcomes by socialising them into new norms through processes of social learning and persuasion. The transnational approach, in contrast, seeks to empower non-state actors in relation to their governments (Schimmelfennig 2007).

Combining the different contents and channels the EU may use, this study follows Börzel et al. (2008b), who identify four ideal-type approaches on how the EU can promote governance reforms (Table 2.1). On the one hand, the EU may place stronger emphasis on either input- or output-related reform goals. On the other hand, it may either target the intergovernmental channel (state actors) or the transnational one (non-state actors).

The first approach of *effective government* addresses the intergovernmental channel and seeks to promote output-oriented objectives, focusing on the administrative core of good governance. The EU could seek to improve governance by enhancing the capacities of the government and its administration or by improving the transparency of decision-making processes. The second approach of *effective governance* also places emphasis on output-oriented reform goals. But it either includes non-state actors in the implementation process to produce better policies by pooling resources and increasing acceptance, or tackles the strengthening of non-state organisations that help to better implement policies. The third approach of *democratic government* again relies on the intergovernmental channel. While promoting input-oriented objectives, the EU targets the

Table 2.1 Four approaches of external good governance support

	Output legitimacy	Input legitimacy
Intergovernmental	Effective government	Democratic government
Transnational	Effective governance	Democratic governance

Source: Börzel et al. (2008b)

state to make it establish and safeguard a public sphere where interests can be articulated and aggregated. The EU could, for instance, promote civil and political rights by supporting the legal framework or independent state institutions that hold the government accountable. The fourth approach of *democratic governance* combines the transnational channel with input-oriented reform objectives. In line with this approach, the EU could support the capacities of non-state actors to empower them to improve the democratic quality of decision-making processes and hold the government accountable.

The EU's Instruments: Cooperative or Confrontational Strategy?

External actors can also seek to impact governance reforms in third countries through different mechanisms and types of instrument. Studies on democracy promotion, external Europeanisation and aid conditionality have suggested various typologies to classify the EU's instruments to promote governance reforms, depending on their different logics of action, mechanisms of influence and different schools of compliance and Europeanisation research (Schimmelfennig and Sedelmeier 2005; Magen and Morlino 2009; Magen and McFaul 2009; Börzel et al. 2008b).

External actors can seek to promote governance reforms through positive or negative *conditionality*, linking material or non-material incentives to the implementation of governance reforms. Conditionality can be used ex-post (i.e. reductions in development aid in response to deteriorations in governance) or ex-ante (i.e. in the EU enlargement process). External actors may use various forms of political or aid policy *dialogues* with a view to changing the preferences of the government or non-state actors in the target country through strategies of persuasion and social learning. External actors may seek to support governance reforms by transferring technical and financial *assistance* to support the human, administrative and financial capacities of state or non-state actors in the target country.

For analytical purposes, and with respect to different underlying mechanisms of influence and logics of action, the literature on EU external governance and democracy promotion generally differentiates between conditionality, dialogue and aid, and often analyses only one of them, for instance the impact of democracy aid on political reforms. In practice, however, external actors generally combine these instruments in different ways. The EU's instruments can respectively be conceived on a continuum ranging from a 'confrontational' to a 'cooperative-rewarding' strategy (Fig. 2.2).

Fig. 2.2 The EU's good governance instruments: between confrontation and rewards
Source: Author's compilation

At one end of the spectrum, external actors can adopt a *confrontational* strategy and merely rely on aid, trade or other forms of sanctions, for instance in response to serious violations of human rights or a *coup d'état*.

Beyond a confrontational strategy and the usage of sanctions, external actors can combine dialogue, governance aid and conditionality in various ways. A cooperative strategy can take different forms, depending on the combination of dialogue, technical and financial assistance, and conditionality that external actors choose. In the case of a *cooperative-conflictive* strategy, the EU would combine governance aid and dialogue with strong negative incentives such as budget-support suspensions to exert pressure on the target government. In the case of a *cooperative-critical* strategy, the EU would combine aid and dialogue with smaller 'sticks' such as critical public statements (shaming) or withholding governance aid to exert pressure on the government. External actors could decide to adopt a purely *cooperative* strategy and rely merely on dialogue and governance aid to promote reforms. Finally, the EU could adopt a *cooperative-rewarding* strategy and combine dialogue and governance aid with positive incentives ('carrots'), such as affirmative public statements or aid modalities such as budget support.

Combining the EU's 'approach' and its 'instruments' allows us to develop a comprehensive framework to analyse the EU's strategies to support governance reforms in individual African countries and over time. The EU could choose to put a strong emphasis on promoting either a narrow or a comprehensive governance agenda. It could choose to merely work with governments or to empower non-governmental actors *vis-à-vis* the government. In addition, the EU could choose not only to rely on dialogue and governance aid but also to combine these instruments with positive or negative incentives to foster an active cooperation on governance reforms. The costs and benefits that the narrow or comprehensive agenda entail for African governments would thus be exacerbated by the EU's usage of confrontational or rewarding governance instruments.

2.2 African Governments' Responsiveness

African governments can respond to the EU's strategies in different ways. First, with regard to the content or substance of the EU's approach, African governments may be more or less willing to engage in a comprehensive or narrow governance agenda. In cases where the EU seeks to promote output- as well as input-related reforms, African governments may be willing to cooperate on a comprehensive agenda, they may be willing to engage only in reforms that improve the effectiveness of government institutions or they may not be willing to cooperate with the EU on governance reforms at all. African governments could be more or less willing to accept EU support for non-state actors and the EU's usage of the transnational channel. Second, African governments can choose to adopt different strategies towards different types of instrument that the EU seeks to employ. For instance, governments may be willing to engage in dialogue (political dialogue or aid policy dialogues), they may be willing to commit to concrete governance reform objectives in exchange for material incentives (positive conditionality), but they may not be willing to cooperate on the implementation of governance aid or vice versa.

African governments' responsiveness towards EU good governance instruments can be conceived on a continuum, ranging from active and willing engagement to indifference. Classifying 'indifference' is relatively straightforward and would entail that African governments do not engage in dialogue, would not agree to implement governance aid and do not comply with EU conditionality. In the case of indifference, African governments would not be willing to engage either in a broad or narrow governance agenda. It is more difficult, however, to discern different forms of 'cooperativeness'. For reasons of simplicity, the analysis will distinguish between reluctant and active cooperation. Active cooperation would entail that African governments are willing to cooperate with the EU on the entire governance agenda that the EU seeks to promote and across all governance instruments that it seeks to apply. Reluctant engagement would entail that governments are willing to engage with the EU only in parts of the agenda that the EU seeks to promote and only in some of the cooperative instruments that the EU applies.

Interaction Effects: EU Good Governance Strategies and African Governments' Responsiveness

The study starts off with a simplified assumption that cooperation on governance reforms is costly for African authoritarian regimes. External support for governance reforms is generally assumed to promote political liberalisation and thereby potentially challenges the propensity of African governments to persist in power (Wright 2009; Cornell 2012). Against this background, one would expect that the more the EU promotes a broad 'content' that seeks to support not only the effectiveness of decision-making processes but also their democratic quality and the more the EU seeks to empower non-state actors in holding the government accountable, the less willing African governments should be to engage with the EU. Further, the more the EU puts pressure on African governments and uses a conflictive approach to support reforms, the less willing African governments should be to engage with the EU.

EU–Africa cooperation on governance reforms is an interactive and iterative situation (Table 2.2). Thus, if the EU narrows or broadens its good governance approach over time, we would expect that governments in African authoritarian regimes become more or less willing to cooperate. For instance, if the EU decides to broaden its approach from a narrow to a comprehensive governance agenda, African governments should become less willing to engage, as reforms geared towards democratic government and governance generate more costs for authoritarian regimes. If the EU narrows its approach and promotes mainly effective government, African governments would be expected to become more willing to engage with the EU since effective government institutions may also be in the interest

Table 2.2 Interaction effects between EU good governance strategies and African governments' response

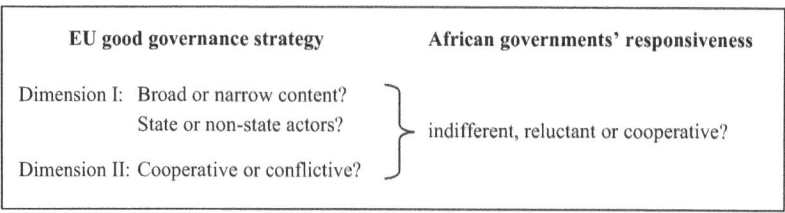

Source: Author's compilation

of African authoritarian regimes. Similarly, if the EU decides to adopt a more conflictive strategy and uses negative conditionality, this should prompt African governments to become more reluctant to engage with the EU. If the EU decides to adopt a more cooperative strategy and to provide positive additional rewards to the governments, this should induce them to become more willing to engage with the EU.

The EU's good governance strategies are only one factor that shapes African governments' willingness to cooperate on governance reforms. In order to develop more specific assumptions on the conditions under which governments are willing to engage, we therefore need to open the 'black box' of domestic politics of African authoritarian regimes.

2.3 Survival Strategies of Governments in Dominant party Regimes

When deciding if they want to cooperate, African governments assess the costs and benefits that the EU's offer entails. Political leaders in dominant party regimes are conceived as rational and self-interested actors seeking to maximise their chances of remaining in power (not too different from their counterparts in democracies). The threat of losing power, and opportunities to increase their chances of staying in power, is thus the basic factor that motivates authoritarian governments to cooperate with the EU on governance reforms. Understanding the costs they want to avoid and the benefits they seek helps to explain their openness to engage with the EU.

Survival Strategies

Autocratic leaders do not remain in office through competitive elections, where they would need to secure support from the majority of the electorate. They therefore always fear being ousted. Put simply, domestic politics in authoritarian regimes can be conceived as a political 'game' between the leadership, members of the ruling coalition (i.e. the ruling party and the military) and the broader society (Bueno de Mesquita et al. 2003). Dominant party regimes have a relatively broad ruling coalition, compared to other autocracies. Whereas military regimes primarily rely on the military, or monarchies on the royal family, political leaders in dominant party systems, instead, have to secure support from members of the ruling party, the military and security forces, and sometimes also strategic business sectors.

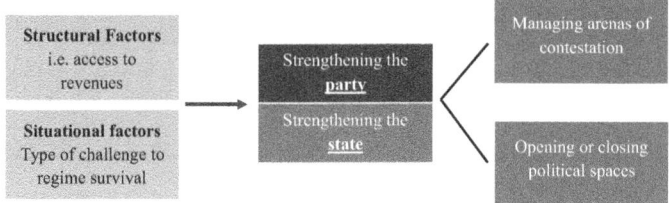

Fig. 2.3 African governments' survival strategies meet EU good governance strategies
Source: Author's compilation

Political leaders in dominant party regimes have at least three basic strategies at hand to increase their chances of retaining power. They can invest in strengthening party or state institutions. They can use arenas of political contestation such as elections or parliaments to mobilise support. They can rely on coercion to open or close political spaces (see Fig. 2.3 for an overview). Research on authoritarianism often examines only one of these strategies and investigates variation across different types of authoritarian regimes. The objective here is to bring these three strategies together and to specify them for dominant party systems.

The Foundation of Political Survival: Strengthening the Party or the State
Political leaders in dominant party systems need strong states or strong parties. Strong state institutions or strong parties are instrumental in effectively managing arenas of contestation and opening and closing political spaces to increase their chances of staying in power. Political leaders in dominant party regimes can decide to particularly invest in building strong political parties, they can invest in building strong states or they can use a mixture of the two. In dominant party systems, the ruling party often fuses with formal state institutions. Ruling parties may almost substitute state functions or vice versa. Those political leaders that have neither strong ruling parties nor strong states are often quickly removed (Levitsky and Way 2010).

Recent research on autocratic regimes has often focused on the role of the ruling party in enhancing regime stability. Political parties in authoritarian regimes provide mechanisms to manage leadership succession (Geddes 2006) and intraelite conflicts (Brownlee 2007). They allow for distributing spoils to regime supporters (Magaloni 2006) and coercing opponents. Moreover, political parties help to develop a support base that the political leadership can mobilise, for instance in case of popular uprising (Geddes 2006). Via access to financial revenues, career opportunities or other perks, the party gives its members a stake in the regime. Through trade unions, youth and women's organisations or cooperatives, well-institutionalised ruling parties extend their influence to a large segment of society (Geddes 2006; Magaloni 2006). Empirical studies suggest that these institutional mechanisms make dominant party regimes more durable than other forms of authoritarian regimes such as monarchies or military regimes (Smith 2005; Geddes 2006; Svolik 2012). Those regimes with relatively strong political parties are found to be most durable (Smith 2005) and often among those economically most successful (Bueno de Mesquita et al. 2003; Faust 2007; Gehlbach and Keefer 2011).

Autocrats can also decide to invest in state institutions. Strong states are one essential factor in securing the stability and longevity of authoritarian rule (Huntington 1969; Levitsky and Way 2010, 57). Authoritarian state institutions may help governments to effectively coerce and repress political opponents. Governments invest in the security apparatus and boost capacities of the army, the police, paramilitary forces or intelligence services. According to Levitsky and Way (2010), the cohesive capacity of authoritarian states, defined as the level of compliance within the state apparatus and the reach of the state, is critical to effectively using coercion. Furthermore, governments also use state institutions as an instrument to provide public goods or to coopt regime opponents. Political leaders may decide to strengthen public administration and the effectiveness of bureaucracies, raise domestic revenues, and improve public goods provision. Modern, rational-legal and meritocratic bureaucracies in the Weberian sense allow for effectively formulating and implementing policies needed to generate economic growth, raise taxes or develop effective healthcare and education systems. On the other hand, governments may use state institutions to distribute perks and spoils. Regime opponents may be coopted by granting access to positions in the government administration. Political leaders may use state institutions to provide spoils to their support group, for instance, their ethnic group or people from their home town.

Managing Political Survival: Effectively Controlling Arenas of Contestation Such as Elections, Parliaments and Courts
Dominant party regimes are not fully closed, but allow for some (albeit limited) political contestation. They establish formal democratic institutions such as elections, parliaments or courts that strongly resemble their

equivalents in democratic regimes. Even though these institutions fulfil different functions than in democratic regimes, effectively managing arenas of contestation is important for incumbents to secure their position in power (Gandhi and Przeworski 2007; Gandhi 2008; Schedler 2009).

Elections are probably most important in this regard. Even though elections in authoritarian regimes are not free and fair, winning elections with a high voter turnout and an overwhelming majority is vital for political leaders (Magaloni 2006). Elections constitute important points in time when opponents inside or outside the ruling elite can directly challenge the incumbent. Opposition parties may seek to mobilise mass movements, for instance if they identify underlying schisms within the ruling elite that they can exploit (Brownlee 2007). Defecting members of the ruling party may decide to use elections to openly challenge the incumbent, for instance during periods of economic crisis (Reuter and Gandhi 2011). In addition, elections allow incumbents to enhance regime stability. Overwhelming electoral victories signal to regime supporters that it pays off to remain loyal to the leadership as the opposition presents no viable alternative. Overwhelming victories also signal to regime opponents that their chances of gaining power are limited (Magaloni 2006, 7ff; Magaloni and Kricheli 2010, 129f). Moreover, election results give some indication about the popular support of the ruling party and about the regional and social distribution of its support base, allowing it to reward supporters with access to government funds and to punish defectors by restricting access to spoils (Magaloni 2006, 9). Political leaders may therefore decide to invest heavily in election campaigns.

Beyond elections, governments in dominant party regimes may decide to use parliaments to solicit cooperation from the ruling party and reduce threats from opposition outside of the ruling elite (Gandhi and Przeworski 2007). Parliaments may provide a forum for the government to grant policy concessions to opposition groups in exchange for regime support (Gandhi and Przeworski 2007). Parliamentary seats may also be allotted to secure the support of members of the ruling elite. Political leaders in autocratic regimes may further invest in the judiciary to promote their interests. Moustafa and Ginsburg (2008, 4), for instance, show how courts are used to strengthen social control and sideline regime opponents: they may be used to promote 'legal' legitimacy; they may facilitate trade and investments; and they may improve compliance of the bureaucracy and elite cohesion.

Managing Political Survival: Opening and Closing Political Spaces
Authoritarian leaders rely on different forms of coercion to open or close political spaces (Wintrobe 2001). Coercion is used as an instrument of sanction against individuals or organisations to reduce threats from the opposition and reinforce their grip on power (see Davenport 2007, for an overview). Following Levitsky and Way (2010) one can distinguish between 'high-intensity' and 'low-intensity' coercion. Dominant party systems are generally found to be less likely to use repression than other types of authoritarian regimes since they depend more strongly on the loyalty of broader segments of society (Davenport 2007; Escribà-Folch and Wright 2015).

Dominant party regimes can be expected to use *high-intensity coercion* to respond to mass protests and challenges from the opposition outside of the ruling elite. Prominent examples of high-intensity coercion would include the killing of protesters in Tiananmen Square in China, in 1989, or more recently in Tahrir Square in Egypt. High-intensity coercion is costly for authoritarian regimes, both economically and politically (Wintrobe 2001; Conrad 2011). It may have medium-term negative effects on economic development as citizens refuse to engage in economic activities and international investments decline in a politically insecure environment (Bueno de Mesquita and Smith 2010). In addition, high-intensity coercion requires autocrats to substantially invest in the security forces to secure their loyalty (Wintrobe 2001). Dominant party regimes would be expected to use high-intensity coercion as a measure of last resort only in situations when the leadership is in a particularly insecure position, facing very strong challenges from the opposition.

By contrast, dominant party regimes can be expected to generally rely on *low-intensity coercion* to gradually close political spaces. Low-intensity coercion can take various forms. Authoritarian regimes may use a variety of formal and legalised or informal strategies to intimidate and harass civil society organisations, and reduce the freedom of the media, opposition parties or individual regime critics (Davenport 2007; Levitsky and Way 2010). Low-intensity coercion may be targeted directly at defecting members of the elite in order to limit their chances of challenging the incumbent. For instance, anticorruption campaigns may be used to marginalise party members who foster a split in the party. On the other hand, low-intensity coercion may be targeted at the broader society to limit the opportunities of defectors to mobilise mass support. For instance, if former party members seek to challenge the incumbent at the ballot box, reductions in press freedom and spaces for opposition parties to campaign may limit the ability of defectors to mobilise support. If low-intensity coercion is successful, it reduces the need to rely on high-intensity coercion (Levitsky and Way 2010).

Structural and Situational Factors That Impact on the Choice of Survival Strategies

Several factors influence political leaders' decisions to use a specific type of strategy to increase their chances of remaining in power. Structural factors constrain the basic choices of political leaders to rely on a certain strategy. For instance, strong parties emerge only under very specific circumstances: conditions related to the founding moment of the regime may considerably shape the incentive for political leaders to invest in party building (Brownlee 2007; Smith 2005). The presence (or absence) of access to easy revenues from natural resources is found to affect the willingness of political leaders to invest in strong parties and effective states (Smith 2005; Ross 1999) and to use coercion and cooptation. Moreover, research on East Asian developmental states has illustrated that not only does access to revenue shape the willingness of political leaders to invest in strong states, but the presence of external security threats has also been identified as a necessary condition for strong state institutions to emerge (Doner et al. 2005).

Furthermore, a leadership's political survival can be challenged by situational factors. Notably, opponents from outside or inside the ruling elite can confront the incumbent at a specific point in time. Challenges to regime survival constitute defining moments in the life of ruling parties and can induce substantial changes in survival strategies (Reuter and Gandhi 2011; Conrad 2011). First, political leaders can be under threat from groups *outside* of the ruling elite, such as opposition parties and mass movements (Ulfelder 2005; Geddes 2006; Gandhi and Przeworski 2007). In Africa, for instance, mass movements and civil society protests played an important role in regime liberalisations and transitions in the late 1980s and early 1990s (Bratton and Van de Walle 1997). Second, persons *inside* the ruling elite, such as individual members or factions of the ruling party, can decide to defect and to challenge the leadership by presenting themselves as a political alternative (Magaloni 2006; Reuter and Gandhi 2011; Svolik 2012). Finally, officials of the party or security forces may decide to defect without directly attempting to challenge the leadership. If that happens, it signals that the regime is weak, possibly prompting further erosion of the support coalition, which may eventually result in mass mobilisation and opposition.

In summary, governments in dominant party systems can decide to invest in the party or the state. They need to control arenas of contestation and can decide to open or close political spaces to strengthen their grip on power. Strong state institutions or strong ruling parties are instrumental for governments in dominant party systems to effectively manage arenas of contestation and use coercion to open or close political spaces (Fig. 2.3). Whether the government decides to invest more strongly in the state or in the party and how it uses arenas of contestation and coercion is influenced by a set of structural and situational factors.

EU Good Governance Strategies Meet Dominant Party Regimes

We assume that cooperation on governance reforms can generate *costs* as well as *benefits* for authoritarian governments. Depending on which survival strategies governments use, EU demands to engage in governance reforms can converge or diverge with authoritarian governments' preferences. The size of the costs and benefits that cooperation involves can vary significantly across countries and over time.

This basic proposition that cooperation on governance reforms can generate not only costs but also benefits contrasts with some of the research on good governance support. Some start by assuming that the implementation of governance instruments mainly entails *costs* for authoritarian governments. Studies that focus on the 'input dimension' of good governance and analyse, for instance, the effect of democracy aid on political reforms usually start by assuming that democracy aid fosters political liberalisation and thereby entails costs for the target government (Wright 2009). Governments in relatively stable authoritarian regimes with good chances of remaining in power are then expected to accept some democracy aid as they can afford higher levels of political liberalisation without losing power (Cornell 2012). Moreover, studies focusing on the 'output dimension' of good governance argue that most target governments accept aid geared towards promoting effective institutions merely as 'signals – to garner short-term support from the international community' (Andrews 2013, 215). Governments' interest in receiving development aid, rather than a genuine interest in engaging in governance reforms is identified as the main driver for cooperation (Andrews 2013).

The previous section developed a comprehensive picture of possible survival strategies. African governments' cooperation with the EU on governance reforms touches only upon parts, but not all, of these strategies.

Recall from Sect. 2.1 that EU good governance strategies are directed towards supporting the effectiveness of government institutions or the democratic quality of decision-making processes; moreover, the EU can strengthen the capacities of non-state actors or empower them in holding the government accountable. Cooperation with the EU on the implementation of governance instruments may therefore be relevant for (a) building strong and effective state institutions; (b) managing arenas of contestation such as elections, parliaments or courts; and (c) open or close political spaces (Fig. 2.3). On the other hand, since the EU mainly engages with African governments and the state more broadly, the EU's good governance strategies have limited relevance for political leaders' decisions to build strong ruling parties. Under what conditions does cooperation with the EU on governance reforms then involve costs or benefits for authoritarian governments (Table 2.3)?

Table 2.3 The costs and benefits of cooperating on governance reforms

Survival strategies	*Costs and benefits of cooperation*
I. Building effective states	
The more governments use and invest in strengthening state institutions to generate economic growth and provide *public goods*...	...the higher the *benefits* to cooperate with the EU
The more governments use formal state institutions mainly to *distribute private goods and spoils*....	...the higher the *costs* to cooperate with the EU
II. Managing arenas of political contestation	
The more governments are confident about winning elections without significant fraud...	...the higher the *benefits* to cooperate with the EU
The more governments are afraid of facing challenges from the opposition during elections...	...the higher the *costs* to cooperate with the EU
III. Opening or closing political spaces	
The more governments decide to *open political spaces* to *prevent* opposition challenges...	...the higher the *benefits* to cooperate with the EU
The more governments decide to use low-intensity coercion to *gradually close political spaces* to *prevent* opposition challenges...	...the lower the *costs* to cooperate with the EU
The more governments decide to use high-intensity coercion to *close political spaces* to *respond to imminent threats* to regime survival...	...the higher the *costs* to cooperate with the EU

Source: Author's compilation

Building Effective States

For governments that decide to invest in building effective states geared towards promoting economic growth and public goods provisions, cooperation with the EU on governance reforms can be beneficial. Cooperating with the EU may help governments to improve access to domestic tax revenues or to make policy formulation and implementation more effective. EU support for public administration and civil service reform, public financial management and the rule of law are thus expected to resonate well with the preferences of the government. Moreover, even EU assistance to strengthen capacities of non-state actors that support the government in providing basic public services can converge with the government's preferences.

By contrast, authoritarian regimes that have limited interest in building effective states, because they mainly use the state to distribute rents and spoils, have few incentives to cooperate with the EU on governance reforms. EU support geared towards improving the transparency of public finances, anticorruption policies and civil service or public administration reforms run counter to the government's attempts to use government institutions to distribute spoils. In these cases, cooperation with the EU on governance reforms is thus expected to be costly.

Managing Arenas of Political Contestation

EU support geared towards elections, parliaments or courts may also entail costs or benefits. Cooperating with the EU may bolster the external legitimacy of the authoritarian regime;[1] EU technical assistance may help African governments to actually conduct elections. However, EU assistance may also be exploited by the opposition and bolster its position *vis-à-vis* the government.

One would expect that the type of challenge to regime survival that the government faces ahead of elections is an important factor that mitigates the size of the costs and benefits that cooperation entails, and thus African governments' interests in engaging with the EU on elections. Governments that face little challenge from opponents and that can win elections overwhelmingly and relatively easily without resorting to significant fraud are likely to have an interest in cooperating with the EU. In these cases, EU technical assistance may provide important benefits to support the election process: EU public statements after the elections or findings from election observation missions may boost domestic and international legitimacy. In contrast, in cases where the opposition or defecting members of the elite use elections to directly challenge the ruling party, cooperating with the EU may be costly. The EU's critical public statements and its technical assistance to support the media or civil society to monitor the election campaign and election process may be exploited by the opposition and used to further challenge the incumbent.

Opening or Closing Political Spaces
For governments that decide to open or close political spaces, cooperating with the EU on governance reforms may also generate costs and benefits. Cooperation with the EU is likely to accrue some benefits in cases where governments decide to open political spaces to strengthen input legitimacy. The EU may extend technical assistance needed, for instance, to support the media or civil society organisations. Cooperation with the EU may provide additional external legitimacy during periods of political openings.

Instead, for governments that decide to use high- or low-intensity coercion to close political spaces, cooperation with the EU on governance reforms is expected to generate costs. However, the size of these costs varies depending on the measures governments use and the type of challenge to regime survival that authoritarian governments face.

In situations where governments use high-intensity coercion to counter mass opposition, engagement with the EU in governance reforms is costly and the government is least likely to engage. In case of mass opposition, even small steps towards liberalisation and ceasing coercive measures may immediately threaten regime survival. In this context, engaging with the EU in political dialogue, the implementation of governance aid or other EU instruments geared towards supporting governance reforms would be particularly risky for the government.

In cases where governments use low-intensity coercion to respond to party splits or reduce challenges from defecting members of the ruling elite, cooperation on governance reforms with the EU is also risky. Yet, engagement in governance reforms is less challenging here than in cases of mass mobilisation. Finally, if members of the ruling elite defect but do not choose to openly challenge the leadership, the government has more leeway to engage with the EU in governance reforms. While erosion of the ruling elite may signal that the regime is weak, only in the medium- to long-term may opponents seek to exploit this weakness, run in elections themselves, align with opposition groups and mobilise mass opposition.

2.4 African Economic Dependence on the EU

The higher the costs of engaging with the EU in governance reforms, the more African governments take into account their dependence on the EU when deciding if they want to cooperate with the EU. African governments' dependence on the EU is shaped by their vulnerability to EU pressure and actions taken by the EU. According to Keohane and Nye's (1987) seminal definition, 'dependence means a state of being determined or significantly affected by external forces'.

African governments thus weigh costs stemming from the implementation of governance instruments against benefits offered by the EU in the form of development aid or trade and investments. Moreover, they assess how vulnerable the EU is to actions taken by them. The more dependent African governments are on the EU, the more likely they are to cooperate. The less dependent African governments are on the EU, the less likely they are to cooperate if this entails risks for regime survival. While this argument is relatively straightforward, the more difficult (and largely empirical) question is to define how dependent African countries are on the EU.

Dependence on Aid and Other Official Flows

If the EU provides important volumes of external finance, African governments may be willing to engage in governance reforms, even in cases where these reforms are costly. The higher the government's dependence on development aid as a source of domestic revenue and the higher the EU's share in total aid flows to the country, the more willing the government should be to engage with the EU.

African governments may use development aid and loans to divert them to regime supporters. Development aid allows the government to free its own resources and to use them to coopt strategic groups or to avoid taxation of those societal groups that are important for the government to remain in office. Empirical studies find, for instance, that foreign aid increases government spending while reducing government revenue and efforts to raise taxes (Remmer 2004). All types of foreign aid affect the opportunity costs of autocratic leaders to modify the allocation of their own resources. Regardless of whether or not aid is channelled through projects or direct budget support, it is a form of external finance that frees up government resources. Governments can (but do not necessarily do) use these resources to coopt regime opponents.

We need to add several points to this basic picture. African governments assess the short- and longer-term benefits of cooperating with the EU. First, some aid modalities give the government considerably more discretionary power to allocate resources according to its preferences. The government's propensity to free domestic resources in case the EU or other donors provide food aid is considerably lower than in the case of direct budget aid, at least in the short-term. Second, some forms of aid and sectors to which aid is allocated may be much closer to the government's preferences than other sectors, freeing up more domestic resources in the short-term. Third, if the EU decides to stop or withhold development aid, the costs for the African government differ depending on the modalities by which aid is provided. For instance, withholding budget support funds that the government uses to pay the salaries of civil servants may be more detrimental in the very short-term than withholding project aid allocated to constructing rural roads.

Dependence on Trade and Investments

Access to trade and investments set direct and more indirect incentives for African governments to cooperate with the EU. For many African countries, trade taxes account for a large share of overall tax revenues. African governments have often maintained a strong control over strategic export sectors. In addition, many African countries still have only very few export commodities, and their export markets are not very diversified (Di John 2010). The EU as a whole has been the largest trading partner for many countries. Trade with the EU may generate important tax revenues for African governments or revenues for societal groups whose support is particularly important for the government. If export goods cannot easily be shifted to other markets, the vulnerability of the government to potential actions taken by the EU is high.

In addition to trade, direct investments may have direct and more indirect effects. They have an indirect effect if they help to promote economic growth, giving the government more resources that it can use to buy support. If the population associates economic growth with the government, this boosts its legitimacy. Direct investments may also have more direct effects. Investments in strategic sectors, for instance resource extraction, increase government revenues. Direct investments may also create important sources of income for societal groups on which the government relies to remain in power. Foreign direct investments in Africa have been small

Table 2.4 How economic dependence on the EU affects African governments' willingness to cooperate on governance reforms

		Dependence on aid and other official flows	
		High	*Low*
Dependence on trade and investments	High	Incentive to cooperate on governance reforms is **high**	Incentive to cooperate on governance reforms is **medium**
	Low	Incentive to cooperate on governance reforms is **medium**	Incentive to cooperate on governance reforms is **low**

Source: Author's compilation

compared to other regions, but European and North American companies have traditionally been the major sources of direct investments (AfDB, OECD and UNDP 2016, 52ff). The dominance of European companies has been particularly pronounced in some (often resource-rich) countries, often as a result of colonial ties.

We can conclude that through aid, trade and investments, the EU potentially has a strong leverage to set incentives for African governments to cooperate on governance reforms (Table 2.4). The higher the economic dependence on the EU, the more likely the government is willing to engage in governance reforms. However, some notes of caution need to be sounded. All other things being equal, countries that depend on the EU in terms of aid but not trade and investments may have much stronger incentives to cooperate with the EU on governance reforms than countries that depend on the EU in terms of trade and investments but not aid. Empirical evidence suggests that the EU does not condition access to aid and trade in similar ways to governance reforms. For instance, the Cotonou Agreement allows the EU to suspend aid and trade preferences in case of fundamental human rights violations or disrespect of democratic principles (Article 96 of the Cotonou Agreement). Yet, in practice, the EU has mostly used the suspension of aid rather than trade to sanction a breach of the essential element clause Portela (2010).

2.5 The Rise of China: What Effect?

What happens if China becomes a major partner for African countries? Similar to their cooperation with the EU, governments in dominant party regimes also define their interests in engaging with China taking into

Table 2.5 Cooperation with China: what effect on African governments' willingness to cooperate on governance reforms?

		Does cooperation with China reduce economic dependence on the EU?	
		Yes	No
China engaging in survival strategies?	Yes	*Strong effect*	*Medium effect*
	No	*Medium effect*	*No effect*

Source: Author's compilation

account their domestic survival strategies. Economic cooperation with China may reduce African governments' dependence on the EU and thus shape African governments' incentives to cooperate with the EU on governance reforms. China may also offer to cooperate with African governments on shaping their survival strategies, which may equally affect their willingness to engage with the EU (see Table 2.5). China is obviously only one of the emering powers and its engagement with African countries is part of a broader power shift. However, China is by far the most important actor in terms of its economic weight and it is the only actor that potentially provides an alternative development model.

Cooperating with China: Reducing Economic Dependence on the EU?

The basic argument on how the rise of China shapes African governments' openness to engage with the EU in governance reforms is again relatively straightforward. China may provide African governments with access to additional sources of development aid, official flows, trade and investments, thereby reducing the vulnerability of African governments to EU pressure. The more that cooperation with China reduces African countries' economic dependence on the EU, the less likely African governments are to engage with the EU in governance reforms. The much more difficult issue is assessing how and to what extent China affects African governments' dependence on the EU. To measure the relevance of China compared to the EU, one needs to compare the structure of European and Chinese cooperation with African countries against the background of the domestic incentives for African countries to cooperate with the EU and China.

The extent to which aid and official flows from China reduce African governments' dependence on EU aid hinges on several factors. The first factor is the size of Chinese official flows. All other things being equal, one can assume that the more a country has access to official flows from China, the less the African government is willing to cooperate with the EU on governance reforms. The modalities through which official flows are provided and the sectors to which they are provided are a second factor shaping African governments' willingness to engage with the EU. The more China's official flows match the preferences of African governments in terms of modalities and sectors to which they are provided, the less likely the government is to cooperate with the EU. Lastly, the timing of when China starts providing substantial official flows to African countries should have an impact on African governments' vulnerability to EU pressure. If China provides important volumes of official flows at a point in time when the EU attempts to use development aid funds to put pressure on African governments, they can be expected to be less willing to comply with EU demands.

Similarly, the extent to which access to Chinese trade and investments reduces African countries' dependence on the EU depends on the scale and structure of economic cooperation. The diversification of export markets and the opening of markets for new export goods as a result of access to trade with China impact on African governments' interests in cooperating with the EU. Growing trade with China may provide significant windfall profits for African governments. Cooperation with China may create business opportunities for societal groups whose support is crucial for African governments to remain in power.

In addition, if China significantly increases its direct investments in African countries, this may create opportunities for countries that have previously had very little access to foreign direct investments. Or it may diversify sources of direct investments and reduce the dominance of European companies.

China: Alternative Support for Survival Strategies?

African governments analyse the benefits and costs of cooperating with the EU on governance reforms not only in light of their economic dependence on the EU and potential shifts in dependence due to access to cooperation with China. African governments also take into account alternative offers to engage in their survival strategies. The Chinese government does not embrace the promotion of 'good governance' as an objective in its external relations. In contrast, its foreign policy discourse highlights principles of non-interference, projects a traditional understanding of national sovereignty and explicitly rejects the promotion of a development 'model'. Yet, China might still engage with African governments in their survival strategies because of China's own economic and political interests or in response to requests from African governments.

As in the case of cooperation with the EU, African governments assess how cooperation with China fits with their domestic survival strategies. Recall the panoply of strategies and institutions that governments in African dominant party regimes can use to secure their position in power (Sect. 2.3). The Chinese government could provide assistance that resembles EU good governance strategies and targets similar dimensions of African governments' survival strategies as the EU. China could, for instance, assist in improving the capacities and effectiveness of government institutions through training courses or supplying office equipment. China's economic interests may lead the Chinese government to provide technical assistance to address some of the side effects stemming from growing economic interdependencies with African countries. For example, growing Chinese investments may prompt a closer engagement with anti-corruption bodies or support to African countries' regulatory frameworks.

On the other hand, China could also engage with African governments on elements of their survival strategies that the EU does not target. In contrast to the EU, China may engage with African ruling parties. Some have argued that the introduction of inner-party checks and balances, the institutionalisation of leadership succession and perfomance-based incentive systems for party cadres constitute important factors that contributed to sustained economic growth in China (Keefer 2007; Zhao 2010; Gehlbach and Keefer 2011). Despite numerous differences between the Chinese Communist Party (CCP) and African ruling parties, cooperation on inner-party reforms might still be very attractive. Particularly for those African political leaders who seek to substantially invest in reforming and strengthening their ruling parties, China could become an interesting cooperation partner. For China, party-to-party cooperation may be interesting from a political as well as economic perspective. High-level visits by party officials can be one instrument to intensify political relations, for example, with those countries where economic cooperation is limited. Regular dialogue between ruling parties may give important insights into domestic political dynamics in African countries. Party-to-party relations may also open channels to establish and promote business relations.

Very little research exists on China's cooperation with African governments that relates to these governments' survival strategies. Two preliminary propositions can be made. First, the stronger the Chinese economic and political interests in cooperating with individual African countries, the more likely China is to engage with African countries in elements of their survival strategies—either by request of the African government or to ease growing economic interdependencies. Second, the more the Chinese experience with economic and political reforms 'resonates' with African domestic contexts and African governments' survival strategies, the more China's support affects African governments' willingness to cooperate with the EU on governance reforms.

2.6 Map of the Puzzle: Explaining African Governments' Responsiveness

African governments face some tough choices when deciding whether they want to engage with the EU in governance reforms, or not. Drawing the points from this chapter together, we can start to build a picture on the factors influencing African governments' decision to engage with the EU.

First of all, African governments' decision is influenced by the EU's good governance strategies. More specifically, the content or substance of what the EU seeks to promote as part of its good governance agenda and the instruments the EU uses, both shape African governments' willingness to cooperate on governance reforms. Second, African governments weigh up the costs and benefits that cooperation with the EU entails against their chances of remaining in power. The more the EU's offer for cooperation aligns with the domestic survival strategies of African governments, the more likely they are willing to cooperate and vice versa. Third, African governments analyse the costs resulting from their engagement in governance reforms against other benefits of cooperating with the EU. If the EU offers comprehensive and attractive packages of aid and trading opportunities to African countries, African governments may still be willing to engage with the EU in governance reforms, even if this engagement bears certain risks for regime stability. Fourth, African governments do not take their decisions to cooperate with the EU in isolation. Instead, they assess opportunities of engaging with the EU in light of cooperation opportunities provided by other international actors such as China. If China becomes an alternative cooperation partner, reducing African countries' economic dependence on the EU and providing attractive support for African governments' survival strategies, we would expect that African governments become less likely to engage with the EU in governance reforms.

EU-Africa cooperation on governance reforms is an interactive and iterative situation. In this regard, changes in one or several of the four main variables *over time* are expected to result in changes in African governments' openness to engage. For instance, if the EU decides at a specific point in time to broaden the content of its good governance strategy, African governments may become less willing to cooperate. If African governments' survival strategies shift, for example, in response to substantial threats from the opposition, this may reduce their willingness to engage. Finally, changes in African governments' dependence on the EU and changing access to cooperation with China over time may also affect African governments' willingness to engage in governance reforms.

The aim of this book is to explain differences in African governments' openness to engage with the EU in governance reforms by exploring interaction effects between the EU's good governance strategies, the survival strategies of African governments, their dependence on the EU and the rise of China as an alternative cooperation partner.

The following three chapters all proceed in a similar way. For each country case, between two and four time periods are distinguished, depending on whether the EU has modified its good governance strategies in that country. For each time period, the chapters analyse the interaction of the four main variables. The main objective of the within-case analysis is to explain why the responsiveness of the Angolan, Ethiopian or Rwandan government towards EU demands to engage in governance has varied over time. In addition, the case studies use cross-case comparisons to further investigate the relative explanatory power of the four main variables.

Notes

1. See, for instance, Simpser and Donno (2012) for a discussion on the unintended side-effects of election monitoring.

Open Access This chapter is licensed under the terms of the Creative Commons Attribution 4.0 International License (http://creativecommons.org/licenses/by/4.0/), which permits use, sharing, adaptation, distribution and reproduction in any medium or format, as long as you give appropriate credit to the original author(s) and the source, provide a link to the Creative Commons license and indicate if changes were made.

The images or other third party material in this chapter are included in the chapter's Creative Commons license, unless indicated otherwise in a credit line to the material. If material is not included in the chapter's Creative Commons license and your intended use is not permitted by statutory regulation or exceeds the permitted use, you will need to obtain permission directly from the copyright holder.

CHAPTER 3

Rwanda

Between 2000 and 2014, the Rwandan government has been increasingly active in cooperating with the EU on governance reforms. Why has the government reluctantly started to engage and why has it then become more active and at times proactive?

This chapter argues that Rwanda is an example of a country where the EU's good governance strategies largely converge with the preferences of the target government, particularly in the second half of the 2000s. Due to the conjuncture of specific structural conditions, the Rwandan government has a strong interest in building an effective state to improve public goods provision in order to enhance its position in power. It faced some opposition in the early 2000s, but has seen very limited open challenges to regime survival after 2005. The government faced limited difficulties in winning elections and it used mostly low-intensity coercion to *prevent* opposition from emerging.

In this context, EU support for governance reforms that focused on building effective state institutions and strengthening formally democratic ones (instead of empowering civil society actors) generated few costs but largely converged with the preferences of the Rwandan government, particularly after 2006. Moreover, by providing significant amounts of development aid (a large proportion of it as direct budget support between 2006 and 2012), the EU was an attractive partner for the government, outweighing those (albeit limited) costs of cooperating on governance reforms. In contrast, Rwanda had little access to economic cooperation from alternative cooperation partners, such as China. China has not (yet) emerged as an alternative cooperation partner in terms of size of economic cooperation and support for the Rwandan government's survival strategies.

This period of relative convergence between the EU and the Rwandan government's preferences has probably come to an end as of 2012. The EU and other donors' decision to use budget support funds to exert pressure on Rwanda to cease backing rebels in the Democratic Republic of the Congo (DRC) in 2012 and Kagame's decision to change the constitution and run for a third term during the 2017 elections seems to herald a new era in Rwanda's relations with the EU and other donors.

3.1 Structural Factors Shaping Rwanda's Survival Strategies

The Rwandan leadership faces three interrelated structural challenges. First, the core elite on which the leadership relies to remain in power is relatively small. The most influential parts of Rwanda's political and economic elites are former Tutsi refugees from Uganda who fought the war against Hutu extremists in 1994.[1] Returnees settled mainly in urban areas, most of them in Kigali (Ansoms 2009, 293ff). Even today returnees from Uganda still hold key positions in the government (Ansoms 2009; Reyntjens 2010), the military and the security apparatus (Waugh 2004) as well as in the business sector which is dominated by companies owned by the Rwandan Patriotic Front (RPF) (Booth and Golooba-Mutebi 2012). However, while still in exile, the RPF leadership made efforts to expand its support base and to include Hutu in prominent positions. When it took power in 1994, the RPF sought to integrate other (mostly Tutsi) returnees from Burundi, Tanzania and European countries as well as genocide survivors and moderate Hutu who had opposed the radicalisation of the former regime in the early 1990s.[2]

Second, given the circumstances of how it came to power and its narrow, (still) ethnicity-based support group, the Rwandan leadership is confronted with a considerable security dilemma. A regime change could still constitute a substantial security threat to the elite. This security dilemma has several implications. The leadership has reason to expect that mass movements and mass opposition could quickly become uncontrollable. Thus it has a strong interest in not only maintaining support from the elite that sustains it in power, but to make sure that popular dissatisfaction does not grow. Moreover, the Rwandan leadership probably does not expect support from the EU or other international actors to guarantee its security, not least in light of the inactivity of the international community during the genocide in 1994. Thus, the ruling elite supposedly has a strong interest in preserving its independence from international actors despite its strong aid dependence.

The third structural dilemma relates to Rwanda's scarce domestic revenues and weak economic development. As we will see below, Rwanda has benefited from substantial aid inflows, notably from the EU. Yet, while the Rwandan government needs to maintain support from the broader populace as well as the core elite, it has few domestic economic resources that are easy to access and that require little manpower, such as oil or other natural resources. The leadership thus has only a small margin of manoeuvre in maintaining support from the elite by granting spoils and perks. These three challenges—a small core elite, the resulting security dilemma and scarce resources—considerably impact on the leadership's basic choice of strategy to tighten its grip on power.

3.2 Rwanda Reluctantly Engaged with the EU in the Early 2000s

The EU has had limited relations with Rwanda until the genocide in 1994. The genocide left the country with multiple crises: about one-tenth of a population of eight million was killed; two million people fled the country, mostly to the neighbouring DRC; and one fifth of the population was suspected of having been involved in the genocide. Important parts of basic infrastructure were destroyed and the economy was depressed. In the first few years after the genocide, the EU and other donors provided humanitarian aid to support the rehabilitation and reconciliation process. Towards the end of the 1990s, the EU's relations with Rwanda normalised and the EU (and other donors) shifted its support from humanitarian to long-term development aid.

The EU's Good Governance Strategies Between 2000 and 2005

The EU's Approach: Promoting Democratic Government
As part of the EU's shift from humanitarian aid to long-term development assistance, support for governance reforms became a stronger priority of

the EU's policies towards Rwanda. Between 2000 and 2005, the EU put the emphasis on promoting not only the effectiveness of government institutions but also the democratic quality of decision-making processes. The first country strategy paper, signed by the European Commission (EC) and Rwanda in 2002, indicates the importance the EU attaches to supporting democratic institutions, human rights, the holding of elections and the judicial system (Government of the Republic of Rwanda and European Commission 2002). The paper mentions the need to strengthen the involvement of civil society actors in the decision-making process, but the focus clearly lies on enhancing state institutions (ibid).

In the early 2000s, the EU spent the bulk of its aid on rural development and macro-economic support (European Commission and Rwanda 2003, 26ff). It also allotted parts of its aid funds to promoting the effectiveness of government institutions and the democratic quality of decision-making processes. OECD aid data show that the EU allocated similar volumes of aid in support of input and output legitimacy (Table 3.1).

Between 2000 and 2005, the EU focused mainly on the intergovernmental channel to support governance reforms and used the transnational channel to a much lesser extent. It channelled only small volumes of aid to non-state actors through the European Development Fund (EDF). The country strategy paper for the ninth EDF did not identify assistance to non-state actors as a priority for the EU's support to Rwanda (Government of the Republic of Rwanda and European Commission 2002). Only €2 million

Table 3.1 EU governance aid to Rwanda 2000–2014 (in USD million and in per cent)

Rwanda	2000–2005	2006–2010	2011–2014
Total governance aid	49.22	48.56	5.23
Total aid (all sectors)	495.69	646.12	160.66
Governance aid/share in total EU aid	9.9%	7.5%	3.3%
Output legitimacy	22.19	3.54	5.23
Input legitimacy	27.03	45.02	0.00
Output legitimacy/share in total governance aid	45.1%	7.3%	100%
Input legitimacy/share in total governance aid	54.9%	92.7%	0.00

Source: Author's compilation, based on data from OECD DAC Aid statistics (2016) (Query for EU institutions; 'total governance aid' includes all aid reported for the EU institutions under the category '151:I5a: Government & Civil Society-general, Total' to the OECD DAC Creditor Reporting System. 'Output legitimacy' includes public sector and administrative management, public finance management, decentralisation and support to subnational government, anti-corruption organisations and institutions; 'input legitimacy' includes legal and judicial development, democratic participation and civil society, elections, legislature and political parties, media and freedom of information, human rights, women's equality. Data accessible at http://stats.oecd.org; last accessed: 5 October 2016)

was to be allocated to support civil society organisations (out of €12 million reserved to support governance reforms) (European Commission and Rwanda 2003, 30f). The EU proposed to launch a fund for civil society organisations, jointly managed with the government (ibid). It allocated only small aid volumes to Rwanda through the European Instrument for Democracy and Human Rights (EIDHR). Most of these funds were provided to international rather than Rwandan civil society actors (Table 3.4).

The EU's Instruments: Cooperative-Critical
In the early 2000s, the EU promoted governance reforms through dialogue and governance aid combined with some negative conditionality. The EU launched political dialogue under Article 8 of the Cotonou Agreement in 2004. During political dialogue meetings, the EU asked the government to establish benchmarks against which to measure progress on governance reforms (European Commission and Rwanda 2005). Together with other donors, the EU made efforts to establish and institutionalise different forms of aid policy dialogues that developed along with reforms to the international aid architecture in the early 2000s. As part of these dialogues, the EU together with other donors sought to make governance reforms an important topic (Hayman 2006).[3] Beyond political and aid policy dialogue, the EU began to support governance reforms with EDF and EIDHR aid funds (see above).

Furthermore, the EU pressured Rwanda to promote political reforms. Similar to other international actors, the EU criticised the limiting of political space for civil society and the opposition ahead of the 2003 elections, and decided to withhold aid funds dedicated to supporting the elections (Kimonyo et al. 2004; Hayman 2008, 172). During the EDF mid-term review in 2004, the EU argued that it would not increase aid funds due to Rwanda's limited progress on governance reforms (European Union 2004b, 16). The mid-term review rated Rwanda's performance on governance reforms as 'insufficient' (European Union 2004b, 15).[4]

Beyond these material incentives, the EU criticised the governance situation in several public statements and non-public *démarches* (Table 3.2). The EU had issued a common position in 1998, which it renewed several times. The common position identified support for democratic reforms and human rights as a key objective of the EU's policies in Rwanda (European Union 2002). It used declarations and presidency statements to raise concerns regarding the human rights situation. In a strong public statement published in the autumn of 2004, for instance,

Table 3.2 EU statements and *démarches* related to governance reforms 2000–2011

	2000–2005		2006–2011		Total
	Positive	Critical	Positive	Critical	
EU public statements on governance reforms	4	6	3	1	14
Démarches	–	3	–	1	4

Source: Author's compilation, based on EU annual human rights reports and documents published by the Council of the EU

the EU criticised deteriorations in the governance situation (European Union 2004a).

The Rwandan Government's Responsiveness: Reluctant Engagement

In response to the EU's demands to cooperate on governance reforms, the Rwandan government reluctantly started to engage with the EU in the implementation of governance instruments. Already in the early 2000s, the Rwandan government was slightly more forthcoming in engaging with the EU than Ethiopia and Angola, as we will see in the next chapters.

Rwanda's Responsiveness: Political Dialogue and Aid Policy Dialogues
Political dialogue with the EU remained ad hoc and informal until 2004. High-level government officials participated in the dialogue. The government agreed to discuss a broad range of issues related to democratic and effective governance reforms as well as regional peace and security. In contrast to Ethiopia and Angola, the Rwandan government agreed to establish benchmarks to measure progress on governance reforms as part of a formal political dialogue (European Commission and Rwanda 2005; European Union 2004b, 17). The government agreed to hold two Article 8 dialogue meetings in 2005, during which it discussed with the EU the abolition of the death penalty in the context of the Gacaca trials, the transfer of the *génocidaire* from the international criminal tribunal in Arusha to Rwanda and problems related to Interahamwe rebels in Eastern Congo who fled to the DRC after the genocide (Euréval and PRODEV 2006).

Beyond the Article 8 political dialogue, the Rwandan government reluctantly started to engage with donors in governance reforms during aid policy dialogues. Parallel to the international effectiveness agenda, which had emerged from the early 2000s with the Millennium Development Goals and the high-level fora on aid effectiveness, donors started to improve their aid coordination structures at country level and intensified aid policy dialogues with developing-country governments (Whitfield and Fraser 2009). Rwanda was one of the few African countries that agreed early on to institutionalise aid policy dialogues with the EU and other donors (Hayman 2006).[5] As part of these aid policy dialogue meetings, the government reluctantly agreed to address governance reforms.[6] It was slightly more willing to address governance issues as part of its aid policy dialogues with the EU and other donors than Ethiopia and particularly Angola. For instance, in contrast to Ethiopia, the Rwandan government was willing to set up specific aid policy dialogues with an explicit focus on governance reforms, for instance, to discuss the elections, support for the Supreme Court or Gacaca jurisdiction (Euréval and PRODEV 2006).

Rwanda's Responsiveness: Positive Conditionality and Governance Aid
The Rwandan government reluctantly agreed to implement governance aid and to include positive conditionality in its engagement with the EU. Together with the UK, the EU was the driving force in negotiating a new budget support agreement with Rwanda in 2003 (Hayman 2006, 79f). The government accepted benchmarks to assess progress on public financial management and transparency of government finance in the agreement. Yet, despite pressure from the EU and the UK, Rwanda did not agree to include objectives related to democratic reforms, such as free and fair elections (Hayman 2006).

Rwanda reluctantly accepted financial and technical aid from the EU and other donors targeted to promote governance reforms. The government agreed to allocate a portion of funds from the eighth EDF to support governance reforms. An analysis of joint annual reports on the implementation of EU aid to Rwanda (2001, 2002 and 2004) as well as the EDF mid-term review (European Union 2004b, 8) and an independent evaluation of the EU's aid to Rwanda (Euréval and PRODEV 2006) suggests that governance aid projects were implemented relatively smoothly and with few delays. Until the end of 2005, the bulk of EU aid allocated to governance reforms was disbursed (Euréval and PRODEV 2006, 57; European Union 2004b, 8).

Moreover, compared to Ethiopia and Angola, Rwanda was more open to assistance that aimed at supporting the effectiveness and democratic quality of decision-making processes. For instance, the government engaged with the EU in public financial management reform. It agreed to use the bulk of EU aid earmarked for supporting governance reforms for the rehabilitation of the judiciary, prisons, the parliament and other government buildings (European Commission and Rwanda 2003, 51f; 2005, 14).

In addition, the government accepted support from the EU and other donors to assist the constitutional referendum and the parliamentary and presidential elections, for instance, by fostering the human and administrative capacities of the national electoral commission (European Commission 2009). It also welcomed the EU election observer mission to monitor the 2003 elections, and accepted support from the EU and other donors for democratic institutions such as the Human Rights Commission (CNDH) that had been established in 1999, even though the CNDH's budget remained largely financed by the government itself (Kimonyo et al. 2004, 44f, 51f). Government institutions such as the National Commission for Unity and Reconciliation (NURC) also benefited from the EU and other donors' support (Kimonyo et al. 2004). Rwanda accepted support from the EU and other donors for drafting the legal framework for these and other institutions such as the Ombudsman or the Office of the Auditor-General of Public Finance.

To summarise, the EU adopted a relatively broad approach and sought to promote *democratic government* in the early 2000s. The EU not only attempted to support the effectiveness of government institutions, but also the democratic quality of decision-making processes. Moreover, the EU used a *cooperative-critical* strategy and put pressure on the Rwandan government to open political spaces. The Rwandan government, in turn, started to *reluctantly* engage. One would assume that since the EU sought to promote a broad understanding of good governance and used a cooperative-critical approach, cooperation on governance reforms would become quite costly for Rwanda. It is thus surprising that Rwanda reluctantly started to engage with the EU in the early 2000s.

The Rwandan Government's Survival Strategies

Strong Domestic Opposition and Threats to Regime Survival
The EU's demands to cooperate on governance reforms coincided with the end of the transition phase after the genocide. By the early 2000s, the

Rwandan government had re-established basic domestic security and its monopoly on power (Waugh 2004; Reyntjens 2009; Prunier 2009). Basic economic development had resumed; by the early 2000s, economic development in terms of gross domestic product (GDP) had returned to pre-genocide levels (Marysse et al. 2006). Moreover, a referendum on the new constitution and the first presidential and parliamentary elections were finally scheduled for 2003 after having been postponed several times.

At the same time, the Rwandan government faced mounting domestic opposition during the early 2000s. Rwandan (and international) civil society organisations and the media increasingly voiced concern that the peace-building process was not accompanied by higher levels of political liberalisation and political competition. Moreover, several members of the 'government of national unity'[7] defected, suggesting that the Rwandan leadership's attempts to broaden its support base were failing (Waugh 2004; Reyntjens 2013). Some former members of the government—moderate Hutu and Tutsi survivors—went into exile. Others joined the domestic opposition, for instance, the Republican Democratic Movement (MDR), the largest opposition party (Waugh 2004). The former president Bizimungu, a Hutu member of the RPF who became president of the 'government of national unity' in 1994, also openly challenged Kagame. Bizimungu resigned in 2000 to establish his own party, the Parti Democratique pour le Renouveau (PDR), to create a political alternative to the RPF (Reyntjens 2004). In addition, the Rwandan government faced some—albeit limited—external security threats. In 2001, the Forces démocratiques de libération du Rwanda (FDLR), a rebel movement active in the eastern part of the DRC and composed of former Interahamwe and *génocidaire* who fled to the DRC after the genocide, attacked Rwanda (Longman 2004, 75; International Crisis Group 2009).

Survival Strategies: Building the Foundation for State Reform, Managing Arenas of Contestation and Using Low-intensity Coercion
With the end of the transition phase after the genocide, strengthening the effectiveness of government institutions to improve public goods provision became a high priority for the Rwandan government, and it launched a civil service reform (Hausman 2011). The effectiveness of the government slightly improved in the early 2000s and the level of corruption remained low (see Fig. 3.3 later). In addition, the government established several democratic oversight institutions such as the national electoral commission, the Ombudsman's office and the Commission on Human Rights.[8]

Some observers question their impartiality and claim that these democratic oversight institutions remained relatively weak. The first Ombudsman, for instance, was one of President Kagame's closest allies, one of the RPF founding members and later the RPF secretary-general.[9]

The Rwandan leadership responded to the growing domestic opposition by substantially limiting political spaces. Low-intensity coercion was used to secure the RPF's and President Kagame's victory in the elections. The MDR, the most important opposition party, was banned ahead of the 2003 referendum and elections (Reyntjens 2004). The former president Bizimungu could not run in the elections; he was arrested in 2003 and later sentenced to 15 years' imprisonment (Beswick 2010, 235). Finally, press freedom was further restricted (Reyntjens 2004).

The referendum on the new constitution and presidential and parliamentary elections in 2003 constituted an important arena for members of the opposition, civil society and the media to challenge the RPF. While there was little doubt that the RPF and President Kagame would be victorious in the elections, winning with a considerable majority was considered to be important to signal that the RPF and President Kagame had a firm grip on power (Reyntjens 2004). The parliamentary and presidential elections finally resulted in a landslide victory for the incumbent regime. The RPF gained about 73 per cent of the votes and President Kagame was elected with more than 90 per cent.

After the elections, spaces for the media and civil society organisations were further reduced. A new and quite restrictive law that required civil society organisations to register with the government had already been passed in 2001. In June 2004, a parliamentary commission on 'genocide ideology' accused some of the most prominent domestic and international non-governmental organisations (NGOs) of promoting ethnic division. Leading figures of LIPRODHOR (Ligue Rwandaise pour la Promotion et la Defense des Droits de l'Homme), the most important independent human rights organisation, left the country (Longman 2011).

When the EU approached Rwanda to engage in governance reforms in the early 2000s, the government was preoccupied with reinforcing formal political institutions and putting more emphasis on economic growth and public goods provision. EU assistance to support the effectiveness of government institutions thus aligned with the government's preferences. At the same time, ahead of the 2003 elections, the Rwandan government faced growing opposition and political competition from former members of government. The government used low-intensity coercion to respond to the growing opposition. In this context, the EU's attempts to promote input legitimacy have generated substantial costs and only very limited benefits.

Rwanda: Strongly Aid Dependent on the EU in the Early 2000s

The EU started asking the Rwandan government to cooperate on governance reforms during a period when Rwanda was also highly dependent on EU aid. Engaging with the EU in governance reforms thereby yielded important direct economic benefits for Rwanda. The EU is also an important trading partner and source of direct investments. Yet, trade and investments still make up a small share of Rwanda's GDP.

During the past decade, real GDP growth averaged about 8 per cent per annum and Rwanda has been one of the fastest growing economies not only in Africa but also beyond. Yet, GDP growth was, to an important extent, driven by aid inflows (Marysse et al. 2007). Rwanda's aid dependence has been very high if measured by the share of aid to gross national income (GNI). Between 2000 and 2005, development aid accounted for 18–24 per cent of GNI (Fig. 3.1), making Rwanda one of the most aid-dependent countries in Africa. Rwanda is also strongly aid dependent if measured by the share of government revenues. Between 2000 and 2005, development aid accounted for about one-third of government revenues; Rwanda's domestic tax base has been very low in comparison to other African countries.

After the genocide, and particularly since 2000, Rwanda saw a shift in its international relations. Traditional partners such as France or Belgium that had supported the old regime even during the genocide, considerably reduced their engagement. Other donors such as the EU and the UK, in turn, scaled up their support. Between 2000 and 2012, the EU institutions, together with the World Bank, the USA and the UK, have been the largest donors to Rwanda (Fig. 3.2). In terms of financial volume, the EU as a whole (EU institutions and member states) was the largest donor between 2000 and 2005. Aid provided by the EU institutions to Rwanda in that time accounted for about 26 per cent of total OECD DAC donors' aid. The EU institutions started to channel aid through direct budget support in 2003 and directed significant shares of their aid to infrastructure and social services, such as healthcare and education.

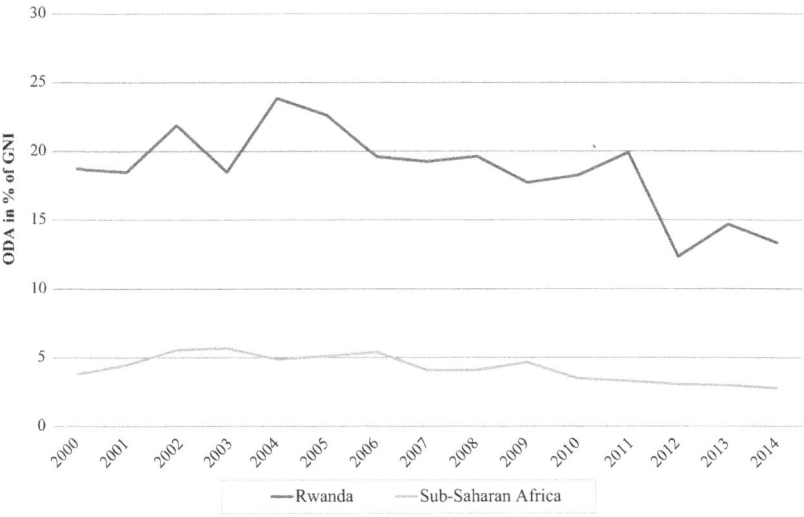

Fig. 3.1 Net ODA as a share of GNI in Rwanda
Source: World Bank (2016a), World Development Indicators; author's compilation

The EU and other Western donors' willingness to substantially increase aid to Rwanda can at least partly be explained by Western feelings of guilt for not intervening in Rwanda during the genocide of 1994. Moreover, the Rwandan government has very actively embraced the international aid effectiveness agenda as it emerged in the early 2000s (Hayman 2009).

The EU was the most important destination for Rwandan exports until the mid-2000s. Yet, the overall volume of exports and its share of GDP has been quite small. Rwanda has a large trade deficit that has grown considerably over time. Some argue that Rwanda was able to finance its imports mainly due to substantial access to development aid (Marysse et al. 2006; IMF 2013); much of it from the EU. By the early 2000s, production of coffee and tea—Rwanda's two major export commodities—was at pre-genocide levels, and exports had resumed (Oomen 2005, 900). Tea and coffee account for more than 50 per cent of Rwanda's exports. Furthermore, the EU has been one of the largest investors in Rwanda. Yet, the overall level of direct investments in Rwanda had been very low in the early 2000s; and substantially below the sub-Saharan African average.

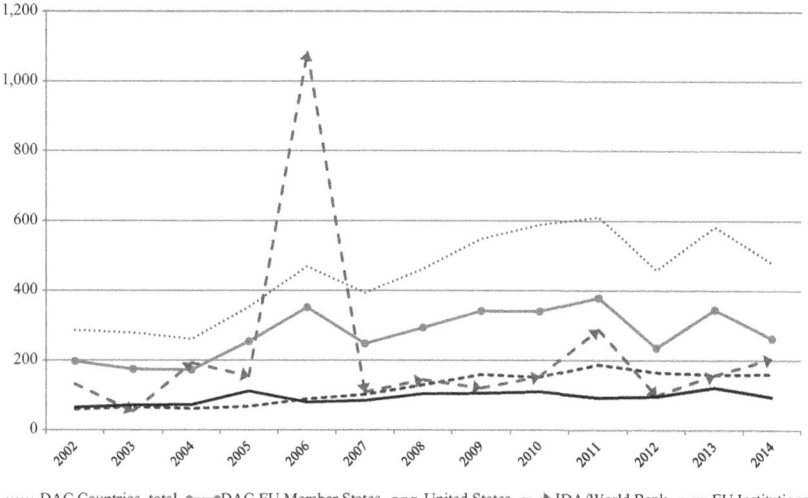

Fig. 3.2 ODA flows to Rwanda (disbursements in USD million)
Source: OECD Development Assistance Committee Aid statistics (2016); author's compilation

In the early 2000s, the EU thus became one of the most important donors to Rwanda. It channelled aid through modalities and to sectors that largely matched the preferences of the Rwandan government. Rwanda therefore had a strong interest in closely cooperating with the EU. These benefits that cooperation with the EU 'beyond' governance reforms entailed compensated for the costs that cooperation on governance reforms produced. Its dependence on EU aid can thus explain why Rwanda reluctantly started to engage in the early 2000s, even though cooperation was risky for regime survival. Yet, this argument would be even stronger if one could control for alternative explanations, such as access to cooperation with China.

China: No Alternative Cooperation Partner in the Early 2000s

In contrast to the EU, China has played a limited role as an economic cooperation partner or as a partner to support the Rwandan government's survival strategies. Between 2000 and 2005, China's cooperation with Rwanda was very limited.

When the EU started to foster cooperation on governance reforms in the early 2000s, bilateral trade between Rwanda and China as well as Chinese foreign direct investments in Rwanda were close to zero (Fig. 3.4). Moreover, Rwanda's access to Chinese grants and loans has been very restricted. China supported a few infrastructure projects, such as road construction, the renovation of the stadium in Kigali and the extension of a nursing school (Table 3.3). The financial volume of Chinese projects is difficult to estimate and directly compare with the EU's aid, as official data cannot be accessed. For the period between 2000 and 2004, interviews with Rwandan and Chinese government officials[10] and a press analysis give no insights into the financial volume of China's aid projects. However, the list of projects (Table 3.3) strongly suggests that the volume of Chinese aid between 2000 and 2005 has been negligible compared to the EU's aid.

Beyond economic cooperation, engagement with China has not provided the Rwandan government with an alternative to the EU with regard to cooperating on the government's survival strategies. Exchanges between the RPF and the CCP have remained relatively limited (Fig. 3.5

Table 3.3 Chinese aid projects 2000–2005

Year	Type of project	Financial volume
2002	Construction of Kibungo hospital and nursing school (Ngoma District); extension of the school (in 2004/2005)	USD 7 million grant
2003	Joint China–Rwanda agriculture cooperation project: Umutara Rice Field Management Project	–
1986	Construction of CIMERWA Cement factory, operated by a Chinese company on behalf of the Rwandan government;	–
2006	privatisation; assistance for expansion of the factory	–
1998	Construction of a national stadium	–
2004	Renovation and repair	–
2001	Construction of Kinyinya-Nyarutarama and Kinyinya-Utexrwa roads in Kigali	–
Various years	Commodities aid (food aid; office equipment and relief)	–
2004	Construction of conference hall 'Prime Holdings'	–
2005	Construction of Ministry of Foreign Affairs	USD 8.9 million grant

Source: Author's compilation, based on data from MOFCOM, aid transparency initiative, *The New Times* and BBC monitoring international reports

below), and China has not assisted Rwanda in strengthening the effectiveness of government institutions, managing arenas of contestation or using coercion.

3.3 Rwanda Proactively Engaging with the EU in the Late 2000s Despite China Looming

Between 2006 and 2011, the EU continued to promote *democratic government*. At the same time it shifted its instruments from a cooperative-critical to a *cooperative-rewarding* strategy. The Rwandan government, in turn, has become very active, and at times proactive about engaging with the EU in governance reforms.

The EU's Good Governance Strategies Between 2006 and 2011

The EU's Approach: Promoting Democratic Government
In the years between 2006 and 2011, the EU continued to promote *democratic government*. The EU highlighted the importance of improving the electoral process, strengthening the separation of powers and enhancing access to justice (Government of the Republic of Rwanda and European Commission 2007). The EU used several channels of communication with the government to address issues of democratic and, to a lesser extent, effective governance reforms. During Article 8 political dialogue meetings, the EU raised concerns regarding limitations of freedom of speech, press freedom and the revision of the media law, shortcomings in the electoral process, judicial reform and the Gacaca or the abolition of the death penalty (European Commission and Rwanda 2008).

OECD aid statistics illustrate that the EU's governance aid remained stable in the second half of the 2000s (Table 3.1). OECD aid statistics also suggest that the EU put a strong emphasis on supporting input legitimacy. Between 2006 and 2010, the EU directed almost all governance aid to support democratic reforms, a large part of which was allocated to support justice sector reform, as will be documented below.

The EU continued to put little emphasis on the transnational channel. In the country strategy paper for the 10th EDF, support to non-state actors was not identified as an explicit objective of the EU's policies, and the amount of assistance allotted to supporting civil society actors through the EDF has been small. Engagement with non-state actors was conceived of as a cross-cutting issue in the strategy paper rather than a direct objective of the EU's aid to Rwanda (Government of the Republic of Rwanda and European Commission 2007, 47). Only around 2010 did the EU start to design a programme to support non-state actors through the EDF.

The EU gave some aid to non-state actors through the EIDHR (Table 3.4). Yet, a significant share of EU aid targeted international NGOs based in France, Germany or Belgium rather than Rwandan NGOs. Furthermore, the EIDHR project descriptions[11] suggest that most EIDHR funds channelled to Rwandan NGOs were used to support justice reform and the reconciliation process. EU support for civil society organisations engaged in the justice sector aimed at supporting the effectiveness and efficiency of the justice system, rather than the independence of the judiciary or other elements of horizontal accountability. In contrast, the EU only provided a limited amount of aid through the EIDHR that focused on promoting freedom of the press or of association.[12]

The EU's Instruments: Cooperative-Rewarding
Around 2005 the EU modified its strategy from *cooperative-critical* to *cooperative-rewarding*. The EU increasingly refrained from putting pressure on Rwanda, but instead rewarded the government through additional development aid, via aid modalities such as budget support and public rhetorical support. By increasing development aid and through its choice of aid modalities, the EU signalled to Rwanda that it viewed the political situation as generally positive.

In 2006, the EU rewarded Rwanda for its compliance with the requirements of the governance incentive tranche with a 30 per cent aid increase. This is the highest possible tranche, received by only five African countries (European Commission and Rwanda 2008, 1). In 2009, Rwanda was the first African country to which the EU offered an 'MDG contract'—a special form of direct budget aid with higher aid levels and long-term predictability.[13] During the 2009 EDF mid-term review, the EU increased aid levels by 30 per cent (€89 million). Rwanda is again one among only eight African countries where the EU raised aid funds during

Table 3.4 EU aid to non-state actors through the EIDHR 2000–2011

	2000–2005	2006–2011	Total
Volume in USD	6,307,588	8,390,594	14,698,182
Share to local NGOs	27%	55%	43%
Number of projects	16	41	57

Source: Author's compilation, based on EIDHR compendia various years (European Commission 1995–2012)

the mid-term review.[14] About 80 per cent of EU aid to Rwanda was spent through direct budget aid. The head of the EU delegation in Kigali, Michel Arrion, explains the decision by the '[...] exemplary progress Rwanda made in recent years in good governance, sustainable development and the fight against poverty and hunger'.[15] In 2009, the EU also decided to channel most of its governance aid through government budgets (as sector budget support), thereby signalling that it appreciates progress on reforms.

In contrast, deficiencies regarding democratic governance did not prompt the EU to exert pressure. The EU never reduced aid or shifted budget support to other aid modalities, unlike some EU member states.[16] In contrast to the early 2000s, it has not used public statements to openly criticise the government (Table 3.2). Around the parliamentary and presidential elections in 2008 and 2010, the EU did not publicly express concern. Instead, it mostly relied on cooperative instruments such as political dialogue and non-public *démarches*.[17]

The Rwandan Government's Responsiveness: (Pro)Active Engagement

Between 2006 and 2011, good governance has been a prominent issue in the Rwandan government's policy documents and its public discourse *vis-à-vis* donors. In public speeches, for instance, during meetings with OECD DAC donors, President Kagame highlighted on a regular basis that governance reforms constitute a key element of the government's development strategy.[18] Compared to the period between 2000 and 2005, the Rwandan government engaged more actively with the EU in the implementation of governance instruments. In contrast to Ethiopia, and particularly Angola, Rwanda has at times even taken proactive initiatives to intensify cooperation on governance reforms with the EU and other donors.[19]

Rwanda's Responsiveness: Political and Aid Policy Dialogues

The Rwandan government continued to engage in a regular and comprehensive formal political dialogue with the EU between 2006 and 2012. It has conducted political dialogue with the EU at the minister of foreign affairs level and invited relevant representatives from other line ministries or government institutions, depending on the issue under discussion. Dialogue took place on a regular basis up to four times a year, a frequency which has reportedly been in the interest of both sides.[20]

During political dialogue meetings, the government has been willing to address a broad range of issues related to regional peace and security, effective government as well as democratic governance reforms. Participants report that the dialogue has been open and frank and has sometimes influenced the government's position, for instance, in the case of the abolition of the death penalty in 2007 (European Commission and Rwanda 2008). The government was also willing to discuss sensitive issues such as reform of the justice sector. It discussed legislative reforms such as the laws on 'genocide ideology', 'divisionism' and the media that have been strongly criticised by human rights organisations and other international observers (European Commission and Rwanda 2008). Even though it is difficult to assess the influence of these dialogue meetings on the government's position, it should be noted that the government has been willing to discuss these issues with the EU.[21] Beyond such formal dialogue mechanisms (and unlike Angola and Ethiopia), the government has allowed the EU (and other donors) very good informal access to decision-makers.

Compared to the early 2000s, Rwanda has also more prominently engaged with the EU in governance reforms as part of its aid policy dialogues. It continued to discuss governance reforms with the EU and other donors during the annual donor–government meetings.[22] During these meetings, Rwanda presented reform progress, for instance, regarding justice sector reform, the fight against corruption, public financial management or decentralisation and agreed with the EU and other donors on reform objectives for the following year. In contrast to Ethiopia and particularly Angola, Rwanda has also maintained regular policy dialogues with the EU and other donors regarding specific policy and institutional reforms, such as justice sector or public financial management reforms as part of the budget support intervention.[23]

Rwanda's Responsiveness: Positive Conditionality
Rwanda defined concrete benchmarks to measure progress on governance reforms together with the EU and other donors. Compared to Ethiopia and particularly Angola, Rwanda has been much more ambitious in defining reform objectives and more actively engaged with the EU.

To comply with the EU's requirements for receiving a 'governance incentive tranche', the government developed a comprehensive 'governance action plan'. This plan was relatively detailed and contained targets related to political rights and civil liberties, the rule of law, the effectiveness of government institutions and the fight against corruption (European Commission and Rwanda 2007). The government updated the plan for the 2008 joint annual report on EU aid to Rwanda (European Commission and Rwanda 2008). According to the EU's assessment, Rwanda made substantial progress in complying with its reform commitments.[24]

Some interviewees suggest that debates on the governance action plan influenced the government's decision to ask the EU and other donors to conduct a 'joint governance assessment'.[25] During a meeting with donors in 2006, President Kagame was critical that Rwanda's rank in international governance indices was outdated and often did not adequately reflect Rwanda's situation. Kagame then asked the EU and other donors to jointly assess the governance situation to develop a shared understanding and more adequate analysis on the state of reforms. The first joint governance assessment was published in 2008 (Government of the Republic of Rwanda and World Bank 2008). The revision was not published until 2011, after lengthy and very controversial discussions between the government and donors (JGA Steering Committee 2011). Yet, despite these difficulties, the government arguably signalled its willingness to engage with the donors (Klingebiel 2011); a very different situation to that of other African authoritarian governments.

Rwanda's Responsiveness: Governance Aid

Between 2006 and 2011, Rwanda also actively engaged with the EU in the implementation of governance aid. The analysis of joint annual reports on the implementation of EU aid to Rwanda for 2006, 2007 and 2008, and interviews with European and Rwandan officials suggest that the government actively cooperated with the EU on the implementation of governance aid. Compared to the period between 2000 and 2005, aid allocated to governance reforms has been disbursed without complications. In contrast to Ethiopia and particularly Angola, Rwanda has engaged with the EU not only on effective but also democratic reforms.

The government agreed to allocate part of the EU's governance aid funds to a programme that supports the Ministry of Finance and Economic Development in strengthening public financial management, the National Authorising Officer[26] and the Rwandan Institute for Statistics (European Commission 2009, 34ff). It agreed to increase the funding for this project from €6.8 million to €10 million in 2010, indicating its support for the project.

Rwanda agreed that a significant share of EU governance aid should support the justice sector. Rwanda had launched the Gacaca system in the early 2000s—an attempt to use traditional community-based instruments of justice for the reconciliation process. Even though different perceptions exist as to whether the initial idea for the Gacaca system came from the government or international actors, Rwanda took an active stance in implementing the Gacaca trials (Oomen 2005). Rwanda's aid policy strategy, published in 2006, requested that the EU remains one of the key donors for the justice sector (together with the Netherlands, Belgium and Germany), indicating a strong preference for EU aid to the justice sector.[27] Moreover, Rwanda developed a comprehensive reform strategy for the justice sector and asked the EU and other donors to channel such support through sector budget support. Even though Rwanda has not always fully complied with all reform objectives agreed upon with the EU and other donors, interviewees and minutes of the aid policy dialogues indicate a general consensus between the government and donors on reform progress.[28]

The government was open to allocating a small share of governance aid to support elections, the media and parliament. Together with other donors, the EU supported the 2008 parliamentary elections. Rwanda agreed that the EU would support the national electoral commission ahead of the 2010 presidential and 2011 local elections (European Commission 2009). It agreed to allocate a small share of EU governance aid to support the capacities of parliamentary committees in fulfilling their function of oversight over the executive. A small share of aid was allocated to support the Great Lakes Media Centre and a vocational training centre for journalists (European Commission 2009).

In contrast to Ethiopia, Rwanda did not openly object to the EU's (arguably very limited) demands to allocate aid to non-state actors through the EDF or the EIDHR. A project to support non-state actors that is managed jointly with the National Authorising Officer was formally launched in 2010 (European Commission 2009). Yet, the calls for proposals to fund civil society organisations were delayed, indicating a rather weak interest in the project on the Rwandan government's side.[29] The government seems to have a clear preference for NGOs involved in the delivery of basic services, rather than advocacy activities that empower NGOs in holding the government accountable.[30]

To summarise, the EU has continued to promote *democratic government* since 2006. However, in contrast to the early 2000s, it has been quite reluctant to put pressure on the Rwandan government. Instead, it has adopted a *cooperative-rewarding* strategy. Whereas in the early 2000s, Rwanda only reluctantly started to engage with the EU, it has been increasingly active in cooperating on the implementation of governance instruments since the mid-2000s. At times, the government has even taken a proactive approach and launched its own initiatives to cooperate with the EU and other donors on governance issues (i.e. the joint governance assessment).

It is surprising that the Rwandan government has even started to proactively cooperate, in spite of the fact that the EU has not narrowed its approach to support merely effective government. The EU's strategies alone can therefore not fully explain the changes in the responsiveness of the Rwandan government. The following sections will show that the Rwandan government's willingness to proactively engage with the EU is influenced by its survival strategies, its dependence on the EU as well as the continuously limited access to cooperation with China.

The Rwandan Government's Survival Strategies

A Period of Regime Stability with Few Threats to Regime Survival
In contrast to the early 2000s, between 2006 and 2011, the Rwandan leadership experienced a period of relative stability with few challenges from domestic political opponents. Even though the leadership's support coalition has further eroded, defecting members of the elite did not substantially challenge the leadership. Particularly ahead of the 2010 presidential elections, several high-level members of the RPF went into exile, suggesting an erosion of the core support base of the regime. Defectors included close allies of President Kagame, senior officers of the armed forces and the intelligence services who played an important role during the RPF's invasion of Rwanda in the early 1990s (Cooke 2011; EIU 2011). Rumours about a *coup d'état* spread in Kigali in 2010, spurred on by a string of grenade attacks. However, former members of the RPF's inner circle made limited attempts to organise a political opposition to Kagame (Cooke 2011; EIU 2011).

Moreover, domestic opposition from outside the ruling elite was limited between 2006 and 2011. No major opposition party was formed and the Rwandan government faced little criticism from domestic NGOs.[31] No major public demonstrations were held, where people expressed their dissatisfaction and openly challenged government policies. Instead, public opinion polls seem to suggest that Rwandans were quite happy with their government.[32] According to Gallup polls (2013), 95 per cent of Rwandans had confidence in their government in 2009 and 94 per cent approved of their government in 2012.

External opposition, such as rebel groups in the DRC, also did not pose a major threat to regime stability. The military strength of the FDLR was considerably reduced.[33] However, the FDLR has remained a political challenge. While the RPF government made substantial efforts to overcome ethnic polarisation, a rebel movement close to the Rwandan border that aims to fuel ethnic tensions, directly challenges this policy.[34] The leadership in Kigali thus has a strong interest in minimising security risks (Silva-Leander 2008; Prunier 2009, 322).

Between 2006 and 2011, the strongest opposition probably came from international NGOs, such as Amnesty International, Human Rights Watch and the International Crisis Group. These NGOs published several very critical and influential reports that accused the Rwandan government of not respecting basic political and civil rights.[35] Yet, most international NGOs have left the country and thus direct their reports at an international rather than domestic audience within Rwanda.

Survival Strategies I: Strengthening the Effectiveness of Government Institutions to Improve Public Goods Provision
Since 2006, the Rwandan government has substantially invested in developing a rational-legal and meritocratic bureaucracy. Reforms of government institutions were geared towards raising more domestic revenues and improving public goods provision.

Rwanda launched a second major civil service and administration reform in the mid-2000s (Hausman 2011). Between 1998 and 2009, the number of central government staff was cut by 90 per cent and salaries for those who remained tripled.[36] A public service commission was created in 2007 to standardise civil service recruitment and to establish safeguards against patronage. To improve service delivery and define policy priorities, the government also introduced annual leadership retreats in the mid-

2000s that bring together high-level officials from various branches of the government (Iyer 2012).

Rwanda initiated reforms to improve the management of domestic revenues. It introduced an ambitious public financial management reform in the mid-2000s to improve all stages of the budget cycle, and it gave the Rwanda Revenue Authority and the Auditor-General more powers (Klingebiel and Mahn 2011). These reforms quickly yielded results. Rwanda considerably improved its performance on the Public Expenditures and Financial Accountability (PEFA) indicators between 2008 and 2010.[37] Observers argue that (in contrast to many other African countries) these reforms were mostly put forward by the government and not enforced by donors (ibid).

Rwanda kicked off a major administrative and fiscal decentralisation programme (Ansoms and Rostagno 2012, 433). Responsibility for the delivery of public services, such as education, healthcare or road construction was partly transferred to the local level (Hausman 2011). Along with the decentralisation efforts, the central government introduced measures to hold local officials accountable for their actions. The so-called *imihigo* performance contracts allow the leadership to condition rewards and resources on local authorities' success in promoting economic growth, and strengthening the efficiency and effectiveness of the bureaucracy. Yet, they also allow the leadership in Kigali to better control local authorities and to expand political influence. For instance, *imihigo* contracts include goals related to voter mobilisation. Critics therefore argue that rather than increasing accountability of local officials towards the population, these performance contracts bolster accountability chains between Kigali and local authorities (Ingelaere 2010, 433; 2011, 67f; Ansoms 2009; Ansoms and Rostagno 2012).

These various efforts to advance the effectiveness of Rwandan government institutions are reflected in considerable improvements in international governance indices. According to the Worldwide Governance Indicators, government effectiveness and control of corruption have significantly ameliorated since 2005. Rwanda is among the best-performing countries across Africa in these areas (Fig. 3.3) and performs better than Ethiopia and particularly Angola.

The government's efforts to enhance the effectiveness of government institutions were geared towards both increasing and improving the delivery of services and the provision of public goods. Since the mid-2000s, the government has considerably increased its spending on social services such as healthcare, education and social protection in line with the priorities defined in its national development strategies. For instance, public spending on healthcare as a share of total government expenditure has been high (more than 10 per cent per annum), according to the World Development Indicators. Rwanda's spending on social services ranks considerably above the average in sub-Saharan Africa, and above Ethiopia and Angola.

The government's efforts to boost public goods provision have shown rapid results. Household surveys conducted between 2000 and 2012 suggest that poverty in urban as well as rural areas has been considerably reduced since the mid-2000s (Ansoms and Rostagno 2012).[38] With a Gini coefficient of 0.49 in 2011, Rwanda is still one of the most unequal countries in the world. Yet, over time inequality has at least slightly decreased, from 0.51 in 2000 and 0.52 in 2006 (Ansoms and Rostagno 2012). Rwanda has been one of the few African countries that achieved most of the MDGs by 2015.[39]

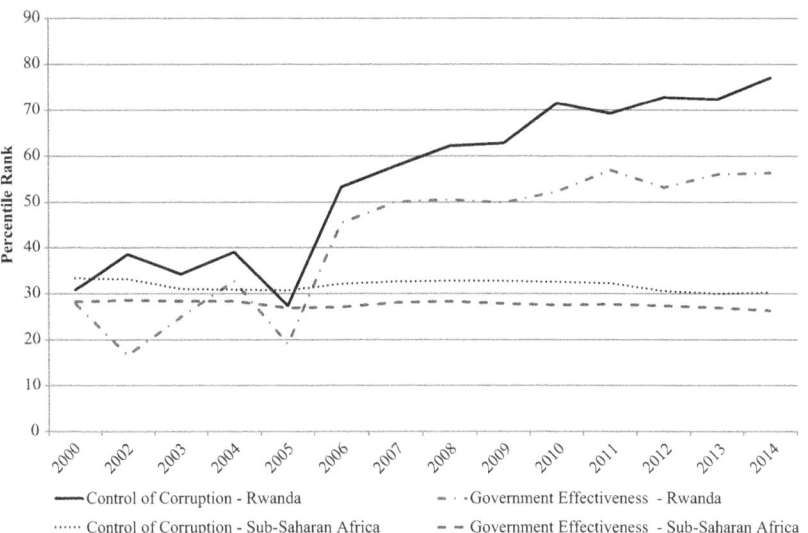

Fig. 3.3 Government effectiveness and control of corruption in Rwanda
Source: Author's compilation, based on World Bank (2016b) Worldwide Governance Indicators

Rwandan citizens also *perceive* the government's policies to be quite successful. According to Gallup polls (2013), 78 per cent of Rwandans had confidence in their healthcare system in 2007; in 2012, 76 per cent of Rwandans were satisfied with their education system. Moreover, 86 per cent of Rwandans felt that the national economy was improving.

Survival Strategies II: Using Arenas of Contestation and Low-intensity Coercion to Prevent Challenges from the Opposition
In the years between 2005 and 2011, arenas of contestation, such as elections or reforms in the justice sector, allowed the government to signal its firm grip on power. Moreover, the government used low-intensity coercion and a gradual closing of political spaces to *prevent* challenges to regime survival.

Parliamentary elections in 2008 and presidential elections in 2010 did not confront the government with a major opposition challenge, but instead allowed the incumbent regime to tighten its grip on power. After banning the Republican Democratic Movement MDR ahead of the 2003 elections, challenges from opposition parties during the 2008 parliamentary elections were very limited (Reyntjens 2010, 11f). Winning the elections with a substantial majority was thus no major difficulty, and international observers found that the election process itself had been relatively free (European Union 2008). Some observers suggest that the government was even *too* successful at the ballot box. They suspect that the RPF actually received almost 98 per cent of the votes, but decided to downplay the official results to 76 per cent to appear less autocratic (Stroh 2008; Hayman 2011; Reyntjens 2010; Longman 2011). The strong results for the RPF signal to regime opponents that organising a political alternative would have limited chances of success. The overwhelming majority in the 2010 presidential elections was also not questioned (Reyntjens 2010). With 93.8 per cent of the votes, Kagame gained a landslide victory.

The Rwandan government made justice sector reforms, and particularly the Gacaca process, a priority (see, e.g. Brown 2010; Samset 2011 for the following). The RPF had arrested about 120,000 people on suspicion of being involved in the genocide. The civil war and the genocide had largely destroyed the judicial system. To cope with the large number of culprits and to establish a system of justice rooted in Rwanda's traditional society, the government initiated the Gacaca processes in 1998; first trial courts were established in 2002. The Gacaca system effectively started in 2005, and by 2010 most detainees had stood trial. The justice system undoubtedly faced tremendous challenges in coping with the consequences of genocide. However, several experts stated that the Gacaca process had been instrumentalised by the ruling party and ultimately reinforced the RPF's grip on power.[40]

The Rwandan government applied various measures of low-intensity coercion to *prevent* potential opposition. It relied on the laws on 'divisionism' (2001), 'genocide ideology' (2008) and a new media law (2009), to limit political opposition, challenges from civil society organisations or the media (Beswick 2010; Samset 2011). In addition to these legal measures, the government also used more informal tactics such as harassment, arrests or 'disappearances' of opposition candidates to further limit political spaces (Beswick 2010; Samset 2011). Ahead of the 2010 presidential elections, for instance, Victoire Ingabire, the most prominent opposition candidate who sought to challenge Kagame at the ballot box was arrested on charges of 'divisionism'. After an internationally contested trial, a Rwandan tribunal sentenced her to eight years in prison in 2012. In January 2014, the court extended her sentence to 15 years' imprisonment.

Between 2006 and 2011, Rwanda has thus experienced a period of limited challenges from the opposition. The government used low-intensity coercion to *prevent* such challenges; it heavily invested in the effectiveness of government institutions and faced limited challenges when managing arenas of contestation such as elections or the judiciary. EU demands to cooperate on strengthening the effectiveness of government institutions and the democratic quality of decision-making processes matched the government's preferences. EU demands to address measures of low-intensity coercion entailed few costs. Analysing Rwanda's interest in engaging with the EU in governance reforms by focusing on EU good governance strategies and the Rwandan government's domestic survival strategies cannot fully explain why Rwanda became not only increasingly active, but at times even proactive, in engaging on governance reforms between 2006 and 2011. One therefore also needs to consider Rwanda's broader interests in cooperating with the EU and opportunities to engage with alternative partners such as China.

Rwanda's Economic Dependence on the EU

Between 2006 and 2011, Rwanda remained strongly dependent on the EU and was as dependent on the EU as it was between 2000 and 2005. It was (again) clearly more dependent on the EU than Angola and Ethiopia.

Aid as a share of Rwanda's GNI slightly reduced compared to the early 2000s. Yet, it still accounted for 18–20 per cent of GNI (Fig. 3.1), making Rwanda one of the most aid-dependent countries in Africa. The share of aid increased to about 50 per cent of government revenues and to 40–50 percent of the government's budget (IMF 2013, 22).

On the other hand, Rwanda's domestic tax base (direct and indirect taxes) stayed quite small. The government's efforts to improve domestic tax systems did, however, bear some fruit. Since 2005, revenues from direct and indirect taxes grew considerably. Yet, they still account for a relatively small share of overall revenue. Rwanda's overall tax revenue also remained below both the regional and sub-Saharan African average (IMF 2013, 21). Rwanda has very little access to non-tax revenues, since it has very few natural resource deposits that can be exploited.

Since the mid-2000s, the Rwandan government has continued to actively embrace the international aid effectiveness agenda. President Kagame has been very vocal in advocating the agenda, for instance, during the high-level meetings in Paris (2005), Accra (2008) and Busan (2011). Rwanda has been among those countries that had made most progress in implementing their international commitments to strengthen aid effectiveness.[41] Rwanda actively used the international aid effectiveness agenda to hold the EU and other donors accountable for the commitments they had made in reforming their aid systems (Hayman 2009). Rwanda was the only African country that published an 'aid policy strategy', identifying direct budget support as Rwanda's preferred aid modality. Donor officials therefore often portray and praise Rwanda as a country with an exceptionally strong 'ownership' of its national development strategy and clear willingness to articulate its policy preferences *vis-à-vis* donors; in contrast to other aid-dependent countries in Africa. Some have argued that Rwanda has considerably more control over its relations with traditional donors than other African countries (Hayman 2009; Whitfield 2009).[42]

Between 2006 and 2011, the EU institutions remained the largest donor to Rwanda, together with the USA, the World Bank and the UK. The EU institutions provided about one-quarter of Rwanda's total aid (Fig. 3.2) and the EU as a whole (EU institutions and member states) was the largest donor to Rwanda. Cooperation with the EU has been attractive to Rwanda not only because of the amount of EU aid, but also because its aid instruments and the sectors it supports match the Rwandan government's preferences. The EU institutions (and the UK) have successively raised the share of direct budget aid, giving the Rwandan government more flexibility on how to spend its aid. Together with the UK, the EU institutions have been at the forefront in negotiating a new budget support framework with the government and establishing direct budget support as an important aid modality in Rwanda (Hayman 2006). By 2010, about half of all aid channelled through government budgets was provided as budget support. Between 2000 and 2010, the EU was the second-largest budget support donor after the UK. In the same period, 35 per cent of all budget support to Rwanda was provided by the EU, most of it after 2005. In contrast, other large donors, such as the USA, gave most of their aid off the budget; humanitarian and food aid still account for most US aid.

The EU and other budget support donors conditioned their budget aid to expenditures on public goods, particularly healthcare and education. The previous section has illustrated that the Rwandan leadership has a clear interest in strengthening public goods provision to enhance support from the broader populace. The EU's priorities thus strongly converge with the preferences of the Rwandan government.

Between 2006 and 2011, the EU was the second most important destination for Rwanda's exports after neighbouring countries in sub-Saharan Africa (Fig. 3.4). Yet, trade still has a low share of Rwanda's GDP. Moreover, exports to the EU have given Rwanda limited opportunities to diversify its export sectors, as exports to the EU mostly consist of coffee and tea. Rwanda's exports—particularly towards East African countries—have increased considerably since 2006, mainly due to stronger economic integration within the East African Community.

Rwanda made considerable progress in improving its regulatory framework and making its business environment more attractive to foreign direct investments. Rwanda's performance in the 'Doing Business' report has improved considerably; it jumped from position 158 in 2005 to position 59 in 2012. However, these efforts have had little effect on the volume of direct investments. According to the World Development Indicators, FDI inflows as a share of GDP have been close to zero (and substantially below the average for sub-Saharan Africa) between 2000 and 2012, with slight increases after 2008. Anecdotal evidence from interviews with Chinese, European and Indian entrepreneurs in Rwanda suggests that several factors influence low levels of investment.[43] As a landlocked country with weak infrastructure links towards neighbouring

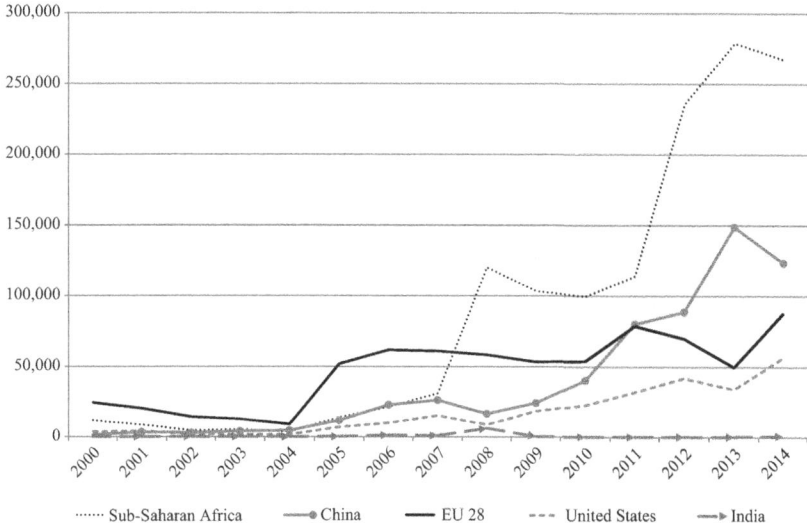

Fig. 3.4 Rwanda's exports to selected countries (in USD thousands)
Source: Author's compilation, based on UNCTAD statistics (2016)

countries, investments in Rwanda are quite expensive compared to other countries in the region. Moreover, even though it has become much easier to start a business in a relatively short time, domestic regulations often change (also retrospectively), making long-term planning difficult for investors.

Rwanda's dependence on development aid as the main source of revenue and the relative importance of EU aid, the EU's choice of aid modalities and the convergence of the EU and the Rwandan government's preferences as to how to spend aid made the EU an attractive partner. Low costs that cooperation on governance reforms involved, in combination with the substantial benefits from overall aid that Rwanda received in return, explain why Rwanda not only reluctantly but even proactively cooperated with the EU on governance reforms between 2006 and 2011. However, this argument would—again—be even stronger if one could control for alternative explanations such as access to cooperation with China.

China: Becoming More Important, But No Alternative Cooperation Partner (Yet)

China's economic cooperation with Rwanda has rapidly intensified since 2006, when the third Forum on China–Africa Cooperation (FOCAC) meeting was held in Beijing. Since then, aid, trade and investments have grown considerably. Yet, as of 2014, China had not (yet) emerged as an economic partner as important as the EU, and has hardly reduced Rwanda's dependence on the EU and other traditional donors. Moreover, China provides little support to the Rwandan government's survival strategies that would compete with EU good governance policies.

China: More Important, But No Alternative Economic Cooperation Partner

After 2006, when the EU and other donors started to substantially raise aid flows to Rwanda and shifted much of their aid to direct budget support, China has also increased its grants and interest-free and concessional loans (Table 3.5). Rwanda has mostly benefited from projects announced under the FOCAC action plans. The two rural schools, the hospital, the agriculture demonstration centre or the USD32 million concessional loan for road renovation in Kigali (Table 3.5) are all part of the 2006 FOCAC package. Beyond activities within the FOCAC framework, Chinese projects in Rwanda include two grants to the Rwandan defence forces or for office equipment for the RPF.

According to Chinese and Rwandan officials, during the past few years, China's annual aid budget for Rwanda was about USD30 million.[44] This would make China a medium-sized donor to Rwanda with an aid budget similar to, for instance, that of Germany, but considerably smaller than that of the EU institutions (about €80 million annually during the past few years). Chinese aid is provided off the budget and information on the volume of aid projects is difficult to access—not only for researchers but also for the Rwandan government itself. China gives aid in the form of turnkey projects, implemented by Chinese companies and with some of the material sourced from China. Some Rwandan officials thus argue that immediate multiplier effects for the Rwandan economy through project implementation are limited. Chinese aid is welcomed with open arms by Rwandan government officials because 'this is something that was not there before',[45] as one official put it. Yet, Chinese aid modalities do not align with the Rwandan government's preference to receive aid channelled through government systems.

Table 3.5   China's aid projects 2006–2012

Year	Type of project	Financial volume
2006	President's office/state house	USD1.5 million grant USD9–10 million grant
2008	Donation for earthquake victims	USD50,000 grant
2008	Two primary rural schools in eastern and northern provinces (Rulindo and Gatsibo)	USD1.6 million grant
2008	Masaka Polytechnic Hospital in Kigali suburbs Supplementary works for the polyclinic hospital	USD4 million–9.9 million grant
2008	Agricultural technical demonstration centre in Rubona, Huye district (rice and mushrooms)	USD4.5–5.3 million grant
2008	CCP donates computer and other office equipment to RPF	USD100,000 grant
2009	Road rehabilitation in Kigali	USD32 million concessional loan
2009	For president Kagame, support for orphans	USD70,000 grant
2009	Confucius Institute in Kigali and grants scholarships	–
2010	Floating dock for Marine regiment; two boats for Rwanda defence forces to protect methane gas plant on Lake Kivu	grants (volume undefined)
2010	Purpose undefined Technical cooperation for bamboo cultivation and craft processing	USD6 million (China Development Bank)
2011	Technical, vocational and educational training centre	USD11 million
2011	Purpose undefined	Yuan 50 million grant; Yuan 50 million, interest-free loan (equal to USD8 million each)
2012	Multinational roads: Rusizi-Karongi-Rubavu lot 4: Mwityazo-Ruvumbu (25 km); lot 5: Ruvumbu-Kibuye (42 km)	USD113 million
12/09/ 2012	Infrastructure projects (to be defined)	USD25 million grants and concessional loans

(*continued*)

Table 3.5 (continued)

Year	Type of project	Financial volume
30/12/ 2012	Projects to be defined (information January 2013)	USD16 million (one or two grants)
		USD19 million interest-free loan
	Scholarships, various years	–

Total committed grants and interest-fee and concessional loans between 2005 and December 2012 (rough estimate) USD245 million

Source: Author's compilation based on: *The New Times*, BBC monitoring international reports, Chinese embassy website, website of Rwanda's Ministry of Foreign Affairs; interviews with Chinese and Rwandan government officials in Kigali March/April 2010 and July 2013, Beijing July 2010 and January 2013; Grimm et al. (2010). If not stated otherwise, the loans listed here are provided by the China EXIM Bank.

Since 2006, China's share in Rwanda's trade has gone up rapidly. China has surpassed the EU in 2011 to become the second most important export destination after exports towards the East African Community (Fig. 3.4). Taking together imports and exports, China is currently the fifth largest trading partner after Kenya, the EU as a whole, Uganda and the USA.

Rwanda mostly exports minerals (ore), coffee and some tea to China. Trade with China has thus allowed Rwanda to increase export volumes and to diversify export markets. Trade with China has not (yet) opened new export sectors and (so far) made little contribution to diversify export products.[46] Rwanda exports ore, coffee beans and tea leaves mostly as raw materials with little value added. The trade preferences that China has granted to African countries do not cover roasted coffee and packaged tea, and thus have allowed Rwanda to export only unprocessed commodities.[47]

Despite Rwandan government efforts to attract more international investments, particularly from China, Chinese investment flows and stocks have remained small. Investment data reported by Chinese and Rwandan officials vary substantially. According to information from the Rwanda Development Board, Chinese investment stock had only been at around USD10 million by 2011; but according to data from the Chinese Ministry of Commerce (MOFCOM), investment stock had been at about USD20 million by 2010. Investment stock from the largest investors—companies from South Africa and Kenya—each totalled about USD100,000. Chinese investments are concentrated in the hospitality sector (hotels and restaurants); some investments also target manufacturing, telecommunications and mining. Very few Chinese investments in Rwanda have seen capital injections from the China Africa Development Fund (CADFund).[48] The CADFund bought shares in a media company that offers digital pay TV.[49] CADFund investments in an assembly plant for mobile phones and in a large hotel in Kigali were under consideration, but have not materialised.[50]

Only since 2011 have private company registrations and investment commitments grown considerably. The volume of investments is thus likely to grow in the medium-term.[51] For instance, a new Chinese textile company has opened in Kigali's special economic zone in 2014. This project has been politically supported by the Chinese government, following a similar precedent in Ethiopia. The project will become another model case for the relocation of Chinese industries towards Africa.[52]

In terms of trade and official flows, China is by far the most important non-traditional partner for Rwanda. According to Rwandan (and Indian) officials, access to financial assistance from India, Brazil or South Africa has remained limited.[53] In 2008, India extended a USD80 million concessional loan for a hydropower plant on the Nyabarongo River. Another USD120 million concessional loan for an irrigation project has been approved. Similar to loans from the Chinese EXIM Bank, concessional loans provided by the Indian EXIM Bank are tied: 75 per cent of the goods and services have to be sourced in India. According to Indian officials, India also gives some technical assistance for capacity building.[54] Rwanda's economic cooperation with South Africa, Brazil or Turkey has remained very limited in terms of financial volume (Grimm et al. 2010).

Chinese 'Model' Attractive, But Little Chinese Support for Rwanda's Survival Strategies
Beyond economic cooperation, engagement with China has not provided the Rwandan government with an alternative to the EU with regard to cooperating on the government's survival strategies. President Kagame has frequently made references to the attractiveness of the 'developmental state' model for Rwanda in public speeches, both domestically and abroad. He has mostly referred to Singapore or South Korea, but has increasingly also mentioned China as a potential 'model' for Rwanda.

However, beyond general public statements, the attractiveness of China's authoritarian capitalism has not yet resulted in a closer engagement between the Rwandan and Chinese elites in how to reform domestic political institutions. China offers little technical assistance for government institutions, for example, to improve the efficiency of government bureaucracy, the regulatory environment or Rwanda's capacity to generate domestic tax revenue. In contrast to countries like Ethiopia, Rwanda sends few high-level officials to China for training. China also offers limited assistance to support economic reforms. For instance, there has been, so far, relatively little exchange on agriculture or private sector development. Moreover, China does not assist the Rwandan government in reducing political spaces. Interviews with Rwandan government officials and an extensive press survey suggest, for instance, that cooperation related to human rights, the media or civil society continues to be very limited.[55]

Exchange between the RPF and the Communist Party of China has been regular but less intense compared to other countries like Ethiopia. The CCP and the RPF have established relations in 1998 and have had regular party-to-party meetings since then (*New Times* 2010). Party-to-party exchanges could open opportunities to discuss leadership succession or the strengthening of party institutions. Yet, visits took place only one or two times a year between 2000 and 2012 (Fig. 3.5). Compared to

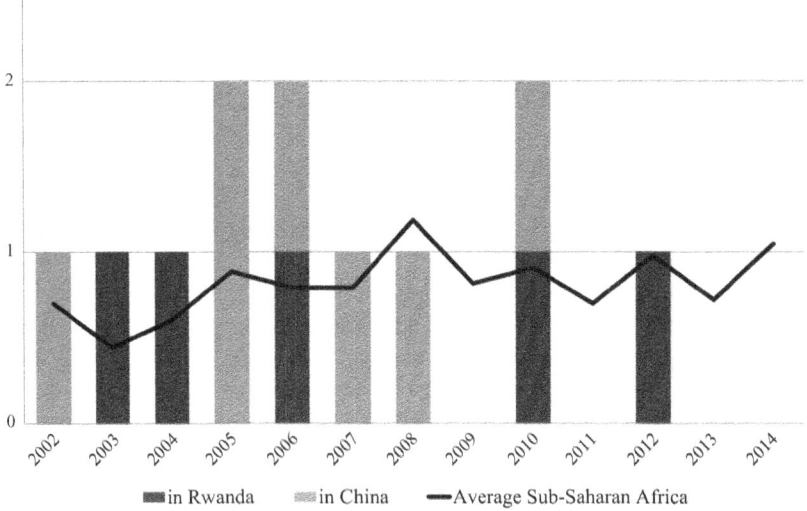

Fig. 3.5 Annual bilateral visits RPF–CCP

Source: Author's compilation, based on news reports from the International Department of the Chinese Communist Party

other African countries, the intensity of the CCP's relations with the RPF figures in the medium range. In 2010, the RPF and CCP signed a memorandum of understanding (MoU) in Kigali (*New Times* 2010). It is unclear, however, to what extent the MoU results in an intensification of bilateral relations.

3.4 A U-turn in the EU's Strategies in 2012 but Little Change in Rwanda's Responsiveness

In the summer of 2012, the EU substantially modified its strategy towards Rwanda. When a report published by a UN panel of experts accused the Rwandan government of backing rebel groups in the Eastern DRC (UN Group of Experts 2012), the EU institutions, the USA and some EU member states such as Germany, the UK and the Netherlands partly suspended or withheld aid funds. The EU decided to postpone decisions regarding new aid commitments to the transport sector (€40 million) and to the MDG contract (€30 million) in September 2012. In light of pressure from some EU member states, the World Bank and the African Development Bank (AfDB) also decided to hold out on the signing of new aid agreements for several months. The EU and most other donors eventually did not reduce aid levels, but started channelling funds through other aid modalities such as sector budget support and project aid.[56]

While the UN panel of experts' report was a main reason for the EU's shift in strategy, the EU's decision was also influenced by its more critical view regarding the governance situation. This more critical perception had gradually built up since the 2010 presidential elections. The EU therefore did not resume general budget support, even when the Rwandan government took a more constructive role in the peace process in Eastern Congo.[57]

Beyond the shift in the EU's policies from a *cooperative-rewarding* to a *cooperative-conflictive* strategy, the EU also slightly broadened the content of its good governance approach after 2012. The negotiations for the programming of funds from the 11th EDF for the period 2014–2020 suggested that the EU wants to make assistance for governance reforms a more prominent issue than before. Moreover, the EU placed a stronger emphasis on supporting non-state actors in holding the government accountable, indicating a gradual shift from *democratic government* towards *democratic governance*.

The Rwandan government vocally criticised the EU and other donors' decision to withhold budget support funds and to use aid funds as leverage.[58] Yet, despite the EU's shift in strategy, the Rwandan government has remained willing to cooperate on governance reforms and engage with the EU in political and aid policy dialogues and the implementation of governance aid.

Rwanda's Survival Strategies and Economic Dependence on the EU

When the EU and other donors decided to use aid funds as leverage to exert pressure on Rwanda, the EU's shift in strategy caused Rwanda substantial challenges. The delayed budget support funds were estimated at totalling about 3 per cent of GDP (IMF 2013). At least in the short-term, the Rwandan government had difficulties in mobilising funds to close the budget gap and struggled to pay civil servants. In 2013, economic growth fell to 4.7 per cent due to donor decisions to freeze aid; between 2000 and 2012 the economy had been growing by 8.2 per cent on average (EIU 2013). Even though the EU (and other donors) did not finally reduce aid levels, the Rwandan government went through a period of great uncertainty as to whether aid would eventually be flowing.

At the same time, when the EU and other donors shifted their strategy, the Rwandan government did not face substantial threats to regime survival and domestic opposition. In contrast to the Ethiopian government in 2005 (as we will see in the next chapter), the Rwandan government had more room for manoeuvre to continue engaging with the EU in governance reforms. We have seen that at least since 2010, the Rwandan regime's support coalition has been eroding further. Members of the Rwandan security apparatus in particular have been defecting (Cooke 2011). Their departure put pressure on the Rwandan leadership to maintain the loyalty of the security apparatus. As there are few sources of easy domestic revenues in Rwanda, allowing the military to exploit natural resources in the DRC may help to maintain support from key segments of the security apparatus. Indeed, observers point to Rwanda's economic rather than security concerns to explain its support of rebel movements in the DRC (Huening 2013; Prunier 2009, 322ff).[59]

Signs of a Gradual Change in China's Policy Towards Rwanda?

Since 2012, the volume of China's assistance and concessional loans has grown. Parallel to disputes over Rwanda's involvement in the DRC between the Rwandan government and traditional donors, China announced an increase of its development aid. In September 2012, a few weeks after EU donors threatened to withhold parts of their aid, President Kagame signed a USD25 million grant and interest-free loan agreement during his visit in Beijing (*New Times* 2012). According to Rwandan officials, the purpose of this loan was not immediately defined and subject to negotiations with the Chinese government. At the end of December 2012, a few weeks after the UN panel of experts had issued its final report, the Chinese ambassador to Rwanda pledged another two interest-free loans amounting to USD35 million that are to be used for infrastructure development in Rwanda (*New Times* 2012). Whereas these grants and loans are relatively small compared to the volume of aid used by traditional donors to pressure the Rwandan government into ceasing its support for rebel movements in the DRC, nonetheless, China's support was timely for the Rwandan government.

The motives of the Chinese government for increasing its aid to Rwanda in 2012 remain subject to speculation. They not only coincide with the disputes between the Rwandan government and traditional donors but also with Rwanda's election to the UN Security Council. Similar to other donors that tend to financially reward non-permanent members of the Security Council (Kuziemko and Werker 2006; Bueno de Mesquita and Smith 2010), China probably had an interest in closer cooperation with Rwanda during this period.

The Rwandan government, in turn, has clearly become more interested in cooperating with China; at least partly as a result of the 2012 crisis.[60] By withholding development aid, the EU and other traditional donors gave the Rwandan government an ever-more prominent indication of the implications of aid dependence. As a result, the Rwandan government has started to explore options for intensifying cooperation with China and other emerging economies.

Outlook: What Prospects for Strengthening Economic Cooperation with China?

Until the end of 2014, China's economic cooperation with Rwanda in terms of aid, trade and investments has been relatively limited compared to Rwanda's cooperation with the EU. What are the prospects for deepening economic relations in the short- to medium-term?

In contrast to other African countries (for instance, Ethiopia and Angola), Rwanda has not (yet) received commercial loans or large-scale concessional loans for sizable infrastructure projects from the China EXIM Bank or the China Development Bank. But plans to support the building of a railway line (and a new airport) have been pushed by the Rwandan government. Not least due to the small size of the Rwandan market and its lack of strategic natural resources, Chinese banks have been reluctant to extend loans in the past. If the Rwandan government engages more closely with other East African countries and presents a vision for making infrastructure projects such as an airport or a railway line economically viable in a regional context, finance may be extended in the future. However, even though the Rwandan government has been quite active in reaching out to China to explore opportunities for receiving more official flows, Rwandan officials also clearly see the limits of how much finance they can expect from China. As one Rwandan government official put it:

> We have very limited means to leverage Chinese finance. Compared to other African countries, Rwanda has few things to offer. We do not play in the same league as countries like Ethiopia or Angola.[61]

A similar situation exists for trade and investments. Due to the size of Rwanda's market, the difficult interregional connectedness and the limited presence of strategic resources, Chinese companies tend to engage with neighbouring countries such as Kenya or Tanzania instead. The Rwandan government has been quite active in developing strategies to strengthen trade and investment relations with China (one example being the new textile company that opened in 2014), but some of the above-mentioned strategic parameters are difficult to address and overcome.

3.5 Conclusions

Rwanda only reluctantly engaged with the EU in governance in the early 2000s, but became increasingly willing and at times proactive after 2006. What explains Rwanda's initial reluctance and the change in the Rwandan government's strategy over time?

2000–2005: Why Was Rwanda Reluctant to Engage with the EU in Governance Reforms?

The EU's strategies to promote governance reforms in Rwanda initially produced only a few benefits but entailed some costs for the Rwandan government. The EU's attempts to promote the *effectiveness* of *government* institutions and to support the establishment of formal democratic institutions partly tied in with the government's preferences. By the early 2000s, the Rwandan government had restored its monopoly on power and basic economic development. Economic growth, public goods provision and the introduction of formal democratic institutions became more important priorities. The 2003 referendum on the new constitution and presidential and parliamentary elections marked the end of the post-genocide transition phase. In this context, EU support for the rehabilitation of parliament, democratic oversight institutions, the judiciary and the reconciliation process thus partly converged with the government's preferences.

At the same time, the EU's attempts to promote *democratic government* and the EU's criticism and pressure to open spaces for civil society and opposition parties were risky for regime stability. The EU began to ask Rwanda to engage in democratic reforms during a period of growing domestic opposition and regime instability. Ahead of the 2003 presidential and parliamentary elections, some members of the 'government of national unity' defected to the opposition to challenge and compete with the RPF. The government responded by banning the MDR, the main opposition party, and by limiting spaces for civil society organisations and the media. The EU's criticism and pressure to open political spaces thus put the government in a difficult position.

In light of these costs and relatively limited benefits that EU good governance strategies generated for the Rwandan government, one would have expected Rwanda to refuse or only very reluctantly accept to cooperate with the EU on governance reforms. However, the challenges that cooperation on governance reforms caused were largely compensated by

Rwanda's broader interests in cooperating with the EU. Since the end of the 1990s, Rwanda's aid dependence was growing rapidly and the EU became one of its largest donors. Rwanda thus had a strong incentive to start engaging with the EU in governance reforms. Moreover, in the early 2000s, Rwanda had very limited access to official flows from China (or other emerging economies) which could have shaped Rwanda's interests in EU development assistance.

2006–2011: Why Did Rwanda Increasingly (Pro)actively Engage?

Between 2006 and 2011, EU good governance strategies caused little cost but some benefit for the government. The EU continued to promote *democratic* and *effective government*. The EU also continued to put little emphasis on using the transnational channel and made few attempts to empower non-state actors. The EU refrained from publicly criticising the Rwandan government or from imposing material pressure. Instead, it *rewarded* Rwanda through higher aid levels and aid modalities such as budget support.

The EU's good governance strategies thereby largely aligned with the preferences of the government. After the end of the transition process, economic growth, public goods provision and state modernisation became even more important pillars for the government's legitimacy. EU demands to cooperate on improving the effective management of state institutions (i.e. public financial management reforms) thus tied in with the Rwandan government's preferences. Moreover, EU support for strengthening democratic government and input legitimacy concentrated on areas where the EU and the Rwandan government's preferences largely converged. EU support for democratic government put a strong emphasis on promoting justice sector reforms, including the Gacaca process, also an important priority of the Rwandan government. Furthermore, the EU provided rhetorical and material support for the elections in 2008 and 2010, which bolstered the domestic and international legitimacy of the regime.

In contrast, between 2006 and 2011, the EU refrained from criticising the gradual closing of political spaces. From the mid-2000s onwards, the Rwandan regime experienced a period of relative stability with few challenges from the opposition from outside or within the country. After banning the main opposition party ahead of the 2003 elections and the crackdown on independent civil society organisations in 2004, domestic opposition was substantially weakened. Members of the inner core of the elite defected (particularly after 2008) and joined the opposition or left the country. The Rwandan government used various strategies of low-intensity coercion and successfully prevented the emergence of a meaningful opposition.

Between 2006 and 2011, EU good governance strategies thus entailed few costs but some benefits for the Rwanda government. Focusing only on the EU's strategies and the Rwandan government's survival strategies, however, cannot fully explain why Rwanda at times even proactively engaged with the EU in governance reforms. One would actually have expected the government to just actively engage.

To explain why Rwanda was even proactive in cooperating with the EU on governance reforms, one also needs to take into account Rwanda's interests in cooperating with the EU 'beyond' governance reforms. While output legitimacy has become more important for Rwanda's strategy to strengthen regime stability, the EU has remained important for Rwanda as a donor. The EU's willingness to provide higher aid levels, to channel increasing shares of aid through the government's budget and to direct aid to social sectors strongly coincided with the Rwandan government's preferences. Rwanda thus had a strong interest in engaging with the EU.

The EU becomes even more attractive as a cooperation partner when taking into account that Rwanda has very limited access to cooperation with China (or other emerging powers). Economic cooperation between China and Rwanda has remained limited compared to economic cooperation with the EU between 2006 and 2011. Since 2011, China has become Rwanda's second-largest trading partner, after the EU, and an important source of direct investments. However, trade and foreign investments continue to account for only a small share of Rwanda's economy. Furthermore, Rwanda's engagement with China in institutional reforms and party-to-party contacts were also limited. Overall, cooperation with China is no alternative to the EU.

The 2012 Crisis and Its Aftermath: Why Has Rwanda Continued to Engage?

The EU shifted its strategy in 2012. It became more critical regarding the governance situation in Rwanda and it used budget support funds to pressure the Rwandan government to cease backing rebels in the DRC. General budget support was not resumed as the EU viewed the governance situation to be more critical and the preparations for Kagame's third term was looming. Even though the EU's shift in policy caused substantial difficulties for the Rwandan government, it continued to actively engage with the EU in the implementation of governance instruments between 2012 and 2014.

The conjunction of three factors explains the Rwandan government's willingness to continue engaging. First, the EU and other donors put very strong pressure on Rwanda. Withholding aid put the government in a precarious position for several months, during which time it was unclear whether donors would eventually reduce aid levels or not. Moreover, the shift from budget support to sector budget support and other aid modalities has caused substantial short-term costs as the government needed to fill the budget gap.

Second, the government could 'afford' to continue cooperating with the EU and other donors since the crisis did not originate in a substantial (domestic) threat to regime survival. The EU and other donors' decision to rescind budget support was not a response to a situation of high-intensity coercion where the government had little room to manoeuvre (as in the case of Ethiopia in 2005, as we will see in the next chapter). Instead, the shift of the EU and other donors' policies results from a gradual change in the perception of the Rwandan regime that has built up since the presidential elections in 2010 and where the UN expert report tipped the scale.

Third, even though Rwanda increasingly has access to cooperation with China, China's grants and loans still remain small compared to the aid volume that the EU and other donors were withholding. China increased its official flows and strengthened its cooperation with Rwanda in 2012 at the height of the conflict between the EU and other donors and the Rwandan government. Moreover, the Rwandan government actively reached out to China (and other emerging economies) to explore options for deepening relations. However, it remains unclear to the government as to what extent China will become a more important economic cooperation partner in the short- to medium-term.

What If...?

Counterfactual arguments are merely a 'thought experiment' (Tetlock and Belkin 1996), but they can make a contribution to strengthening the argumentation. What if the EU had broadened its good governance approach over time from *democratic government* to *democratic governance* and what if the EU had continued to use a *cooperative-critical* approach between 2006 and 2011? If the EU had put more emphasis on empowering civil society organisations *vis-à-vis* the government, EU strategies would have generated substantially more costs for the regime. If the EU had used more critical public statements and withheld aid to put pressure on the government, for instance, after the 2008 or 2010 elections, this would have entailed substantial direct costs for the government and might have empowered opposition and non-state actors.

What if Rwanda had already had much more access to cooperation with China in the early 2000s or at least between 2006 and 2014? The Rwandan government's willingness to proactively engage with the EU (and other donors) in governance reforms was part of its efforts to maximise access to development aid funds. Rwanda was very active in shaping and implementing the international aid effectiveness agenda, at least partly in order to receive more aid. If China had already been a major partner to engage with Rwanda in the early or mid-2000s, the Rwandan government might still have engaged with the EU in governance reforms. However, it is possible that the government would have been less proactive in cooperating on governance reforms.

Outlook

The case of Rwanda documents that the domestic logic of political survival in authoritarian regimes has important consequences for what the EU can achieve with its good governance strategy. Since the mid-2000s, the Rwandan government has very actively embraced the good governance agenda and actively cooperated with the EU (and other donors) on governance reforms, at least partly with a view to position itself as an aid darling and increase access to development aid funds. In countries like Rwanda, where the government has not been politically challenged domestically since 2006, and where the government was generally willing to engage with the EU in governance reforms, the EU (and other donors) may have had more room to manoeuvre in urging for political reforms. Until 2012 the EU has been highly reluctant to pressure the government not to further reduce political spaces. As with other donors, the EU thus contributed little to counter the gradual closure of political spaces since 2006, to avoid the hardening of authoritarian structures and to prevent the constitutional change that has allowed President Kagame to continue in power after 2017.

NOTES

1. According to figures from the UNHCR, about 100,000 refugees returned from Uganda in 1994. Based on OAU and US State Department reports, Sarkin (2001) reports the growing dominance of Tutsi in the government (see also Silva-Leander (2008) and Ansoms (2009, 294)).
2. This observation is consistent with findings on authoritarian regimes. Political leaders generally prefer small coalitions. Yet, in light of mass movements, elite conflicts or severe social conflicts during the early stages of state formation, they are under pressure to broaden their coalition. This argument has been made, for instance, in the case of Asian states (Doner et al. 2005).
3. The minutes of these meetings can be found online at http://www.devpartners.gov.rw/, last access on 3 June 2015.
4. The EU uses three main criteria to decide on the allocation of EDF funds and increases or reductions in EDF funds during the mid- and end-term review: the governance situation, the 'needs' of the country measured in terms of economic and social development, and the country's capacities to absorb aid funds.
5. See Hayman (2006) for an analysis of the aid management framework and the different aid policy dialogue fora in Rwanda in the early 2000s. For an overview of the development of aid policy dialogue between the government, the EU and other donors, also refer to Euréval and PRODEV (2006, 41ff).
6. The minutes of the aid policy dialogue meetings can be found at http://www.devpartners.gov.rw/, last access on 3 June 2015.
7. The government of unity was created after the genocide. It was partly based on the Arusha Accords that were signed in 1993 by the RPF and the Rwandan government to end the three-year civil war (see also Prunier 1997).
8. The national electoral commission was founded in 2000. The Ombudsman office was founded in 2003. See official mandate and legal framework of the Ombudsman online at https://www.ombudsman.gov.rw/, last access on 3 June 2014.
9. See, for instance, the interview with Tito Rutaremara online at http://www.princeton.edu/successfulsocieties/content/data/oralhistory/S7TitoRutaremaraid297/TitoRutaremara.pdf, last access on 3 June 2014.
10. Interviews with Rwandan and Chinese government officials were conducted in Kigali in March and April 2010 and in July 2013 and in Beijing in January 2013.
11. Information on EIDHR projects for various years is available at EIDHR compendia; see European Commission (1995–2012).

12. Some EIDHR funds were used for strengthening the civil society platform that monitored the 2008 and 2010 elections, to support freedom of the press or the human rights advocacy work of NGOs (European Commission 1995–2012).
13. Aid provided under the MDG contract is not made conditional upon specific governance reforms. The main objective is to assist countries in making progress in achieving the MDGs and reducing poverty. Nevertheless, the EU's decision to reward Rwanda with an MDG contract signalled to the government that the EU views the governance situation as generally positive.
14. Results from the mid-term review are published on the website of the European Commission online at www.ec.europa.eu/development, last access on 10 November 2016.
15. EU Press statement, 7 May 2012, online at http://eeas.europa.eu/delegations/rwanda/press_corner/all_news/news/2012/20120507_01_en.htm, last access on 7 May 2013.
16. In response to a UN panel of experts report that accused Rwanda of supporting rebel movements in the DRC, Sweden and the Netherlands shifted budget support to project assistance in 2008 (Hayman 2011, 677f). The EU did not.
17. In addition to these formal channels of communication, the EU used periodic informal meetings with the government to address governance issues.
18. See, for instance, speech by President Kagame at the Ninth Government of Rwanda and Development Partners meeting—Kigali, 4 November 2010, online at http://www.paulkagame.com/2010/index.php?option=com_content&view=article&id=214:speech-by-president-kagame-at-the-9th-government-of-rwanda-and-development-partners-meeting-kigali-serena-november-4-2010-&catid=34:speeches&Itemid=56&lang=en, last access on 3 June 2014.
19. In addition to the documents cited, the following section has been particularly informed by interviews with officials from EU institutions, EU member states and the Rwandan government. Interviews were conducted in Kigali in March and April 2010 and July 2013, and in Brussels in October 2012.
20. Interviews with officials from the EU institutions, member states and the Rwandan government, Kigali March and April 2010.
21. Whereas issues related to governance reforms are brought onto the agenda mainly as a result of the EU's initiative, the Rwandan government has been particularly interested in discussing the extradition of genocide suspects who have sought refuge in the EU. Broader international issues such as the aid effectiveness agenda or political developments in the EU were appar-

ently not discussed during formal Article 8 dialogue meetings. Interviews with officials from the EU institutions, member states and the Rwandan government, in Kigali in March and April 2010 and in Brussels in October 2012.
22. During the meetings the government discussed with donors its overall development strategy, progress achieved and areas of disagreement. The minutes of all meetings can be found online at http://www.devpartners.gov.rw/, last access on 5 December 2015.
23. The minutes of the meetings can be found online at http://www.devpartners.gov.rw/, last access on 5 December 2015.
24. Interviews with officials from the EU institutions, member states and the Rwandan government, Kigali March and April 2010, July 2013 and in Brussels October 2012.
25. Ibid.
26. The National Authorising Officer is located within the Ministry of Local Government and manages the implementation of EDF funds.
27. The aid policy strategy defines the government's position on aid and seeks to clarify the responsibilities of different national and international actors in implementing aid (Government of Rwanda 2006). In this strategy, the government asks other donors, such as Sweden, to shift aid from the justice sector to other policy fields.
28. See minutes of sector budget support meetings accessible online at http://www.devpartners.gov.rw/, last access on 3 January 2013 as well as interviews with officials from the EU institutions, member states and the Rwandan government, in Kigali in March and April 2010.
29. Interviews with EU officials in October 2012.
30. Limiting the political space for non-state actors caused a number of international NGOs to leave the country, rendering EU support for NGOs even more difficult.
31. Most Rwandan civil society organisations focused on service delivery and supported the implementation of government policies rather than seeking to hold the government accountable (Longman 2011).
32. In a political context where freedom of expression is severely restricted, public opinion polls have to be viewed with great caution, of course. This is equally relevant for opinion polls in Ethiopia and Angola.
33. Whereas exact figures are difficult to obtain, the FDLR was estimated as having about 10,000 troops in the early 2000s (Waugh 2004). By 2008 it suffered an erosion of its military strength and the number of troops was reduced to 6000 (Prunier 2009, 322ff, International Crisis Group 2009). According to UN figures, it had as few as 1500 to 1800 troops by December 2013. See, for instance, Voice of America, 11 December 2013,

online at http://www.voanews.com/content/un-targets-fdlr-fighters-in-eastern-congo/1808451.html, last access on 3 June 2014.
34. Moreover, the RPF came to power as a result of a situation not too different: it was established in Uganda by armed refugees who had fled the crisis in Rwanda in the 1960s.
35. See, for instance, Amnesty International (2010) or Amnesty International (2012).
36. The 2006 reform reduced staff numbers from 10,000 to about 2000. Salaries that made up 73 per cent of government expenditure at the end of the 1990s were cut to 33 per cent. The percentage of civil servants with university degrees rose from 6 per cent in 1998 to almost 80 per cent in 2005 (Hausman 2011).
37. PEFA seeks to assess the quality of the budget process. In 2010 Rwanda scored 'good' or 'very good' on 18 out of 28 PEFA indicators. The results for the PEFA analysis can be found online at http://www.pefa.org/, last access on 3 June 2016.
38. The rate of primary school completion increased from 76 per cent in 2009–2010 to 79 per cent in 2010–2011. The gross enrolment rate for secondary education also increased (African Development Bank et al. 2011).
39. According to the MDG monitor, Rwanda achieved all goals except for goal 2 (universal primary education) and goal 8 (global partnership for development), where not enough information is available.
40. The RPF successfully resisted pressure to look back on human rights abuses and killings it carried out during the civil war in the early 1990s, during its military advance into Rwanda in 1994 as well as in the early years after the genocide (Prunier 1997, Longman 2004, 77). The RPF's refusal to take responsibility and to be accountable for gross human rights abuses is seen as an important obstacle to long-term peace-building and stability (Longman 2004).
41. The 2007 report on Rwanda's progress in meeting the principles set out by the Paris Declaration can be found online at http://www.oecd.org/dac/effectiveness/42155403.pdf, last access on 10 December 2016.
42. This 'exceptionalism' is also probably a result of Rwanda's domestic survival strategies and the basic threats to regime stability that the government faces.
43. Interviews with Rwandan, Chinese and Indian entrepreneurs in Kigali in July 2013, in Delhi in July 2013 and in Beijing in July 2013.
44. Information here and in the following is based on interviews with Chinese and Rwandan officials in Kigali in March 2010 and July 2013 and in Beijing in January 2013.

45. Interview with Rwandan government official, Kigali July 2013.
46. One-third of Rwanda's exports is composed of metals and ore like tin, coltan, wolfram and cassiterite. Since the mid-2000s, the volume of ore exports has substantially increased, most of which goes to China (see UN Comtrade data).
47. In June 2013 China started to allow roasted coffee to be imported and may thus set incentives for Rwanda to roast and package the coffee domestically before exporting it to China.
48. The CADFund is an equity fund set up by the China Development Bank after the 2006 meeting of the Forum for China–Africa Cooperation in Beijing. For more information on the CADFund, see, for instance, Sanderson and Forseythe (2013).
49. *New Times* (2011), Digital TV firm to add more channels, online at http://www.newtimes.co.rw/news/index.php?a=44509&i=14728, last access on 3 June 2014.
50. See also Joseph Mudingu 'China and Rwanda celebrate years of economic and trade cooperation', *New Times*, 29 October 2008, reprinted by BBC monitoring international reports.
51. The information on FDI flows and stocks was kindly provided by the Rwanda Development Board in an e-mail exchange in July 2013.
52. See 'Chinese firm to set up new textile plant in Rwanda', *The East African*, 19 July 2014, online at http://www.theeastafrican.co.ke/business/Chinese-firm-to-set-up-textile-plant-in-Rwanda/2560-2389932-lx4x90z/index.html
53. Interviews with Rwandan and Indian government officials in Kigali in July 2013 and in Delhi in July 2013.
54. Interviews with Rwandan and Indian government officials in Kigali in July 2013 and in Delhi in July 2013.
55. Interviews with Rwandan and Chinese government officials in Kigali in March and April 2010 and in July 2013.
56. For AfDB see, for instance, IGIHE, 4 April 2013 'AfDB Gives US$ 39.44 M to Rwanda's Specific Sector Budget', online at http://en.igihe.com/business/afdb-gives-us-39-44m-to-rwanda-s-specific-sector.html, last access on 3 June 2014.
57. Conversations with officials from the EU and EU member states in June 2013.
58. International observers were divided over the question of whether aid should be cut or not. The former UK Prime Minister Tony Blair (who is known as a strong supporter of President Kagame) and the philanthropist and politician Howard Buffett argued against cutting aid. They reasoned that Rwanda is not the only party to be blamed for the crisis in the Eastern DRC, and aid cuts would therefore be one sided. Furthermore, they argued that aid has a

huge positive impact on poverty reduction in Rwanda; aid cuts would therefore not only hurt the poor but would also not contribute to solving the crisis. See Blair and Buffett (2013) 'Stand with Rwanda. Now is not the time to cut aid to Kigali'. The Howard Buffett Foundation has even published its own, very critical assessment of the UN panel of experts report and the methodology used for that report (The Howard G. Buffett Foundation 2013).
59. Reports published by the UN group of experts in 2001, 2005 and at the end of 2008 accused members of the Rwandan government of supporting rebel movements in the DRC (Huening 2013, Prunier 2009, 322ff). Findings of the report from the UN group of experts were contested and criticised, for instance, by Tony Blair and Howard Buffett.
60. Interviews with Rwandan government officials in Kigali in July 2013.
61. Interview with Rwandan official in Kigali in July 2013.

Open Access This chapter is licensed under the terms of the Creative Commons Attribution 4.0 International License (http://creativecommons.org/licenses/by/4.0/), which permits use, sharing, adaptation, distribution and reproduction in any medium or format, as long as you give appropriate credit to the original author(s) and the source, provide a link to the Creative Commons license and indicate if changes were made.

The images or other third party material in this chapter are included in the chapter's Creative Commons license, unless indicated otherwise in a credit line to the material. If material is not included in the chapter's Creative Commons license and your intended use is not permitted by statutory regulation or exceeds the permitted use, you will need to obtain permission directly from the copyright holder.

CHAPTER 4

Ethiopia

Over the past decade, the Ethiopian government has remained hesitant to engage in governance reforms with the EU. It reluctantly started to engage in the early 2000s, and became more open ahead of the 2005 elections. After the 2005 election crisis, it at first refused to cooperate and then until the 2010 elections only reluctantly engaged. Between 2011 and 2014, the government has again become slightly more open to cooperation. What explains this overall reluctance and the slight changes over time?

This chapter argues that Ethiopia is an example of a country where the EU's good governance strategies only partly converge with the preferences of the government. Due to specific structural conditions, the Ethiopian government generally has a strong interest in building an effective state and investing in public goods provision, not unlike Rwanda. Similar to Rwanda, the government faced opposition from within the ruling elite in the early 2000s. In response, the Ethiopian government also invested in making state institutions more effective. In contrast to Rwanda, however, the Ethiopian government faced mass opposition and direct threats to regime survival, notably during the 2005 elections. In the aftermath of the crisis, it used low-intensity coercion as a response to opposition. Moreover, the leadership used the state as an instrument of cooptation and expanded the influence of the party on the state and society. In this context, the EU's good governance strategies caused some costs in the early 2000s and substantial difficulties after 2005.

© The Author(s) 2018
C. Hackenesch, *The EU and China in African Authoritarian Regimes*, Governance and Limited Statehood,
https://doi.org/10.1007/978-3-319-63591-0_4

Ethiopia is considerably dependent on aid. In the early 2000s, the EU became one of the largest donors to Ethiopia. In the aftermath of the 2005 election crisis, Ethiopia's aid dependence slightly increased as output legitimacy became more important for the government. Moreover, the EU raised aid levels, providing aid through aid modalities and to sectors that matched the preferences of the government. Ethiopia's (aid) dependence thus explains why the government continued to at least reluctantly engage with the EU in governance reforms after 2005, even though cooperation generated significant costs.

Access to cooperation with China was limited in the early 2000s. Since the 2005 election crisis, however, China has become an alternative partner for the Ethiopian government. Yet, the Ethiopian government has continued to at least reluctantly engage with the EU, which gives substance to the argument that the presence of China only had a small effect on the willingness of African governments to engage with the EU in governance reforms between 2000 and 2014.

4.1 Structural Factors Shaping Ethiopia's Survival Strategies

When the EPRDF[1] overthrew the militarist Derg regime in 1991 after 17 years of armed struggle, the new regime had to transform the state and the economy from a feudal system into a modern state. The new government embarked on an economic reform and modernisation programme. It inherited a relatively efficient bureaucracy that was prepared to work for the successor regime. The army was replaced by the armed wing of the Tigrayan People's Liberation Front (TPLF) and the new government quickly gained the monopoly on power over most of the territory (Clapham 2009, 185; Young 2004).

The Ethiopian leadership faces several interrelated structural challenges that impact on the government's basic choice of strategies for remaining in power. The political coalition that sustains the EPRDF regime is relatively broad compared to its predecessors: the militarist Derg regime and the monarchy under Haile Selassie. The core elite consisted primarily of the TPLF—those Tigrayans who led the struggle against the Derg. However, to broaden its support base and to expand its influence throughout the country, the TPLF developed alliances with several regional parties in the early 1990s. Under the umbrella of the EPRDF, the TPLF thus took charge of a party coalition rooted in different regions (Clapham 2009, 184f; Young 2004, 35ff; Vaughan 2011, 626ff).[2] The EPRDF and particularly its TPLF members remained influential in the security forces and the army (Lyons 2011, 11). The EPRDF has a key role in economic activities through its influence in parastatal companies,[3] party-affiliated companies[4] and cooperatives (Vaughan and Gebremichael 2011; Furtado and Smith 2009; Altenburg 2010). Beyond the core elite, the EPRDF's main constituency are peasants; the EPRDF sees neither the (relatively small) private sector nor the urban middle classes in Addis Ababa as its natural allies (Vaughan and Gebremichael 2011, 26).

Territorial integrity constitutes an important challenge to the Ethiopian leadership. In a multi-ethnic state and within a region prone to insecurity, state failure and violent conflicts, national unity is one of the main pillars of the EPRDF's legitimacy. Between 1998 and 2000, Ethiopia and Eritrea fought a war, during which about 100,000 people were killed and one million displaced. Since then, the conflict has remained deadlocked (Clapham 2009, 186).[5] Domestically, the government maintains its monopoly on power over most of the territory, except for the Ogaden region close to the border with Somalia where the government has been fighting a counter-insurgency campaign (Abbink 2009, 20).

While the Ethiopian leadership needs substantial means to sustain its relatively broad support base, the government has little access to natural resources to generate revenues. Some oil and natural gas deposits may be situated in the Ogaden region. However, prospecting has only progressed slowly, not least due to the difficult natural environment and insecurity in that region.

In light of these interrelated challenges, the Ethiopian government has a fundamental preference for building effective state institutions to generate revenues and provide public goods. However, the following sections will show how imminent threats to regime survival during the past decade further shaped the government's survival strategy and its willingness to engage with the EU.

4.2 Ethiopia Reluctantly Engaging with the EU in the Early 2000s

The EU's relations with Ethiopia were limited in the 1990s. However, after the end of the war with Eritrea, in light of Ethiopia's strategic importance in the war on terror after 9/11, and due to the Ethiopian government's willingness to align with the priorities of the MDGs and the international aid effectiveness agenda, the EU intensified its cooperation with Ethiopia in the early 2000s. In parallel, support for governance reforms became more important in the EU's engagement with Ethiopia.

The EU' Good Governance Strategies Between 2000 and 2005

The EU's Approach: Promoting Democratic Government
Between 2000 and 2005, the EU adopted a broad strategy, promoting *democratic government* with some elements of *democratic governance*. The country strategy paper, signed by the EU and Ethiopia in 2002, reflects a broad understanding of good governance (Ethiopia and European Community 2002). The EU sought to promote input legitimacy by strengthening democratic institutions that hold the government accountable to national and international laws, by supporting elections, justice sector reform and the independence of the judicial system. It promoted output legitimacy by supporting public financial management and civil service reforms. The EU earmarked USD36 million in aid funds to advance these objectives (Table 4.1). Food security, transport, macroeconomic reform, healthcare and education accounted for the largest shares of EU aid to Ethiopia (Ethiopia and European Community 2002, 2007).

Table 4.1 EU governance aid to Ethiopia 2000–2014 (in USD million and in per cent)

Ethiopia	2000–2005	2006–2010	2011–2014
Total governance aid	36.02	48.29	49.03
Total aid (all sectors)	1437.36	1578.41	639.64
Governance aid/share in total EU aid	2.5%	3.1%	7.7%
Output legitimacy	22.82	21.17	22.48
Input legitimacy	13.19	27.12	26.55
Output legitimacy/share total in governance aid	63.4%	43.8%	45.8%
Input legitimacy/share total in governance aid	36.6%	56.2%	54.2%

Source: Author's compilation, based on OECD DAC Aid statistics (2016) (Query for EU institutions; 'total governance aid' includes all aid reported under the category '151:I5a: Government & Civil Society-general, Total' to the OECD DAC Creditor Reporting System. 'Output legitimacy' includes public sector and administrative management, public finance management, decentralisation and support to subnational government, anti-corruption organisations and institutions; 'input legitimacy' includes legal and judicial development, democratic participation and civil society, elections, legislature and political parties, media and freedom of information, human rights, women's equality. Data accessible at http://stats.oecd.org; last access: 5 October 2016)

In the early 2000s, the EU hardly used the transnational channel. The country strategy paper presented civil society organisations as important partners in promoting governance reforms in Ethiopia. Yet, only little aid was allocated to support civil society actors. With funds from the Ninth EDF, the EU started building up a small Civil Society Fund to strengthen NGOs' capacities for service delivery, human rights, governance and conflict prevention and to empower them *vis-à-vis* state actors (Ethiopia and European Community 2002; MWH, ODI, and ECDPM 2004, 40f). Civil society organisations that promoted human rights and helped prepare the 2005 elections received some assistance through the EIDHR (European Commission and Ethiopia 2009, see also Table 4.3).[6] Compared to other traditional donors, the EU was not very active in defending the cause of civil society organisations (MWH, ODI, and ECDPM 2004, 40).

The EU's Instruments: Cooperative-Critical
Similar to Rwanda, the EU also adopted a *cooperative-critical* strategy in Ethiopia in the early 2000s. The EU made governance reforms a key issue during both the formal political dialogue meetings that were launched in 2001 and its aid policy dialogues (Ethiopia and European Community 2008).

In 2004, the EU and other donors agreed to substantially increase the share of aid channelled through budget support (Schmidt 2005). Besides, the EU publicly raised concerns about the governance situation and issued several critical statements regarding the human rights situation, for instance, in the UN Human Rights Commission (Table 4.2).

Table 4.2 EU statements and *démarches* related to governance reforms 2000–2012

	2000–2005		2006–2012		Total
	Positive	Critical	Positive	Critical	
EU public statements on governance reforms	3	8	3	7	21
Démarches	–	5	3	8	

Source: Author's compilation, based on EU annual human rights reports and documents published by the Council of the EU

The Ethiopian Government's Responsiveness: Reluctant Engagement Between 2000 and 2005

The Ethiopian government reluctantly started to engage with the EU in the implementation of governance instruments in the early 2000s. It has been slightly less willing to engage than Rwanda, but more forthcoming than Angola.

Ethiopia's Responsiveness: Political and Aid Policy Dialogues

The government agreed to launch a formal Article 8 political dialogue in 2001. Until 2005, Ethiopia agreed to hold dialogues on a regular basis and to send high-level representatives. Dialogues took place twice a year with Prime Minister Meles and twice a year with the Minister of Foreign Affairs (Ethiopia and European Community 2007). Dialogues covered a broad range of issues including human rights, governance and democratisation, the establishment of democratic institutions such as the Ombudsman and the Human Rights Commission, the upcoming elections in 2005, the death penalty or the ratification of the Rome statute. Regional peace and security issues, notably Ethiopia's relations with Eritrea, also figured prominently in the dialogue (Ethiopia and European Community 2007). Official documents indicate that both the EU and the Ethiopian government considered the quality of political dialogue to be relatively good and steadily improving: It was perceived to be open and mutually beneficial (European Commission and Ethiopia 2002). Ethiopia explicitly highlighted the importance it has been attaching to political dialogue (European Union 2004).

In the early 2000s, the Ethiopian government agreed—albeit very reluctantly—to address governance issues as part of its aid policy dialogues with donors. Similar to Rwanda, Ethiopia and the EU started to institutionalise different formats of aid policy dialogues alongside commitments made under the international aid effectiveness agenda (Furtado and Smith 2009). However, Ethiopia was clearly less willing to address governance reforms as part of these aid policy dialogues than Rwanda. For instance, the Ethiopian government was very reluctant to engage in questions related to governance reforms during the budget support policy dialogue. Only after the first two dialogue meetings did the government agree at least to address questions related to public financial management reforms or the fight against corruption and the atmosphere of the dialogue subsequently improved (Schmidt 2005, 61f; 101f). Moreover, similar to

Rwanda, the EU and other donors initiated specific dialogue formats to better coordinate their aid to governance-related sectors, such as justice reform, civil society organisations or democratic institutions. In contrast to Rwanda, Ethiopia refused to engage with donors in these meetings (DAG 2005b).

Ethiopia's Responsiveness: Positive Conditionality and Governance Aid
In the early 2000s, the Ethiopian government reluctantly agreed to engage in the implementation of governance aid and inclusion of positive conditionality in its engagement with the EU.

The government hesitated to include indicators related to democratic reforms in its agreement with the EU and other donors on direct budget support. The EU and other donors insisted on introducing indicators on elections and human rights (Schmidt 2005; Bergthaller and Küblböck 2009). Yet, the government objected to these requests and the final agreement that was signed in April 2004 had no targets related to democratic reforms (Schmidt 2005).

Ethiopia was reluctant to cooperate with the EU on the implementation of governance aid. Annual reports on the implementation of EU aid and secondary sources indicate that the implementation of governance aid faced considerable difficulties. Similar to Rwanda, the Ethiopian government was willing to engage in the implementation of aid geared at supporting the effectiveness of government institutions. Compared to Rwanda, Ethiopia was less willing to cooperate on the implementation of aid targeted to support democratic reforms.

One case in point is the justice sector. While the government insisted that the EU should support the justice sector by funding the Public Service Capacity Administration Programme (PSCAP), which also entails capacity-building for justice institutions, the EU was hesitant to increase support for justice sector reform through PSCAP, as this programme mostly aims at strengthening technical and financial capacities rather than the independence of the judicial system. As a result of these diverging preferences, most of the EU's aid earmarked for justice sector reform between 2000 and 2005 was not disbursed.[7]

Another example is the EU's assistance for democratic institutions. With support from the EU and other donors, the government developed the legal foundation for establishing a Human Rights Commission and an Ombudsman's office in the late 1990s (MWH, ODI, and ECDPM 2004). The Ethiopian parliament passed the relevant legislation in July 2000. The EU and other donors subsequently urged the authorities to proceed in appointing the Commissioner and the Ombudsman (European Commission and Ethiopia 2004). Yet it took until late 2004 for both to be appointed, only a few months ahead of the 2005 parliamentary elections (Government of Ethiopia and United Nations Development Programme 2007). Some observers argue that the delay resulted from the government's reluctance to support these institutions, as it had to expect criticism for its human rights record (Rahmato and Ayenew 2004, 42f).

The government was clearly reluctant to engage with the EU in the implementation of aid geared towards civil society organisations. The EU issued feasibility studies to design a strategy on how to support civil society in Ethiopia, but the proposed Civil Society Fund could only be launched in 2006 (Ethiopia and European Community 2002; European Union 2004).

We can conclude that between 2000 and 2005, the EU sought to promote *democratic government*. The EU aimed at promoting input legitimacy by strengthening democratic institutions that hold the government accountable to national and international laws, by supporting elections, justice sector reform and the independence of the judicial system. The transnational channel did not play a prominent role in the EU's strategies. The EU mostly used public statements and declarations to criticise the governance situation in the country. The Ethiopian government started to *reluctantly* engage. Whereas the government became more forthcoming in cooperating with the EU ahead of the 2005 parliamentary elections, the post-election crisis marked the end of this period.

The Ethiopian Government's Survival Strategies

Strong Threats to Regime Survival: A Split in the Ruling Elite

In the early 2000s, the EU's strategies to support governance reforms in Ethiopia coincided with a period of domestic instability, a reorganisation of the regime's support base and a restructuring of the relationship between the EPRDF and the state. Disagreements within the TPLF, and more generally the EPRDF, about the war with Eritrea (1998–2000) caused a split in the TPLF central committee in 2001 (Tadesse and Young 2003; Tronvoll 2009). A majority within the TPLF favoured an aggressive military strategy towards Eritrea to assert Ethiopia's strong position on the Horn of Africa and to demonstrate that Ethiopia does not give in to Western pressure. Instead, Prime Minister Meles supported a moderate approach and a negotiated settlement of the border dispute rather than the elimination of the Eritrean regime by military means. Meles was apparently more vigilant about the economic and diplomatic repercussions that the war had on Ethiopia and the regime's stability (Tadesse and Young 2003, 396; Tronvoll 2009, 465). The crisis positioned Meles as the undisputed ideological leader of the party and the government.

Survival Strategies I: Subordinating the Party to the State
In response to the split in the TPLF central committee, the Ethiopian leadership embarked on a state modernisation programme and carefully allowed for political liberalisation ahead of the 2005 general elections. The 2001 split in the TPLF leadership thus did not only affect power relations within the EPRDF but also altered the relationship between the EPRDF, the state and society (Tronvoll 2009, 466; Tadesse and Young 2003, 401).

The split in the central committee and the expulsion of the dissidents were followed by a comprehensive 'cleansing' of the political and military apparatus during which thousands of their (suspected) supporters were eliminated (Tronvoll 2009, 465). The way that internal disagreements were handled alienated important segments of the population in Tigray—Prime Minister Meles' core support base—where many of the dissidents were popular due to their participation in the armed struggle against the Derg and the Eritrean war (Tronvoll 2009, 466).

After the 2001 split, the EPRDF leadership carefully introduced several measures to enhance formal state institutions and to secure the preeminence of the state over the party. To bolster the EPRDF's power base in rural areas, local state structures were reinforced to bring the state closer to the people and to make government service provision more effective. The district level (Woreda) received more influence in implementing social services and spending financial resources that were formerly managed by the regions (Furtado and Smith 2009; Peterson 2010, 9f). On the other hand, power and control of the local and regional level was again more strongly centralised within the state and in Addis Ababa (Vaughan 2011, 629ff).

Among the measures to strengthen the state, 'capacity-building' gained particular prominence. The leadership developed a comprehensive civil service reform programme that entailed reforms related to urban management, greater prevalence of information technology, the justice sector and tax and public financial management. This civil service reform programme was later developed into the PSCAP project that the government jointly managed with the World Bank, which the EU and other donors supported (Vaughan 2011, 630f; Peterson 2010). Similar to Rwanda, some experts point out that external support for tax and public financial management reform in Ethiopia was more successful than in other African countries because these reforms were designed by the government and not by the donors (Peterson 2010). Overall, the government's reforms quickly showed results. In the early 2000s, the effectiveness of the Ethiopian government considerably improved if measured in terms of Ethiopia's ranking in the WGI (Fig. 4.1).

New government institutions such as the Federal Ethics and Anti-corruption Commission of Ethiopia (FEAC) were created in the wake of the split in the central committee. One of the FEAC's first measures was to purge high-level party members on the basis of corruption charges. Corruption charges have therefore been widely perceived among the general public as politically selective (Vaughan and Gebremichael 2011, 30). In the early 2000s, the level of corruption did not improve as a result of building up institutions to fight against it (Fig. 4.1).

Tadesse and Young (2003, 401) recapitulate the measures induced after the party split: 'As a result of the defeat of the dissidents, the state is now unquestionably the dominant organ of governance in Ethiopia and the party is assuming the role of servant to the state'.

Survival Strategies II: Managing Arenas of Contestation and Low-Intensity Coercion

Opposition parties had boycotted the parliamentary elections in 1995. The 2000 parliamentary elections were therefore the first elections where opposition parties participated. While the government firmly controlled political spaces, the opposition was relatively unorganised. Opposition parties therefore clearly did not constitute a viable threat to the ruling EPRDF in 2000. They only gained 12 seats in the House of Representatives, indicating the EPRDF's strong grip on power (Tronvoll 2009, 454, 464).

In the early 2000s, the Ethiopian government used measures of low-intensity coercion to limit opportunities for the media, civil society organisations or opposition parties to challenge the EPRDF. The regime change in 1991 had clearly not been accompanied by higher levels of political liberalisation. After the party split in 2001, the government relied on low-

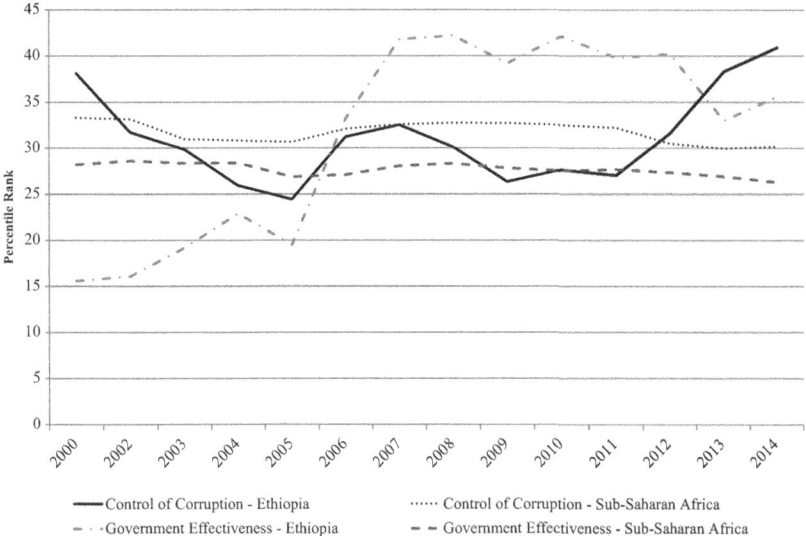

Fig. 4.1 Government effectiveness and control of corruption in Ethiopia
Source: Author's compilation, based on World Bank (2016b), Worldwide Governance Indicators

intensity coercion to limit the chances of defecting party members and other opponents to mobilise mass support.

Just ahead of the 2005 elections, the Ethiopian government slightly opened up political spaces. The campaign for the 2005 parliamentary elections saw a relatively free debate and slightly more openness than previous elections, generating a spirit of optimism (Abbink 2006, 176; Tronvoll 2009, 454f; Aalen and Tronvoll 2009, 194ff). The Ethiopian government invited a number of international observers, including those from the EU. They noted shortcomings with regard to respect for human rights, the rule of law and basic democratic principles during the election campaign. However, opposition parties had unprecedented possibilities to engage, particularly in Addis Ababa and other urban areas. Furthermore, the opposition was much better organised and stronger than during the previous elections in the mid-1990s and in 2000 (Tronvoll 2009, 464).

In the years between 2000 and 2005, the EU and other donors' demands for political liberalisation only partially aligned with the EPRDF's strategy to reorganise state-party relations. Those parts of EU governance aid geared towards strengthening *effective government*—for instance, support for anti-corruption institutions, public financial management or decentralisation—were largely in line with government priorities. However, other activities that were more clearly targeted towards *democratic government* caused considerable adaptational pressure. It is surprising that the Ethiopian government still, albeit reluctantly, started to engage with the EU in these activities. One therefore also needs to consider Ethiopia's interest in engaging with the EU 'beyond' governance reforms.

Ethiopia's Economic Dependence on the EU Between 2000 and 2005

Ethiopia has been strongly dependent on development aid. It has historically received low aid volumes compared to other African countries. As it has never been colonised, it had no special relationship with a former colonial power (Furtado and Smith 2009). Aid flows increased when the EPRDF came to power in 1991. However, during the Ethiopian–Eritrean war, most donors went back to limiting assistance to humanitarian aid. Since Ethiopia viewed Eritrea as the aggressor, the Ethiopian government felt it was punished unjustly (Furtado and Smith 2009).

The end of the war between Ethiopia and Eritrea in 2000 coincided with the beginning of reforms in the international aid system. Similar to the Rwandan President Kagame, Prime Minister Meles also took a very active stance in the international aid effectiveness agenda from the very beginning and sought to use the reform dynamic to attract greater aid flows (Furtado and Smith 2009). In the early 2000s, donors rapidly scaled up aid and the government's aid dependence increased considerably. The share of aid in GNI peaked at 19 per cent in 2003 (Fig. 4.2). Grants constituted the second-largest share of government revenue between 2000 and 2005, after trade taxes.

The EU institutions were one of the largest donors to Ethiopia between 2000 and 2005, providing about 17 per cent of total DAC donors' aid (Fig. 4.3). Moreover, the modalities by which the EU provided aid largely matched the preferences of the Ethiopian government. In 2002, shortly after the end of the war, the EU resumed general budget support. Similar to Rwanda, the EU was one of the driving forces among the budget sup-

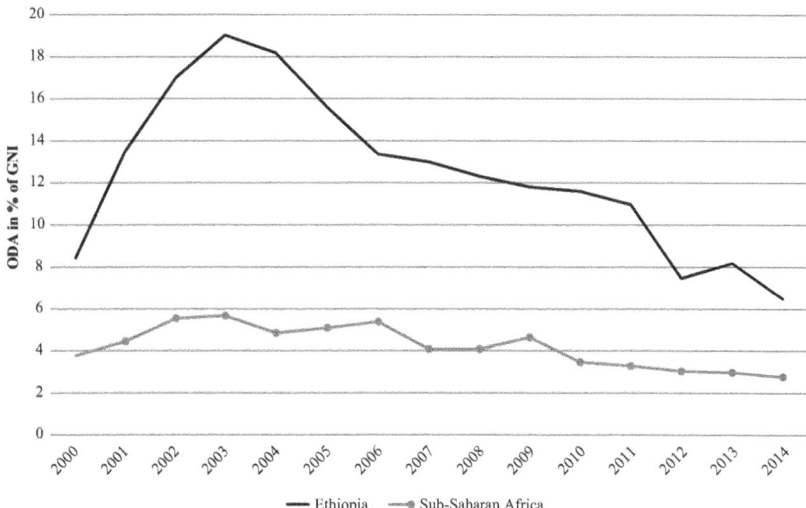

Fig. 4.2 Net ODA as a share of GNI in Ethiopia
Source: Author's compilation, based on World Bank (2016a), World Development Indicators

port donors to negotiate a new harmonised budget support contract with the Ethiopian government (Schmidt 2005; Bergthaller and Küblböck 2009). In 2004, only one year before the 2005 elections, the EU and other donors reached an agreement with the Ethiopian government on a new budget support contract. The share of aid channelled through budget support was supposed to rise considerably as a consequence of the agreement (Schmidt 2005; Bergthaller and Küblböck 2009).

Between 2000 and 2005, the EU had been the most important destination for Ethiopia's exports. Ethiopia exported more to the EU than to the rest of sub-Saharan Africa. Exports to the USA were marginal (Fig. 4.4). Moreover, companies from Europe—if taken together—were the largest investors in Ethiopia. Trade and investments, however, constituted a small share of GDP.

In the early 2000s, when the EU's support for governance reforms did not entail substantial costs, Ethiopia's access to EU development aid and to a lesser extent trade and investments easily outweighed the risks of

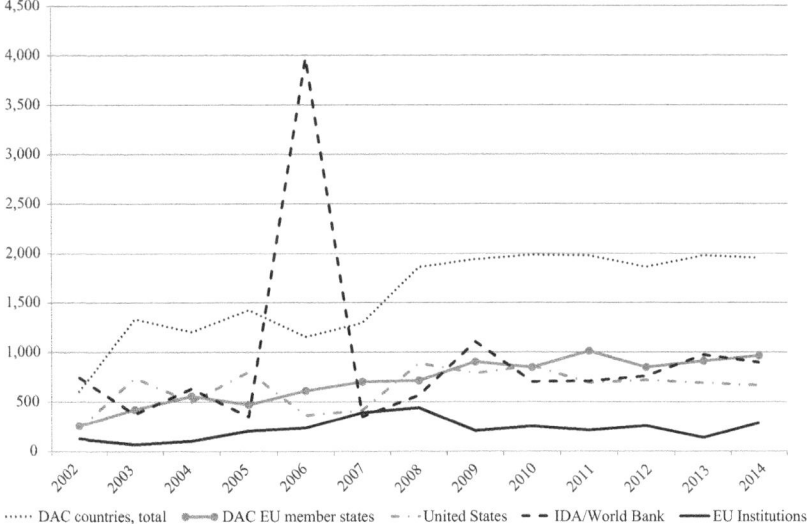

Fig. 4.3 ODA to Ethiopia, selected donors (disbursements in USD million)
Source: OECD CRS aid statistics (2016), author's compilation

engaging in governance reforms, which explains why the Ethiopian government did reluctantly start engaging with the EU.

China: Limited Engagement Between 2000 and 2005

At the turn of the century, when the EU started to make support for governance reforms a more prominent issue in its cooperation with Ethiopia, the government had very little access to economic cooperation with China. China was no alternative partner.

Ethiopia has not only actively sought to strengthen economic cooperation with the EU and other traditional partners but also with China and other emerging economies. Ethiopia's external relations strategy identified China as one of its key partners as early as 2002 (Information 2002). Moreover, according to Ethiopian and Chinese officials, Ethiopia was a driving force behind the FOCAC meetings from the beginning. The second meeting in 2003 took place in Addis Ababa.

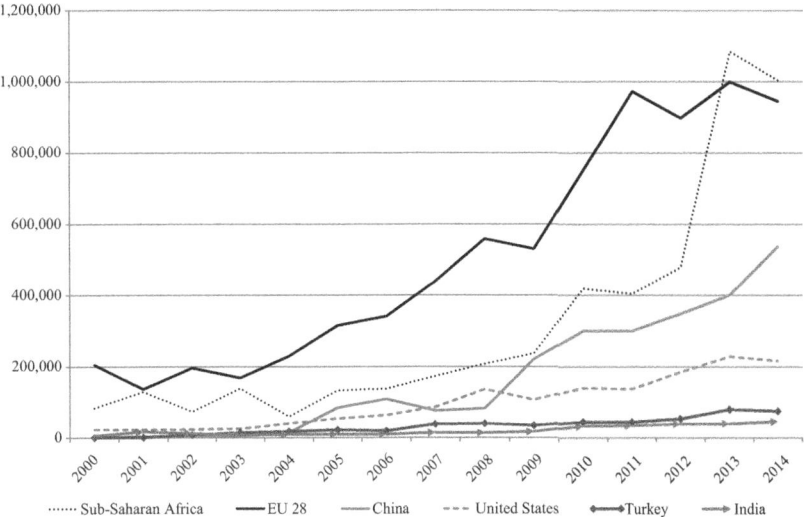

Fig. 4.4 Ethiopia's exports to selected partners (in thousands of USD)
Source: Author's compilation, based on UNCTAD statistics (2016)

Ethiopia co-hosted the third meeting that took place in Beijing in October 2006.

The Ethiopian government's attempts to reinforce its relations with China did not immediately result in closer economic cooperation. In the 1990s, economic exchange mostly consisted of a few aid projects, for instance, to improve water supply (Hawkins et al. 2010). In the early 2000s, the Chinese government financed some road projects and other infrastructure development in Addis Ababa, and it sent medical teams. But Chinese aid remained limited. Chinese direct investments and bilateral trade were also insignificant in the early 2000s (Fig. 4.4). According to the MOFCOM, Chinese investment stocks in Ethiopia stood at less than USD50 million in 2005.

The EPRDF and the Communist Party of China established relations shortly after the EPRDF came to power in 1991. However, if measured in terms of the number of bilateral visits, contact has been relatively limited during the 1990s and between 2000 and 2005 (Fig. 4.5).

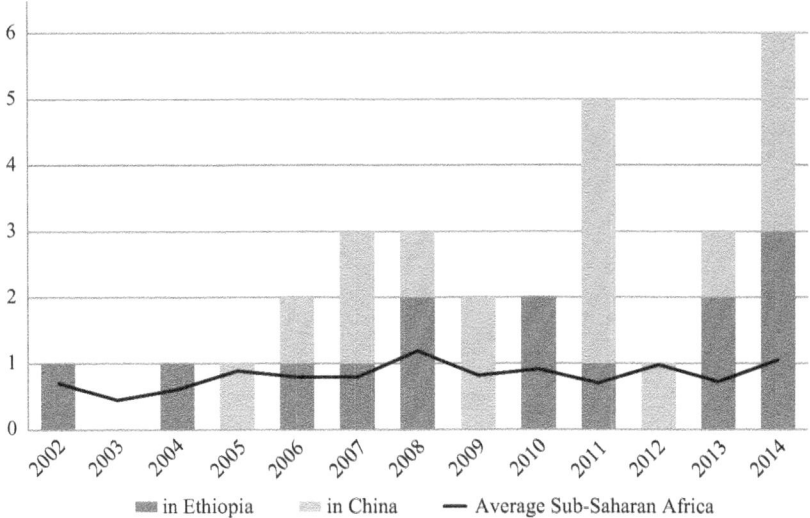

Fig. 4.5 Annual bilateral visits EPRDF–CCP
Source: Author's compilation, based on analysis of New Reports; International Department of the Chinese Communist Party

4.3 The 2005 Election Crisis: A Turning Point in EU-Ethiopia relations

In 2005, the EPRDF leadership was for the second time seriously challenged. In contrast to the party split in 2001, this time it was not by members of the core elite, but by the political opposition outside the EPRDF. The parliamentary elections in May 2005 thus marked a watershed for the Ethiopian government and for the EU's strategies for engaging with Ethiopia.

After a doubtful process of recounting and revoting in some constituencies, the national electoral board declared an EPRDF victory. Yet, according to the official figures the opposition gained about one-third of the votes. The Coalition for Unity and Democracy, the largest opposition party, received about 20 per cent of the seats, the United Ethiopian Democratic Forces most of the other 10 per cent (Tronvoll 2009, 455). When the National Electoral Board announced the results, turmoil broke out. During protests in June and November 2005, about 200 people died, and 20,000–30,000 opposition members and sympathisers were jailed (Tronvoll 2009, 455; Abbink 2006).[8]

The EU's Good Governance Strategy

The Ethiopian government's response to the crisis took the EU and other donors by surprise. After the end of the war with Eritrea, Ethiopia was perceived by donors as a 'model pupil'. Ethiopia made progress in poverty reduction and increased spending in social sectors, in line with the international development paradigm as it had evolved with the MDG agenda. The government emphasised the importance of good governance in its relations with donors; initiatives such as the PSCAP programme suggested that the government indeed had a strong interest in capacity-building. Moreover, it very actively engaged in the international aid effectiveness agenda, the G8 meetings and other international fora (Furtado and Smith 2009).

In response to the crisis, the EU used a *cooperative-conflictive* approach. It tried to mediate (Abbink 2006), while also putting substantial pressure on the government. As the crisis escalated, the EU postponed a decision regarding a €155 million aid agreement for the transport sector in autumn 2005. In December 2005, the EU decided to freeze the remaining €95 million in budget support. Other donors also suspended their budget aid (Ethiopia and European Community 2008).

The Ethiopian Government's Response: Indifference

The Ethiopian government showed little willingness to reconcile with the opposition in response to the EU and other donors' pressure. Moreover, it refused to engage with the EU and suspended political and aid policy dialogues. Tim Clarke, head of the EU delegation summarises the situation:

> The door is closed....It takes two to tango. A dialogue requires trust and I can understand that on their side they were wounded. Suddenly the doors were closed, or at least half closed, and although we have been pushing for openness and a dialogue, we haven't seen that happening as fast as we want.[9]

Prime Minister Meles in turn set conditions for resuming political dialogue:

We are eager to engage the donor community in dialogue, but we would want to establish that dialogue on the basis of a number of principles...the first is predictability. Development assistance should not be turned on and off.[10]

The Costs and Benefits for Ethiopia of Ceasing to Engage with the EU

For the Ethiopian government, engaging with the EU and other donors during the crisis and complying with their demands to cease coercive measures and release political prisoners were perceived as a direct threat to regime survival.

The strong gains for the opposition during the elections took the EPRDF by surprise (Abbink 2006, 179f; Aalen and Tronvoll 2009, 196). In spite of irregularities in the run-up to the elections, on election day and during the vote counting, available data do not suggest that the opposition actually won the elections (Tronvoll 2009, 463). Still, the election results demonstrated that the EPRDF had considerably under-estimated the dissatisfaction with its political record and the perception within the population that economic achievements were poor and biased towards the EPRDF, particularly in rural areas. The elections confirmed that the EPRDF had little support from the middle class and in urban areas of Addis Ababa as well as from the private sector. However, particularly the loss of support from the peasants, its core power base, shocked the EPRDF (Abbink 2006, 179f; Arriola 2008). Due to the government's control of the local level and its declared commitment to agricultural policies and rural development, it expected that the peasants and rural population—who make up about 85 per cent of the total population—would vote for the EPRDF. It had thus not expected that opening political spaces in urban areas would turn out to become a potential challenge to regime survival (Aalen and Tronvoll 2009, 197). Some point out that the EPRDF was so confident to emerge victorious in rural areas that it had barely campaigned there prior to the elections (Lefort 2010, 440).[11]

In this context, the Ethiopian government perceived engaging with the EU as a direct threat to regime survival. In an open letter published in the *Ethiopian Herald* on 28 August 2005, Prime Minister Meles criticised that the presence of the EU election observer mission had encouraged opposition demonstrations and that the EU had thus contributed to fuelling the crisis. The EU election observer mission was perceived to be siding with the opposition candidates and thereby bolstering the opposition's domestic legitimacy. Moreover, preliminary results from the election observer mission were leaked before the government published its final results. The opposition used the mission's report to claim having won the elections.

On the other hand, the Ethiopian government had reason to expect that donors would not cut aid altogether, not least because Ethiopia had become an important international partner for the EU institutions and some member states such as the UK during the previous years (Furtado and Smith 2009). Indeed, the EU institutions did not reduce aid funds, but channelled budget support through other aid modalities with stronger earmarking and monitoring procedures attached. Yet, the usage of aid as a lever for change put the Ethiopian government in a precarious situation—at least in the short- to medium-term. Not only had aid dependence considerably increased during the previous years; the shift towards general budget support also meant that as a result of the EU withholding funds, the government could not cover parts of its expenditure. Moreover, threats to cut budget support funds came in the midst of the Ethiopian budget planning process and thus exposed the government to a great deal of uncertainty (Bergthaller and Küblböck 2009).

China's Support During the 2005 Election Crisis: Reducing Donor Pressure

Largely unnoticed by the EU and other traditional donors, China extended its first substantial loan to Ethiopia in early 2006, a few weeks after the EU and other donors had decided to freeze budget support. Alongside the EU and other traditional donors' decision to suspend general budget support and before the Ethiopian government agreed with donors that budget aid should be rechannelled to a new programme, China offered Ethiopia a loan facility. In January 2006, Ethiopia's Minister of Finance, Sufyan Ahmad, travelled to China (BBC 2006).[12] China extended a mixed loan facility, amounting to USD500 million and consisting of grants, interest-free loans and concessional loans. The Ethiopian government presented a list with potential projects; but the precise activities financed with the loan were agreed upon only later. The volume of USD500 million equalled the volume of funds that the Ethiopian government would have been losing if the EU and other donors had not only withheld but actually cut development aid. Relatively unobserved by the EU and other traditional donors,[13] economic cooperation with China thereby reduced Ethiopia's dependence on its traditional partners at a critical point in time.

4.4 ETHIOPIA RELUCTANTLY ENGAGING WITH THE EU IN THE LATE 2000S DESPITE CHINA'S STRONG PRESENCE

Between 2006 and 2010, the EU broadened its approach towards promoting *democratic governance* and has again adopted a *cooperative-critical* strategy. The Ethiopian government, in turn, was highly reluctant to engage in governance reforms.

EU Good Governance Strategies and Ethiopia's Responsiveness

The EU's Approach: Promoting Democratic Governance
After the 2005 election crisis, the EU redoubled its efforts to promote input legitimacy. Governance reforms became a more important issue in EU–Ethiopia relations. In the country strategy paper, governance reforms were highlighted as an important area for bilateral relations; support for governance and macro-economic reform became the third focal sector of the EU's aid to Ethiopia.[14] The EU sought to promote elections, justice sector reform, the independence of the judiciary and the involvement of civil society organisations (Ethiopia and European Community 2007; annual joint reviews EU aid to Ethiopia, various years).

OECD DAC data indicate that the EU has slightly increased the volume of aid that it has allocated to governance reforms since 2006 (Table 4.1). Whereas in the early 2000s the EU had spent most of its governance aid on output legitimacy, it has committed most of its governance aid to input-related reforms since the mid-2000s.

In pushing its good governance agenda, the EU has increasingly relied on the transnational channel. The EU finally launched the Civil Society Fund, financed through the EDF (about €10 million for 2008–2013). The fund seeks to support the capacities of NGOs with a view to empowering them to engage in dialogue on policy and political reforms with the government at the national, regional and local level (Ethiopia and European Community 2007). The EU has also sought to enable NGOs to participate in the political dialogue between the EU and the Ethiopian government. Beyond direct assistance and the inclusion of civil society organisations in its dialogue with the government, the EU has pushed for improvements in the institutional environment in which Ethiopian NGOs operate. The EU raised concerns when the Ethiopian government issued a new NGO law shortly before the 2010 parliamentary elections, because the law was perceived to restrict the space of civil society organisations to engage in governance issues.

The EU's Instruments: Cooperative-Critical
After the election crisis, the EU resumed its strategy of promoting governance reforms through a *cooperative-critical* strategy. The EU made several attempts to strengthen political dialogue and address governance reforms as part of aid policy dialogues. In parallel, the EU continued to put pressure on Ethiopia, signalling to the government that the EU does not agree with the governance situation. In contrast to Rwanda, the EU allocated only a medium-sized governance incentive tranche to Ethiopia in 2006. It argued that budget support could only be resumed once the governance situation had improved, even though Ethiopia meets all other eligibility criteria (Ethiopia and European Community 2008). In the mid-term review for the 10th EDF, the EU justified its decision not to increase EDF funds by referring to the difficult governance situation. The EU made several critical public statements (Table 4.2). It criticised the closing of an independent journal, raised concerns that the new civil society law substantially limits spaces for civil society, and that the 2010 parliamentary elections did not meet international standards. However, the EU clearly did not move beyond a 'cooperative-critical strategy': the EU did not reduce aid and it did not threaten to reduce aid if the governance situation was not improving.

Ethiopia's Responsiveness Between 2006 and 2010: Reluctant Engagement

Immediately after the 2005 election crisis, the Ethiopian government was almost indifferent towards EU demands to engage in governance reforms. Only towards the 2010 elections did the government again agree to at least reluctantly engage. It was clearly more willing to engage with the EU on *effective* as opposed to *democratic* governance. In the late 2000s, Ethiopia was visibly less open for cooperation than Rwanda but more forthcoming than Angola.

Ethiopia's Responsiveness: Political Dialogue
Even though formal Article 8 political dialogue eventually resumed at the end of 2006, it did not take place very often in the following years. In contrast to Rwanda, Ethiopia has been definitely more reluctant to engage

in dialogue since the mid-2000s. Between 2007 and 2010, the Ethiopian government held dialogue only once and sometimes twice a year (Ethiopia and European Community 2007). During those meetings, Ethiopia engaged at the highest political level—with the prime minister or the minister of foreign affairs. In the course of dialogue meetings, the government agreed to address a broad range of issues, including the human rights situation, media reforms, the rule of law, economic governance issues, migration as well as regional peace and security. The government also discussed sensitive and difficult issues, such as the new civil society law or the 2010 election process.

Participants and observers of the political dialogue meetings describe the atmosphere as frank; the government has been willing to address sensitive issues even if no consensus could be reached.[15] However, some European participants and observers perceive the dialogue as having very little impact on the government's position. Ethiopia has not agreed with the EU on concrete reform objectives during dialogue meetings. While democratic governance issues had been brought onto the agenda mainly at the request of the EU, the Ethiopian side appears to have been more interested in discussing regional peace and security issues.[16]

Ethiopia's Responsiveness: Aid Policy Dialogues
The Ethiopian government reluctantly agreed to discuss governance reforms during aid policy dialogues. Statements by interviewees, public documentation of these meetings and secondary literature suggest that Ethiopia was clearly less prepared to institutionalise aid policy dialogues on governance reforms with the EU and other donors between 2006 and 2011 than Rwanda.

One case in point are the high-level forum (HLF) meetings. They brought together the government and donors between one and four times a year. The government accepted making governance issues a topic on the agenda, for instance, after the proclamation of the new civil society law (DAG 2011). The HLF meetings, however, mostly provide a forum for the EU and other donors to convey messages to the government, rather than to actually engage in *dialogue* (Furtado and Smith 2009).

More importantly, the Ethiopian government has not agreed to set up a specific governance dialogue with the EU and other donors.[17] Aid policy dialogues related to healthcare, education or transport take place regularly and are perceived to be functioning fairly well (Furtado and Smith 2009). Yet, despite the EU and other donors' explicit demand for it, Ethiopia refused to set up a specific governance aid dialogue.[18] Relevant line ministries, such as the Ministry of Justice, also showed no great interest in setting up regular dialogues with the EU and other donors (DAG 2012, 25; European Commission 2009).

Finally, the shifting of modalities from direct budget support to the World Bank-administered Protection of Basic Services (PBS) programme closed another potential channel for dialogue on governance reforms. Even though budget support dialogue mostly focused on overall macro-economic issues, it also gave an opportunity for the EU and other donors to address issues of democratic governance. Policy dialogue under the new PBS programme instead mostly focused on budget issues at the regional and local levels (von der Heijden 2007, 3; ECO Consult et al. 2012). Some observers argue that this setting allowed the government to keep donors at arm's length and avoid dialogue on sensitive issues. The government has therefore also not appeared to be too interested in the resumption of general budget support (Bergthaller and Küblböck 2009; von der Heijden 2007).

Ethiopia's Responsiveness: Positive Conditionality and Governance Aid
Between 2006 and 2010, the Ethiopian government has remained very reluctant to engage in the implementation of EU governance aid and to include positive conditionality in its engagement with the EU.

The Ethiopian government has been highly reluctant to develop a comprehensive 'governance action plan' to comply with the EU's requirements for receiving a 'governance incentive tranche'. The EU's request for a governance action plan came at a point in time when the relationship between the government and donors was particularly tense as a result of the 2005 election crisis. The government was also in a process of drafting its new poverty reduction strategy paper (PRSP). At least partly in response to donor pressure, the government finally agreed to include some objectives related to governance reforms in its PRSP. These objectives were also used as a basis for the governance action plan for the EU (DAG 2005a, 2006, 2009). EU officials argue that the governance incentive tranche thus contributed to convincing the government to include governance indicators in the new PRSP.[19] The government's definition of 'governance reforms', however, was quite narrow and limited to capacity-building of government institutions (Government of Ethiopia 2006; Ethiopia and European Community 2007). Ethiopia's governance action plan was clearly less ambitious than in the case of Rwanda.

After the election crisis, the Ethiopian government only reluctantly engaged with the EU and other donors in the implementation of governance aid. Interviews with EU and Ethiopian officials, an analysis of annual reports on the implementation of EU aid as well as an independent evaluation of EU aid, indicate that the implementation of governance aid met with considerable challenges. The government remained open for engaging with the EU in the implementation of aid geared to support the effectiveness of government institutions. However, compared to the early 2000s, it was even less willing to implement aid targeted at supporting the democratic quality of decision-making processes.

Consider the example of the PSCAP project. It became Ethiopia's flagship programme for reinforcing the effectiveness of government institutions at the regional and local level. Among others, the programme has sought to promote civil service reform, strengthen revenue and tax administration, information and communication technology development as well justice sector reform. Observers highlight that the government had a strong interest in implementing this programme, particularly components related to the effectiveness of government institutions.[20] In contrast, those PSCAP projects related to input legitimacy such as justice sector reform made limited progress.[21]

Another illustration is the support for democratic institutions. The Ethiopian government agreed to allocate €3 million to the democratic institutions programme, which it managed jointly with the United Nations Development Programme (UNDP). The objective of the programme is to strengthen the capacities of the Human Rights Commission, the Federal Ethics and Anti-corruption Commission of Ethiopia or the parliament. The EU and other donors would have preferred to use aid to strengthen the independence of these institutions and to empower them to hold the government accountable.[22] Ethiopia, in turn, had a clear preference for concentrating on the technical and institutional capacities of these institutions.

The Ethiopian government was very hesitant to invite another EU election observer mission for the 2010 parliamentary elections. It finally allowed a mission to monitor these elections. At the same time, it has not authorised the mission to present its final report in Addis Ababa —as had been planned (European Union 2010). In a press statement, the Ethiopian Ministry of Foreign Affairs criticised that the election observer mission had 'chosen to publish a report which is nothing but a preconceived and biased political analysis on Ethiopia' (Ministry of Foreign Affairs 2010). The EU thus could only present its report to an international audience in

Brussels in November 2010. Ethiopia is the first country where the government prevented EU election observers from presenting their final report to the domestic audience in the host country.

Most visible and debated was probably Ethiopia's resistance to accept aid geared towards supporting civil society organisations. The new civil society law, the Proclamation on Charities and Societies (CSO law), passed by parliament in 2009, initially put the EU's (and other donors') aid to civil society at risk entirely. For instance, the CSO law considerably challenged the implementation of the Civil Society Fund that the EU had set up. The CSO law restricts the amount of international funds for Ethiopian NGOs engaging on human rights, democracy or the rule of law to 10 per cent of their budget. Only after difficult negotiations did the Ethiopian government finally agree to grant the EU a legal exemption for the EU Civil Society Fund by considering it Ethiopian national funding.[23]

The civil society law also affected EU support channelled through the EIDHR. As assistance through EU budget lines is considered international funding, the CSO law reduced the EU's possibilities to use EIDHR funds to support civil society in Ethiopia. The volume of EIDHR funds had already dropped between 2006 and 2010 (Table 4.3) and reduced further after 2010 due to the CSO law. Furthermore, the Ethiopian government has been very hesitant to accept aid for civil society organisations spent through other projects, such as the Protection of Basic Services programme. The implementation of the PBS' civil society component faced considerable difficulties.[24]

We can conclude from this review that governance reforms have become a more important but also much contested issue in EU–Ethiopia relations between 2006 and 2010. The EU has slightly broadened its approach from *democratic government* to *democratic governance*. Moreover, similar to the early 2000s, the EU used a *cooperative-critical* strategy. The Ethiopian government, in turn, was highly reluctant to engage with the EU and other donors in the aftermath of the 2005 election crisis. The

Table 4.3 EIDHR projects in Ethiopia

	2000–2005	2006–2010	Total
Volume in USD	4,489,651	1,970,890	6,460,541
Number of projects	11	23	34

Source: Author's compilation, based on EU compendia EIDHR projects, various years (1995–2012)

government only hesitantly resumed political dialogue. Compared to the early 2000s, it has accepted higher volumes of EU aid to be spent on governance reforms, but it has sought to direct governance aid towards capacity-building of government institutions to strengthen their efficiency rather than empowering them to fulfil their role in policy-making processes. Government initiatives such as the civil society law had a direct and negative effect for EU attempts to empower civil society organisations to hold the government accountable.

The Ethiopian Government's Survival Strategies

After the 2005 elections and the resulting political crisis, public support for the government was at an all-time low. According to Gallup polls, only 32 per cent trusted the government in 2007 (Gallup 2013). To regain stability and prevent further challenges from the opposition, the government sought to broaden its support base and to reinforce the influence of the party at the local and regional levels. Moreover, the government introduced a series of legal measures to restrict political spaces.

Survival Strategies I: Subordinating the State to the Party
Shortly after the elections, the EPRDF started to reinforce its party structures. It expanded its membership from 760,000 in 2005 to about four million members in 2008 and five million by 2010 (Aalen and Tronvoll 2009, 203; Vaughan 2011, 633). With a view to both increasing compliance of party members and coopting opponents, the EPRDF conditioned access to state employment and public services on party membership (Tronvoll 2009, 469; International Crisis Group 2009). At the rural level, the EPRDF coopted the leading farmers to expand its power base among the peasants (Lefort 2007). Mass youth and women's organisations and trade unions were revived and expanded, forging a link between the party, the state and the people (Vaughan 2011, 634; Lyons 2011, 10). Furthermore, the Ethiopian government made less effort to invest in the effectiveness of state institutions; in contrast to Rwanda, the level of government effectiveness stagnated after 2007 (Fig. 4.1).

In the years between 2006 and 2010, the Ethiopian government expanded its investments in social services, not unlike Rwanda. After the election crisis, government spending on social services and infrastructure rose to over 60 per cent of government expenditure. For instance, the share of healthcare in government spending increased substantially from about 11 per cent in 2006 to about 19 per cent in 2011, according to the World Development Indicators.

However, in contrast to Rwanda, along with growing investments in public services, Ethiopia also expanded state employment in the social sectors. According to figures from the Ministry of Health and Education, the number of teachers and health education workers more than doubled from about 120,000 in 2004/2005 to over 250,000 by 2010 (Vaughan 2011, 643f). At the same time, access to basic services and university education has at least partly been conditioned to EPRDF membership (Abbink 2009, 17). Reports by Human Rights Watch (2010) and media reports (BBC 2011; IRIN 2013) argue that access to food aid and basic government services has been used to generate support for the EPRDF. In contrast to Rwanda, despite higher government spending, public satisfaction with social services remained quite low according to Gallup polls. In 2007, only 19 per cent were confident in the healthcare system; only 43 per cent were satisfied with the education system (Gallup 2013).

After the elections, the government faced a considerable dilemma. On the one hand, it needed to make more public investments in order to regain popular support. On the other hand, it could not easily raise more taxes to finance public expenditure. In a country where per capita GNI was as low as USD280 in 2008, the tax base is arguably highly limited. Furthermore, in light of the crisis, the government could not alienate strategic support groups any further by increasing taxes. In the first few years after the elections, the government reduced presumptive taxes to strengthen public support (Prichard 2010, 259f). Between 2005 and 2007, overall tax revenues fell sharply, at least in part due to the reluctance of the government to punish tax evasion (Prichard 2010). Only after 2008 did the government again make efforts to increase tax revenue (Prichard 2010, 262) and direct and indirect taxes rose considerably.

In light of the 2005 crisis, economic growth has become an even more important pillar of the regime's legitimacy. The Ethiopian government's poverty reduction strategy papers, published shortly after the 2005 election crisis and then again in 2010, put a much stronger emphasis on economic growth and investments in large-scale infrastructure, such as roads, power generation and telecommunications, than previous government strategies. Furthermore, heated discussions on the official growth rate figures between the opposition, the government, the World Bank and other donors illustrate how important economic growth is to the regime as a pillar of its legitimacy.[25] Whereas government figures suggest that growth rates have been high since 2005, the International Monetary Fund (IMF) and members of the opposition openly questioned these figures (EIU 2012).

Survival Strategies II: Managing Arenas of Contestation and Using Low-Intensity Coercion
Along with strengthening party structures and increasing public expenditure, the government reduced political spaces through a series of new laws. The press law (2008), party law (2008), anti-terror law (2009), and particularly the civil society law (2009) have considerably limited the freedom of opposition parties, the media and civil society organisations. For example, the CSO law requires that NGOs have to register with the newly established Charities and Societies Agency. Organisations that receive more than 10 per cent of their funding from abroad are not allowed to engage in human rights, conflict resolution, justice and law enforcement activities. As most local NGOs rely heavily on international funding, the law has a tremendous impact. Two prominent civil society organisations—the Christian Relief and Development Association (CRDA) and the Ethiopian Bar Association (Ethiopian association for law professionals) faced particularly severe restrictions (Aalen and Tronvoll 2009, 199–202).

Moreover, in light of the 2005 election crisis, winning subsequent elections with substantive majorities was important for the government to regain stability. The local (Kebele) and district (Woreda) elections were widely perceived as a 'test run' for the government. They were at first delayed but then finally held in 2008. During these local elections, the opposition did not pose any considerable challenge for the EPRDF, partly because the opposition failed to reorganise and partly because the government had tightened its grip on local administrative structures (Aalen and Tronvoll 2009, 202–203). The EPRDF thus won the local elections with an overwhelming majority.

The run-up to the 2010 elections was marked by a tense atmosphere and severe restrictions on civil society organisations' ability to campaign. The civil society, anti-terror and media laws (see above) were passed relatively shortly before the elections and allowed the government to limit political spaces. On the other hand, the main opposition parties were also less organised than ahead of the 2005 elections. The government eventually won the elections in a landslide victory and secured the EPRDF all but two seats in parliament. This almost Stalinist outcome signalled to opposition members or anyone among the elite who might have considered

pillar of its legitimacy.[25] Whereas government figures suggest that growth rates have been high since 2005, the International Monetary Fund (IMF) and members of the opposition openly questioned these figures (EIU 2012).

Survival Strategies II: Managing Arenas of Contestation and Using Low-Intensity Coercion
Along with strengthening party structures and increasing public expenditure, the government reduced political spaces through a series of new laws. The press law (2008), party law (2008), anti-terror law (2009), and particularly the civil society law (2009) have considerably limited the freedom of opposition parties, the media and civil society organisations. For example, the CSO law requires that NGOs have to register with the newly established Charities and Societies Agency. Organisations that receive more than 10 per cent of their funding from abroad are not allowed to engage in human rights, conflict resolution, justice and law enforcement activities. As most local NGOs rely heavily on international funding, the law has a tremendous impact. Two prominent civil society organisations—the Christian Relief and Development Association (CRDA) and the Ethiopian Bar Association (Ethiopian association for law professionals) faced particularly severe restrictions (Aalen and Tronvoll 2009, 199–202).

Moreover, in light of the 2005 election crisis, winning subsequent elections with substantive majorities was important for the government to regain stability. The local (Kebele) and district (Woreda) elections were widely perceived as a 'test run' for the government. They were at first delayed but then finally held in 2008. During these local elections, the opposition did not pose any considerable challenge for the EPRDF, partly because the opposition failed to reorganise and partly because the government had tightened its grip on local administrative structures (Aalen and Tronvoll 2009, 202–203). The EPRDF thus won the local elections with an overwhelming majority.

The run-up to the 2010 elections was marked by a tense atmosphere and severe restrictions on civil society organisations' ability to campaign. The civil society, anti-terror and media laws (see above) were passed relatively shortly before the elections and allowed the government to limit political spaces. On the other hand, the main opposition parties were also less organised than ahead of the 2005 elections. The government eventually won the elections in a landslide victory and secured the EPRDF all but two seats in parliament. This almost Stalinist outcome signalled to opposition members or anyone among the elite who might have considered

share of healthcare in government spending increased substantially from about 11 per cent in 2006 to about 19 per cent in 2011, according to the World Development Indicators.

However, in contrast to Rwanda, along with growing investments in public services, Ethiopia also expanded state employment in the social sectors. According to figures from the Ministry of Health and Education, the number of teachers and health education workers more than doubled from about 120,000 in 2004/2005 to over 250,000 by 2010 (Vaughan 2011, 643f). At the same time, access to basic services and university education has at least partly been conditioned to EPRDF membership (Abbink 2009, 17). Reports by Human Rights Watch (2010) and media reports (BBC 2011; IRIN 2013) argue that access to food aid and basic government services has been used to generate support for the EPRDF. In contrast to Rwanda, despite higher government spending, public satisfaction with social services remained quite low according to Gallup polls. In 2007, only 19 per cent were confident in the healthcare system; only 43 per cent were satisfied with the education system (Gallup 2013).

After the elections, the government faced a considerable dilemma. On the one hand, it needed to make more public investments in order to regain popular support. On the other hand, it could not easily raise more taxes to finance public expenditure. In a country where per capita GNI was as low as USD280 in 2008, the tax base is arguably highly limited. Furthermore, in light of the crisis, the government could not alienate strategic support groups any further by increasing taxes. In the first few years after the elections, the government reduced presumptive taxes to strengthen public support (Prichard 2010, 259f). Between 2005 and 2007, overall tax revenues fell sharply, at least in part due to the reluctance of the government to punish tax evasion (Prichard 2010). Only after 2008 did the government again make efforts to increase tax revenue (Prichard 2010, 262) and direct and indirect taxes rose considerably.

In light of the 2005 crisis, economic growth has become an even more important pillar of the regime's legitimacy. The Ethiopian government's poverty reduction strategy papers, published shortly after the 2005 election crisis and then again in 2010, put a much stronger emphasis on economic growth and investments in large-scale infrastructure, such as roads, power generation and telecommunications, than previous government strategies. Furthermore, heated discussions on the official growth rate figures between the opposition, the government, the World Bank and other donors illustrate how important economic growth is to the regime as a

establishing a political alternative that the ruling party had regained its strength (Vaughan 2011; Tronvoll 2010).

From the mid-2000s onwards, the EU's good governance strategies have clearly diverged from the Ethiopian government's preferences. The EU's support for *effective government* still matched the preferences of the government. But improving the effectiveness of state institutions had become less important compared to expanding party structures and coopting regime opponents and followers through these structures. On the other hand, EU support for *democratic government*, for instance, by assisting the Human Rights Commission or the parliament, induced considerable costs for the Ethiopian government. Moreover, the EU's attempts to empower civil society actors clearly diverged from the government's preferences. Only by closely involving the government in the management of the Civil Society Fund, was the government eventually persuaded to give the EU an exemption, allowing it to support civil society organisations. In light of the experience of the 2005 elections, inviting in another EU election observer mission for the 2010 elections could cause considerable threats to regime survival for the Ethiopian government. The government's strong reluctance to invite this observer mission and its decision not to allow the mission to present its final results in Addis Ababa demonstrates how fragile the government's position still was ahead of the 2010 elections. At the same time, it also suggests that EU support for the elections was perceived as potentially being dangerous to regime survival.

Ethiopia's Economic Dependence on the EU

Ethiopia's economic dependence on the EU slightly increased following the election crisis. Ethiopia is fairly dependent on development aid, and the EU has remained one of its largest donors. Ethiopia's exports to the EU increased and the EU continued to be an important source of direct investments. Moreover, due to considerable challenges from the opposition during the 2005 elections and very low popular support for the regime after the election crisis, output legitimacy through economic growth and the provision of social services has been even more important for the government since 2005 (see previous section). In this regard, aid, trade and investment from the EU (and other external actors) have become clearly more important for the Ethiopian government compared to the early 2000s.

If measured as a share of government revenue, Ethiopia's aid dependence remained very high. Since 2006, Ethiopia has had more access to development aid. Between 2006 and 2010 grants still constituted the second-largest source of government revenue after trade taxes. However, the share of aid to GNI successively declined to 11 per cent in 2011, despite rising inflows of aid (Fig. 4.1).

Together with the USA, the World Bank and the UK, the EU institutions are the largest donors to Ethiopia (Fig. 4.3). Between 2006 and 2010, the EU institutions have again provided about 17 per cent of total DAC aid to Ethiopia. Compared to Rwanda, Ethiopia has a larger number of donors from which it receives development aid. Almost all EU member states are also involved in Ethiopia. The bulk of aid by European donors is provided by the EU institutions and the UK, and to a lesser extent by Germany, France and others. The EU as a whole (EU institutions plus member states) had been the largest donor to Ethiopia between 2006 and 2010 (Fig. 4.3). For the EU institutions (and several member states), Ethiopia has emerged as one of the largest aid recipients in Africa and also worldwide. Even though the EU and other donors put considerable pressure on the Ethiopian government during the 2005 election crisis, in the end, they did not reduce the financial volume of development aid. The EU institutions even slightly increased aid in the following years (Fig. 4.3).

Moreover, the modalities of how the EU provides development aid have largely converged with the preferences of the Ethiopian government. For instance, the EU has supported the PBS programme which has been quite important to the government. The PBS that replaced the direct budget support has functioned quite similarly to direct budget aid (Bergthaller and Küblböck 2009; Borchgrevink 2008), and the government apparently did not have a strong interest in resuming budget support (ECO Consult et al. 2012). PBS funds help the government in providing basic services at the local level. Similar to direct budget support, funds are channelled through the government. However, in contrast to budget support, PBS does not involve a high-level macro-economic dialogue with the government in Addis Ababa. Critics posit that PBS (and some other aid programmes) are used by the government to strengthen its grip on power (BBC 2011; IRIN 2013). Human Rights Watch (2010), for instance, argued that the provision of basic services at the local level is conditioned to support for the EPRDF. Some are critical that programmes, such as PBS, thereby boost the government's authority structures, since funds are directed at regional and local government institutions, most of them controlled by the ruling party (Human Rights Watch 2010).

For the Ethiopian government, economic cooperation with the EU beyond development aid was also attractive. Since 2006, the EU has continued to be the most important destination for Ethiopian exports (Fig. 4.4) and the second-largest source of its imports. Ethiopia still exports only a few products; almost 80 per cent of these are (unprocessed) agricultural goods, most of it coffee. According to UN Comtrade statistics (2010), Germany has been the largest destination for Ethiopia's coffee exports ahead of Saudi Arabia and the USA. Ethiopia's coffee export markets are comparatively diversified. In recent years, Ethiopia could open some, albeit very few, new export sectors with respect to the EU, notably horticulture (flowers).

Ethiopia did not attract high levels of direct investments between 2006 and 2010. According to the World Development Indicators, direct investments accounted for less than 5 per cent of GDP. For most of the past decade, direct investments as a share of GDP were lower in Ethiopia than in the rest of sub-Saharan Africa. If companies from EU member states were taken together, the EU would still be the largest source of direct investments (European Union 2012). However, no single EU member state is among the top10 investors in Ethiopia (unlike China, as we will see below).

To sum up, the EU kept its position as one of the most important donors to Ethiopia since 2006. The sectors to which the EU provides its aid and the modalities by which it provides aid, largely match the preferences of the Ethiopian government. The EU, taken as a whole, is still the largest market for Ethiopia's exports (mainly coffee) and the largest source of investments. One can thus argue that in the late 2000s, the Ethiopian government even had a stronger interest in cooperating with the EU beyond governance reforms. After the election crisis, however, the EU's demands to cooperate on governance reform clearly diverged from the preferences of the Ethiopian government. In contrast to the early 2000s, access to EU aid could thus only partially compensate for the cost that cooperation would have generated, explaining why the government only very reluctantly resumed cooperation on governance reforms. This argument, however, would be even stronger if one could control for alternative explanations, such as Ethiopia's access to cooperation with China.

China: Alternative Cooperation Partner Since 2006

China's economic cooperation with Ethiopia has been rapidly expanding. By 2012, China had emerged as an alternative partner for the Ethiopian government. It does not only extend official flows on a par with EU aid. China also offers new trading opportunities and direct investments, much needed by the Ethiopian government to raise domestic revenues, promote economic growth and provide public goods. Moreover (and in contrast to Rwanda and Angola), China engages with Ethiopia in reforms of the ruling party and other parts of the government's survival strategy.

China: Becoming an Alternative Economic Cooperation Partner

Since 2006, Ethiopia has gained considerable access to official flows from China. Chinese official flows do not only align with the Ethiopian government's preferences. They also target sectors and policy fields that receive less support from the EU and other traditional donors.

Chinese aid and loans have rapidly increased up to USD7 billion until 2012 (Table 4.4). By 2014, loans further surged to a total of USD12.2 billion, making Ethiopia the second-largest recipient of Chinese loans in Africa, after Angola (Brautigam and Hwang 2016). The former Chinese ambassador in Addis Ababa highlights that Ethiopia is the only African country that benefited from all eight FOCAC policy measures announced in Beijing in 2006 (Gu 2008); a clear indication of Ethiopia's political importance in China's Africa policy. Most of the projects and technical assistance provided under the FOCAC framework—such as rural schools, a malaria prevention centre, a technical and vocational training centre, an agriculture demonstration centre or scholarships for students to study in China—would be counted as aid under the OECD DAC definition.

Chinese official flows have also grown beyond the scope of these development aid projects, particularly since 2008. Although preferential and commercial loans are extended below market rates, they would not be counted as aid in the OECD definition, as they are aimed at supporting Chinese exports or their level of concessionality is not low enough. According to Ethiopian officials, preferential and commercial loans are allocated to large-scale productive projects; they have only been provided since 2008. Most of the official flows are allocated to large-scale infrastructure investments (Table 4.4). As part of the FOCAC measures, the EXIM Bank financed an expressway from Addis Ababa to Dukem with a USD350 million concessional loan. In 2006, the China Development

ETHIOPIA 131

Table 4.4 Chinese official flows to Ethiopia 2006–2012

Year	Type of project	Financial volume
2000–2004	Road construction in Addis Ababa: Parts of the Addis Ring Road	USD87 million
	Sino-Ethiopia Friendship Avenue	–
2006	More than 11 projects financed under a mixed loan facility, including: Mugher Cement factory; Fan Hydropower Station	Total: USD500 million (combination of grants, interest-free loan and concessional loan) USD100 million
2006	ZTE investment in Ethiopian Telecommunication Corporation	USD1.5 billion (export seller's loan, China Development Bank)
2006	Gotera highway in Addis Ababa	China covers 75%
2006–2012	FOCAC projects: three rural schools, technical vocational training centre (2008), hospital (2008), agriculture demonstration centre (2008), anti-malaria treatment centre (2008), malaria medication, China-Ethio Polytechnical College (USD14 million) including teachers	G
	Expressway Addis-Dukem	USD350 million (CL)
2008–2012	Various hydro-power projects and transmission lines, Ethiopian Electric Power Corporation	USD2–3 billion (PL, ComLo)
	Office equipment for several Ethiopian ministries	
	African Union building	USD200 million (G)
2010	Nine vessels for Ethiopia Shipping Lines (ESL)	USD294 million, EXIM Bank covers 80%
2011	Energy projects (hydro, solar, biogas) and anti-malaria medication	Birr203 million, 127 of this G
	Water supply project for Addis Ababa	USD100 million loan
2011	During Meles' visit in China, EXIM Bank announces loan for various projects	USD 500 million loan
2010–2011	Constructing parts of new railway system for Ethiopia Railway Corporation (ERC); 317 km Addis-Miseo CREEG 339 km CCECC	USD1.1 billion, part of it covered by China and GoE USD1.2 billion total, 60% Chinese soft loan
2011	37 km light railway system in Addis implemented for Addis City Roads Authority by CRECC	USD400 million total costs, China covers 60%, GoE rest
	4.3 km Meskel Square-Bole bridge, CRBC	USD60 million EXIM Bank

(*continued*)

Table 4.4 (continued)

Year	Type of project	Financial volume
2012	Maintenance hangar for Ethiopian Airlines	USD100 million, no information which bank, unclear G/L
2012	China extends USD612 million over first six months of the fiscal year for various projects; USD300 million master loan facility for GTP; USD100 million loan for water supply to Addis	
2012	65 guest cars, 25 coaches	Birr108 million (G)
2012	Infrastructure development (28 January 2012) not clear if this is for a range of projects. Early in 2012, seven agreements are signed to cooperate on railway, sugar, telecommunication and currency exchange agreement with CDB	USD3 billion loan

Total volume of projects, very rough estimate: USD7 billion (excluding 2012 loan)

Source: Author's compilation based on interviews conducted in Addis and Beijing, information from MOFED and MOFCOM, aid transparency initiative, BBC monitoring international reports and Ethiopian newspapers (Ethiopian News Agency, *Ethiopian Herald*, *Addis Fortune*, *Ethiopian Capital*)

G Grant, *IFL* interest-free loan, *CL* concessional loan, *PL* preferential loan, *ComLo* commercial loan. Most loans are provided by the EXIM Bank

Bank granted a USD1.5 billion loan for telecommunication (as an export seller's loan). Chinese policy banks, mostly the EXIM Bank, but increasingly also the CDB and ICBC, have provided several loans to support hydro-power projects or transmission lines.

China extends some loans to Ethiopian parastatal companies—Ethiopian Road Authority, Ethiopian Electric Power Corporation, Ethiopian Airlines, Ethiopian Shipping Lines, Ethiopia Telecommunication Corporation and the Ethiopia Railways Corporation (Table 4.4). Some of these public enterprises also receive development aid from traditional donors. For instance, the EU and several others support the Ethiopian Road Authority; the World Bank finances hydropower projects for the Ethiopian Electric Power Corporation. However, many projects supported by China would not be funded by the EU and other traditional donors, because the required financial volume is too large or because their economic and social impact is contested (large-scale dams, for instance). Furthermore, China gives assistance to some parastatal companies that have not had access to official or private capital flows from other international actors such as Ethiopia Shipping Lines. While official figures are not available, interviews with Chinese officials indicate that for the Chinese EXIM Bank, Ethiopia has become one of the largest recipients of loans in Africa and one of the countries with the most diversified project portfolio.[26]

Chinese support for infrastructure projects managed by Ethiopia's parastatal companies gives the Ethiopian government access to strategic rents. Moreover, it expects that loans from China will play a key role in financing its ambitious development strategy, as outlined in the Growth and Transformation Plan.[27] In light of the government's strong focus on economic growth and infrastructure investments since 2005, official flows from China have become an important alternative to the EU and other donors' development aid.

Since 2006, cooperation with China has not only yielded important official flows for the government's investments in infrastructure. Engagement with China has also generated revenues through trade and, to some extent, direct investments. While the EU has traditionally been Ethiopia's largest trading partner, trade structures have changed considerably in the past few years. China was Ethiopia's largest source of imports. Ethiopia imports electronic equipment, textiles, machinery and vehicles from China. On the other hand, China's importance as an export destination has grown considerably, particularly since 2008 (Fig. 4.4). Given the pace at which exports have grown in recent years, China may overtake the EU as the main destination of exports in the next few years. Ethiopia's exports to China (similar to those to the EU) mainly consist of raw materials. China has not yet become a major market for coffee exports.[28] Ethiopia's exports to China include traditional export goods, such as leather, grain and gum.

Trade with China has also generated new export sectors, notably for oilseeds. Within a few years, Ethiopia has become the largest grower of sesame seeds in Africa and one of the largest in the world.[29] Oilseeds overtook coffee as Ethiopia's largest export product in 2007. Oilseeds from Ethiopia are mostly exported to China.[30] In contrast to Rwanda, in Ethiopia, trading with China has thus provided the government with an important windfall. Foreign currency earnings from sesame seed exports are put in a bank account at the state-owned Commercial Bank of Ethiopia; they are then transferred to an escrow account with the China EXIM Bank to pay back Chinese loans for construction projects.[31] While the surge in sesame seed exports opens important additional sources of revenues, concentrating on China as the main export market is not without risks. Anecdotal evidence from interviews with Chinese traders suggests that Ethiopia's exports of sesame seeds faced difficulties in competing with China's domestic production and are only imported in case of a poor sesame harvest in China.[32]

According to the MOFCOM (2010), Chinese investment stock in Ethiopia jumped from about USD100 million in 2006 to about USD360 million in 2010. The Ethiopia Investment Agency estimates Chinese investments to be considerably higher (about USD1 billion). Between 2005 and 2009, Chinese companies were the third largest foreign investors to Ethiopia, after Saudi Arabia and India, and ahead of Sudan and Turkey. Chinese companies mostly engage in manufacturing, and Chinese investments are spread across a wide range of projects (Geda and Meskel 2009; Ethiopian Economic Association 2009). A special economic zone that has been established outside Addis Ababa is likely to attract more investments from China (and other countries). The CADFund, an equity fund managed by the China Development Bank, opened an office in Addis Ababa in 2010 and began supporting Chinese investment projects in Ethiopia, for instance, a glass factory. Chinese small- and medium-sized enterprises and private companies see the country as a promising market and a 'launch pad' for their engagement in the wider region (Geda and Meskel 2009; Ethiopian Economic Association 2009). According to Chinese officials and business representatives, Ethiopia is an important market for Chinese provincially and centrally state-owned construction companies—partly financed by Western donors.

Other emerging economies, such as India or Turkey, have also invested in Ethiopia. Figures are difficult to obtain. Interviews with the Ethiopian Ministry of Finance and Economic Development, the Indian embassy in Ethiopia and the Ethiopian embassy in India indicate that compared to China, India's assistance is still small and concentrated in a few policy fields, such as education[33] (see also Greenhill et al. 2013). Investments are concentrated in agriculture, and particularly the sugar industry, where the India EXIM Bank supports several projects totalling USD700 million (India EXIM Bank 2013). Turkey, Qatar or Saudi Arabia also boosted their investments in Ethiopia. Even though the Ethiopian government actively looks for support from other actors, China thus appears to be the most important partner among the emerging economies in terms of assistance, trade and loans.

Attractiveness of the China 'Model' and Support for Survival Strategies
In public speeches, but also in internal party debates, Prime Minister Meles repeatedly emphasised that China's development provides important lessons for Ethiopia. From 2000 onwards, the Ethiopian government's development strategy has been strongly inspired by development trajectories of East Asian countries—particularly China and South Korea (Fourie 2012). In public speeches and internal party documents directed towards both a domestic and international audience, Prime Minister Meles emphasised the importance of learning from China in order to promote development in Ethiopia. The Ethiopian leadership has sought inspiration from China's economic development trajectory as well as its political institutions. The learning process is facilitated by close cooperation between the Chinese and Ethiopian governments and ruling parties.

China gives some technical assistance to support the capacities of the Ethiopian government. However, this assistance differs from the EU's governance aid. China offers training programmes for various segments of the Ethiopian elite. Representatives from Ethiopian regional and national administrations or the media are sent to China for between 10 days and one month. According to Chinese officials, between 2006 and 2010, around 200 Ethiopians took part in these programmes every year.[34] After a government reshuffle, China may invite all newly appointed senior officials for a study tour.[35] Many participants of these training and exchange programmes are greatly impressed by China's economic development. At the same time, several participants describe these exchanges as 'visiting tours' rather than training courses. The courses are probably helpful for improving knowledge about China and fostering both a positive attitude among larger parts of the Ethiopian elite and a supportive environment for Sino-Ethiopian relations. As systematic analyses on their effects are still lacking, their impact is unclear. According to Chinese and Ethiopian officials, beyond training and advice, China also offers material assistance to some ministries, for instance, office equipment for the Ministry of Foreign Affairs or the Ministry of Information. The volume of this aid was small between 2006 and 2012.

In contrast to the EU, the Chinese government has hardly relied on the transnational channel and engages very little with Ethiopian civil society organisations. Civil society organisations are not included in the negotiation and implementation of Chinese projects. The Chinese government started to invite NGO representatives for short-term visiting tours. In private discussions, some representatives from Ethiopian NGOs have voiced concern about Chinese engagement and highlight that China opens alternative sources of financial support that further empowers the government to the detriment of opposition forces. In the media and public debates, however, the government does not allow for controversial discussions on China's engagement, and criticism is raised in private conversations only.

Party-to-Party Relations
In contrast to the EU's cooperation with Rwanda, party-to-party cooperation constitutes one important channel for China–Ethiopia relations. Since 2005, the number of party visits increased considerably. Between 2006 and 2011, Ethiopia's Minister of Information, Simon Bereket, was been the most prominent actor engaged in EPRDF relations with the CCP; he led most official EPRDF delegations to China.[36]

In 2005, shortly after the election crisis and alongside efforts to reinforce the influence of the party, the EPRDF established an office for foreign relations and started to intensify its engagement with other ruling parties. According to Ethiopian officials, the CCP has become the most important international partner for the EPRDF. For the CCP, the EPRDF is also one of the most important partners in Africa. If measured in terms of the number of bilateral visits, the EPRDF clearly figures above the average for sub-Saharan Africa (Fig. 4.5). Ethiopia is also one of few African countries where the CCP has dispatched a representative to the Chinese embassy.

Upon request by the EPRDF, both parties signed a MoU in October 2010 to further institutionalise and intensify party-to-party contacts. Not least in light of the EPRDF party reforms after the 2005 election crisis, for the EPRDF, party-to-party relations open an important channel to discuss experiences on development, the relationship between the party and the state, strategies on how to organise leadership succession, how to manage intraparty transition from one generation to the next or the role of mass movements, such as women's and youth associations. As many of the party cadres who fought the liberation struggle are about to retire, maintaining loyalty and compliance within the party becomes a key concern for the EPRDF leadership. Upon request by the EPRDF, the CCP supported the establishment of the central party school. The CCP itself also has a strong interest in the relationship. Close party-to-party relations are perceived as an important foundation to strengthen economic and political cooperation between the two countries. Moreover, due to Ethiopia's political influence in the region, cooperation with the EPRDF allows the CCP to learn more about African politics in general.

4.5 Brief Breeze of Change in EU–Ethiopia Cooperation Between 2011 and 2014

After the 2010 elections, the EU slightly modified its good governance strategy. It continued to promote governance reforms by supporting *democratic governance*. It continued to target not only the government, but also used the transnational channel, for instance, through the Civil Society Fund. The EU proceeded to support not only the effectiveness but also democratic quality of decision-making processes. However, at the same time, the EU shifted its strategy from cooperative-critical towards *cooperative*. The EU became more hesitant in issuing critical public statements and using aid funds to exert pressure on the Ethiopian government to open political spaces and cease coercive measures. Instead, between 2011 and 2014, the EU has mainly relied on political dialogue and governance aid to support reforms.

Between 2011 and 2014, the Ethiopian government has apparently once again become more forthcoming in engaging with the EU in governance reforms. It agreed to hold dialogue more frequently and to include the heads of relevant line ministries, such as the Minister of Justice or the Minister of Agriculture, depending on the specific topic under discussion. Moreover, the Ethiopian government has agreed to engage with the EU and other donors in a regular dialogue with civil society representatives (DAG 2012, 3).

What can explain Ethiopia's renewed openness to cooperation? The landslide victory in the 2010 elections showed both the leadership and opposition parties that the EPRDF was clearly back in power. In light of the relatively secure position of the Ethiopian leadership and the EU's modification of its good governance strategy, engaging in governance reforms with the EU was less challenging between 2011 and 2014 than it was before the 2010 elections. Moreover, although the sudden death of Prime Minister Meles in August 2012 could have put the party in a difficult position, the change in the leadership did not result in open power struggles or a split within the ruling party.

China has become even more important as a cooperation partner since the 2010 elections. The Chinese government started to assist key sectors of Ethiopia's Growth and Transformation Plan, such as railways, a light railway in Addis Ababa and additional hydro-power projects (Table 4.4). In the second half of 2012, China extended loans amounting to USD612 million, making it the largest loan provider to Ethiopia (Tadesse 2012; Ministry of Finance and Economic Development 2013, 23). Financed by the CADFund, two Chinese companies set up a joint venture to invest USD2 billion to produce shoes in Ethiopia in 2012. The project created several thousand jobs and is one of the largest CADFund projects, according to Chinese officials.[37] Other emerging economies such as India have also become slightly more important in recent years. In addition to previous loans for the development of the sugar industry, India has approved a loan of USD300 million for the development of the railway system (India EXIM Bank 2013). However, as cooperation on governance reforms was less costly between 2011 and 2014 compared to the period between 2006 and 2010, China's growing presence had limited effects on the Ethiopian government's openness to engage with the EU in governance reforms.

4.6 Conclusions

Ethiopia only reluctantly engaged with the EU in governance reforms in the early 2000s. It became slightly more open to cooperation ahead of the 2005 elections. After the elections, Ethiopia was initially indifferent towards EU demands to cooperate. Towards the 2010 elections, the government again agreed to at least reluctantly engage. Only after the 2010 elections has it again become more open. What explains Ethiopia's overall reluctance and these slight changes over time?

Why Has Ethiopia Only Reluctantly Engaged in Governance Reforms Between 2000 and 2005?

Ethiopia's willingness to reluctantly engage with the EU in governance reforms in the early 2000s can be explained by a partial convergence of the EU and the Ethiopian government's preferences, Ethiopia's high economic dependence on the EU and the absence of alternative cooperation partners such as China.

In the early 2000s, the EU's strategies to promote *effective* and *democratic government* and to use a *cooperative-critical* strategy produced some benefits, but also caused difficulties for the Ethiopian government. EU demands to cooperate on governance reforms came at a time of political instability, caused by the split in the TPLF central committee after the war with Eritrea. The Ethiopian leadership's response to strengthen state institutions, to introduce decentralisation and promote output legitimacy partly matched EU demands to cooperate on *effective* government. However, its strategy to use low-intensity coercion to reduce the risk that defecting members of the elite mobilise mass support made cooperation on *democratic* government quite costly. In contrast to Rwanda, ahead of the 2005 elections, the Ethiopian government cautiously opened up political spaces for opposition parties, civil society and the media, allowing for some (limited) cooperation on democratic government.

In the early 2000s (and similar to Rwanda), the Ethiopian government also started to reach out to the international donor community—including the EU—to attract higher levels of development aid. Prime Minister Meles actively embraced the international aid effectiveness agenda from the very beginning. The EU's willingness to increase development aid to Ethiopia was highly welcome and gave incentives to the government to reluctantly engage in governance reforms, despite the costs involved. On the other hand, Ethiopia still had very limited access to official flows from China and other non-traditional donors in the early 2000s, which potentially could have reduced Ethiopia's interests in engaging with the EU.

The 2005 Elections: Cooperating with the EU on Governance Reforms Threatens Regime Survival

The 2005 elections marked a turning point for the stability of the regime as well as for Ethiopia's openness to cooperate with the EU. During the 2005 election crisis, cooperating with the EU generated a fundamental threat to regime survival. The relatively strong election result for the opposition caught the EPRDF by surprise and significantly altered domestic political dynamics in Ethiopia. The government blamed cooperation with the EU for having contributed to the crisis. The EU election observer mission was accused of siding with the opposition, thereby encouraging the opposition to take its protests to the streets. Moreover, the EU and other donors' decision to withhold budget support put significant pressure on the government. During a period when the government had to set up its budget and when output legitimacy became more important than ever, the EU and other donors' decision to use aid funds as leverage put the government in a precarious situation.

Largely unnoticed by the EU and other traditional donors, the 2005 election crisis marked the starting point for China's closer economic and political cooperation with Ethiopia. Simultaneously with the EU and other donors' decision to withhold general budget support funds, the Chinese government extended its first substantial loan facility to Ethiopia, whereby it significantly reduced the Ethiopian government's vulnerability to the EU and other traditional donors' pressure. However, in 2005 it was still unclear to the Ethiopian government to what extent this *ad hoc* engagement would result in better access to economic cooperation with China in the medium to long-term.

Why Ethiopia Continued to Reluctantly Engage Between 2006 and the 2010 Elections

The 2005 election crisis had not only short-term effects but also increased the costs for the Ethiopian government to engage with the EU in the medium-term. In the aftermath of the 2005 election crisis, the Ethiopian government abruptly closed political spaces and expanded the influence of the EPRDF. The government used measures of low-intensity coercion, such as new laws on media, terrorism and civil society that substantially limited the freedom of the opposition. The EPRDF expanded its membership base. It introduced measures to link access to civil service and some public goods to party membership to broaden its support base and improve compliance. At the same time, and as political spaces narrowed, state modernisation and the provision of public goods became even more important to secure regime stability. In this context, the EU's decision to broaden its good governance strategies and to promote not only *democratic government* but to also assist and empower civil society actors *vis-à-vis* the government entailed risks for the Ethiopian government. Moreover, the EU's decision to combine *cooperative* with *critical* instruments, inflicted considerable costs as EU criticism tied in with domestic reform pressure and regime instability.

As cooperation with the EU on governance reforms was challenging for the government after the 2005 election crisis, one would have expected that Ethiopia would be indifferent towards EU demands to engage. To understand why the government *still* reluctantly engaged with the EU between 2006 and 2010, one thus needs to take into account its broader interests in cooperating with the EU. While output legitimacy became even more important for the Ethiopian government, the EU remained one of the largest donors to Ethiopia, one of the most significant sources of direct investment and an important trading partner. The Ethiopian government thus could not 'afford' to ignore EU demands to cooperate on governance reforms despite the fundamental costs that cooperation entailed.

However, since the 2005 election crisis, China also successively emerged as an alternative economic cooperation partner, reducing Ethiopia's dependence on the EU and other traditional donors. Moreover, China has become an important partner for the Ethiopian government to support its survival strategies and the main partner of the EPRDF to engage in party reforms. In the case of Ethiopia, China has thus clearly emerged as an alternative cooperation partner to the EU between 2005 and 2011.

In this context, one would have expected that Ethiopia would refuse to cooperate with the EU on governance reforms, when China emerges as an alternative cooperation partner. However, Ethiopia has continued to at least reluctantly engage, going against the argument that China's presence in Africa substantially influences African governments' willingness to cooperate with the EU on governance reforms.

Why Has Ethiopia Again Become More Forthcoming to Engage Between 2011 and 2014?

After the 2010 elections, the EU has continued to promote *democratic governance*. But it has also modified its strategy from a cooperative-critical towards a *cooperative* strategy. The Ethiopian government has again become slightly more forthcoming and willing to cooperate on governance reforms. However, the slight modifications in the EU's strategy alone cannot account for the changes in the government's responsiveness. Instead, this change can be explained by greater domestic regime stability. The 2010 elections brought a landslide victory for the EPRDF, winning all but two seats in parliament. This overwhelming victory signalled to both the regime and the opposition that it had (at least partly) regained its strength, also giving it more confidence to engage with the EU and other donors in the aftermath of the elections.

What If...?

At least two counterfactual conjectures should be explored. First, what if the EU had continued to promote mostly *democratic government* or even narrowed its approach to *effective government* instead of broadening its good governance approach to *democratic governance* since 2006? In this case the Ethiopian government may have been more forthcoming in engaging with the EU. Parts of the EU's good governance approach matched the preferences of the Ethiopian government. EU attempts to strengthen the effectiveness of government institutions and support capacity-building, for instance, in the context of the PSCAP programme, was very welcome to the Ethiopian government. Moreover, Ethiopia may have been more willing to engage in political and aid policy dialogues on governance reforms, if the EU had issued fewer critical public statements. As one EU official describes the dilemma: 'We can have a political dialogue meeting with the minister or we can publish a critical statement, but we can't have both'.[38] It can thus be argued that the Ethiopian government might have been more active in engaging with the EU in governance reforms, if the EU had narrowed its good governance approach and had refrained from adopting a *cooperative-critical* strategy. However, this would also have considerably limited the EU's means of influencing political reforms.

Second, what if China had not emerged as an alternative cooperation partner since the mid-2000s? China's growing role as a provider of official flows, a trading partner, a source of direct investments, and as a partner to cooperate on governance reforms has reduced the incentives for the Ethiopian government to engage with the EU. However, it seems unlikely that in the absence of China, the Ethiopian government would have been much more forthcoming and would have actively or even proactively engaged with the EU in governance reforms, given the high risk that this cooperation involved after the election crisis. This (again) illustrates the importance of the domestic survival strategies as the determining factor to explain differential response strategies towards EU demands to cooperate on governance reforms.

Outlook

As is the case with Rwanda, the example of Ethiopia demonstrates that the domestic logic of political survival in authoritarian regimes has important consequences for what the EU can achieve with its good governance strategy at a certain point in time. In Ethiopia, political spaces have also gradually reduced since the mid-2000s. However, Ethiopia was much less willing than Rwanda to engage with the EU (and other donors) in governance reforms. The Ethiopian government thus made it very hard for the EU (and other donors) to put governance reforms on the agenda of bilateral relations. Given that the government considerably depends on output legitimacy for which EU aid also plays a prominent role, the EU institutions—in close cooperation with EU member states and other donors—might have used their leverage more strategically and applied more pressure on the government not to close political spaces further. Providing large sums of development aid to Ethiopia without exerting substantial pressure for political reforms, while the government gradually closes political spaces and does not allow for any opposition, engagement of CSOs or debates in the media, raises serious questions regarding the EU's contribution to medium- to longer-term prospects of inclusive and sustainable development in the country.

Sadly enough, recent events in Ethiopia seem to confirm those sceptics who argue that authoritarian regimes that focus on strong institutions and public goods provision while reducing political spaces will not be stable in the medium to long-term. The 2015 parliamentary elections demonstrated the EPRDF's firm grip on power and a hardening of authoritarian rule: the EPRDF won all seats. This overwhelming victory thus signalled to the EPRDF and opposition members that the it has not lost its strength, in spite of the death of Prime Minister Meles in 2012. As formal channels to express dissatisfaction through the media, civil society engagement or opposition parties in parliament were no longer available, protesters took to the streets. The upsurge in demonstrations against the government since the end of 2014 indicates a strong dissatisfaction and public dissent with government policies. The government's violent response illustrates the extent to which it is shaken by the protests.

These recent dynamics in Ethiopia thereby second the argument that the EU and other actors should not one-sidedly focus on enhancing the effectiveness of government institutions, but should in parallel promote the democratic quality of decision-making processes. In other words, these recent dynamics underscore the need for the EU to make support for democratic governance an integral part of its policies in order to positively contribute to sustainable and inclusive policies in the long run, particularly in cases where the EU at the same time provides large sums of development aid and by doing so—in any case—has an effect on domestic politics.

Notes

1. The EPRDF is a party coalition consisting of the TPLF, Amhara National Democratic Movement (ANDM), Oromo People's Democratic Organization (OPDO) and Southern Ethiopian People's Democratic Movement (SEPDU). Parties closely affiliated with the EPRDF are SPDP, ANDP, BGPDP and GPUDM. Trigray represents only 6 per cent of the population.
2. However, in contrast to the TPLF that had fought the struggle against the Derg and already established new state structures in the liberated territories, other parties within the EPRDF coalition were more loosely anchored in their respective regions (Clapham 2009; Young 2004; Vaughan 2011).
3. In several key sectors such as transport, energy, telecommunication or shipping, parastatal companies operate on behalf of the government. Not much information exists on most of these parastatal companies. Their budget is not part of the state budget, which makes effective parliamentary oversight difficult. As one European donor official put it: 'They [these companies] are a black box to us'.
4. Party-affiliated companies control important parts of the economy—particularly in Tigray region—buttressing the political power of the EPRDF (Abbink 2009, 11; Vaughan and Gebremichael 2011).
5. The government has not used the war to broaden its political support base, since it was largely fought within Tigray region (Clapham 2009, 186).
6. Reviewing the EIDHR projects in Ethiopia between 2000 and 2006 indicates that the EU focused on strengthening media and press freedom, basic human rights and capacity-building of parliaments.
7. Interviews with officials from the EU and member states in Addis Ababa in October 2009 and November 2010.
8. Only the United Ethiopian Democratic Forces that had gained 52 seats, took up their positions; the Coalition for Unity and Democracy did not take up the seats in parliament and other elected offices, such as that of the Mayor of Addis Ababa (Tronvoll 2009, 458).
9. BBC News, 1 August 2006, *The politics of aid in Ethiopia*, online at http://news.bbc.co.uk/2/hi/africa/5233352.stm, last access on 1 January 2013.
10. Ibid.
11. Due to the restructuring of the party and particularly party-state relations after the leadership split in 2001, the capacity of the EPRDF to organise an election campaign at the local level was limited. Moreover, the purge of opposition forces from the ruling coalition in 2001 had delegitimised the EPRDF (Tronvoll 2009, 466f).

12. Ethiopia's minister for information and secretary-general of the EPRDF Simon Bereket had also been travelling to China in February 2006.
13. Various interviews with European donor officials suggest that European actors had no notice of the agreement between the Ethiopian government and China.
14. The CSP states that €49 million representing about 8 per cent of the 10th EDF should be allocated to democratic governance reforms. Of these €49 million, the country strategy paper provides €29 million for supporting capacity-building of democratic institutions and the judicial system. Both in terms of its absolute volume and its relative share of overall EU assistance to Ethiopia, aid for governance reforms has increased significantly compared to the Ninth EDF (Ethiopia and European Community 2002, 2007).
15. Interviews with Ethiopian government officials in Addis Ababa in November 2010 and June 2013 and interviews with officials from the EU and member states in Addis Ababa in October 2009, November 2010 and June 2013 and in Brussels in April 2010 and December 2012.
16. Beyond Article 8 dialogue, the Ethiopian government agreed to meet with the Group of Ambassadors on a regular basis to discuss various issues of regional peace and security, economic development, but also governance reforms.
17. The discussion here and in the following is also based on interviews with Ethiopian government officials and EU and member states' officials in Addis Ababa in October 2009 and November 2010 as well as with EU officials in Addis Ababa in June 2013.
18. See also DAG annual reports, various years. Relevant line ministries, such as the Ministry of Justice, have met with sub-groups to the donors' governance technical working groups, that is, to work on justice sector reforms, human rights or civil society, but the government agreed to meet with donors only on an ad hoc basis and in response to specific requests (DAG 2010, 16ff).
19. Interviews with EU officials in Addis Ababa in November and October 2009.
20. Interviews with EU officials in Addis Ababa in November 2010 and in December 2012.
21. Only after lengthy negotiations did the government agree in 2009 to allocate €4 million of the €10 million earmarked for supporting justice sector reform under the 10th EDF to strengthen the capacities of the 'Justice Organs Professional Training Centre' (European Commission 2009). Despite the EU's requests, the Ministry of Justice has not been willing to combine the provision of technical and financial assistance for justice reform with a regular dialogue on such reforms (European Commission

2009). This was also confirmed during interviews with EU officials in Addis Ababa in November 2010.
22. Interviews with officials from the EU institutions, EU member states and other international donors in Addis Ababa in November 2010.
23. The objective of the Civil Society Fund is to strengthen the participation of NGOs in the dialogue between the EU and the Ethiopian government, for instance during the preparation and implementation of the National Indicative Programme (European Commission 2009).
24. Already during the negotiations to launch the PBS programme, the government rejected the civil society component (Furtado and Smith 2009). The new NGO law negatively affected support to civil society through this programme. Only recently had the government decided to consider aid through the PBS national funding, thereby giving national NGOs access to it (ECO Consult et al. 2012).
25. In 2012, the IMF suspended its programme over disagreements with the Ethiopian government about growth rates and about the ability of the government to generate enough capital needed for investments in infrastructure (EIU 2012).
26. Interviews with Chinese officials in Beijing in July 2010, March 2011 and July 2013.
27. See also Ministry of Finance and Economic Development, press statement 2011 'China plans to double its development assistance to Ethiopia', online at http://www.mofed.gov.et/English/NewsandUpdates/Pages/ChinaPlanstoDoubleitsDevelopmentAssistancetoEthiopia.aspx, last access 3 June 2014.
28. Information based on United Nations Commodity Trade Statistics Database (2010).
29. See *The Guardian* 10 July 2013 'Ethiopia's sesame seed trade with China—a partnership of equals?', online at http://www.theguardian.com/global-development/poverty-matters/2013/jul/10/ethiopia-sesame-seed-trade-china, last access on 3 June 2014.
30. China went from being a net exporter to a net importer of sesame seeds.
31. Brautigam quoted by Bloomberg, 'Ethiopia's bank-secured sesame seed-sales seen boosting exports', 6 December 2012, online at http://www.bloomberg.com/news/2012-12-06/ethiopia-s-bank-secured-sesame-seed-sales-seen-boosting-exports.html, last access on 3 June 2014.
32. Interviews with Chinese business men in Beijing in July 2010 and in Addis Ababa in December 2010.
33. Interviews were conducted in Delhi in July 2013 and in Addis Ababa in December 2010.
34. Interview with Chinese official in Addis Ababa in November 2010.

35. This happened for instance in 2010 according to an Ethiopian senior government official; interview in Addis Ababa in November 2010.
36. This is shown by various press statements on relations between the CCP on the EPRDF as indicated on the website of the CCP International Bureau, online at http://www.idcpc.org.cn/, last access on 3 June 2014.
37. See also *Capital Ethiopia* 'Chinese firm to spend $2 billion in leather sector', 5 March 2012, online at http://www.capitalethiopia.com/, last access on 5 November 2012.
38. Interview with EU official in Addis Ababa in June 2013.

Open Access This chapter is licensed under the terms of the Creative Commons Attribution 4.0 International License (http://creativecommons.org/licenses/by/4.0/), which permits use, sharing, adaptation, distribution and reproduction in any medium or format, as long as you give appropriate credit to the original author(s) and the source, provide a link to the Creative Commons license and indicate if changes were made.

The images or other third party material in this chapter are included in the chapter's Creative Commons license, unless indicated otherwise in a credit line to the material. If material is not included in the chapter's Creative Commons license and your intended use is not permitted by statutory regulation or exceeds the permitted use, you will need to obtain permission directly from the copyright holder.

CHAPTER 5

Angola

The Angolan government started to very reluctantly engage with the EU in governance reforms in the early 2000s. Over time it has become increasingly indifferent in its response to EU demands to cooperate.

This chapter demonstrates that—in contrast to Ethiopia and Rwanda—Angola is an example of a country where the EU's good governance strategies mostly entail costs for the government. Due to specific structural conditions (notably the Angolan government's access to abundant oil resources), the government has very little interest in building effective state institutions. Instead, in light of its access to easy revenues, it mostly uses state (and party) institutions to coopt regime supporters and opponents. The Angolan government faced little opposition in the first few years after the civil war. Since 2008, however, dissatisfaction within the party fermented and opposition outside of the party has grown. In response, the leadership has expanded party institutions, cooptation mechanisms and low-intensity coercion.

In this context, EU support for governance reforms was risky and generated almost no benefits. The Angolan government's decision to still, albeit reluctantly, start engaging in governance reforms in the early 2000s can be explained by its interest in receiving EU support for the reconstruction process. However, in 2004 when China appeared on the horizon as an alternative economic cooperation partner and Angola's interest in cooperating with the EU 'beyond' governance reforms faded away, the EU was left with no 'carrots or sticks' to persuade the Angolan government to address governance issues.

The example of Angola thus illustrates the limitations of the EU's good governance strategies in cases where the government has no genuine interest in cooperation and where it is not dependent on EU aid. Since the EU's instruments to support governance reforms are mainly operationalised in the field of development policy, the EU is left with limited options to engage in these contexts.

5.1 Structural Factors Shaping Angola's Survival Strategies

After the end of the civil war in 2002, the MPLA under President Eduardo dos Santos fostered its position as the dominant political force in Angola. Almost 30 years of civil war left the country devastated, with basic infrastructure destroyed and millions of people displaced. The government faced several challenges: it needed to transform the economy from a war- to a peace-time economy. It had to demonstrate that it was not only able to bring about peace but also an economic and social 'peace dividend' for its supporters. Furthermore, it needed to maintain support from key segments of the elite, such as the military and security forces, the MPLA party apparatus, the state oil company Sonangol and members of the presidential family.[1]

The Angolan government can rely on enormous revenues from oil exports. Some have argued that the 'resource curse' creates incentives for politicians to dismantle state institutions to seize rents, rather than to actually strengthen state institutions (Ross 1999). This argument also holds true in the case of Angola. The MPLA-governed state has often been described as a 'successfully failed state' (Soares de Oliveira 2011; Sogge 2009). On the one hand, formal state institutions were (and still are) quite weak or absent. The state has not been fulfilling some of its most basic functions in terms of guaranteeing human security and delivering basic services to its citizens. On the other hand, the Angolan leadership has established a highly efficient oil industry capable of generating vast amounts of rent that are necessary for regime survival. During the civil war, the state-owned company Sonangol had already gained a positive international reputation for its efficiency and aptitude in negotiating with international oil businesses (Soares de Oliveira 2015).

5.2 Angola Reluctantly Engaging in Governance Reforms in the Early 2000s Despite China Emerging

Until the end of the civil war in 2002, the EU's engagement with Angola had been limited. Throughout the 1990s, the EU mostly provided humanitarian and food aid, depending on the intensity of the conflict and humanitarian crisis (Republic of Angola and European Community 2003). After the end of the war, the EU sought to establish closer relations, and regular EU development assistance quickly resumed.

The EU's Good Governance Strategies Between 2000 and 2005

The EU's Approach: Promoting Democratic Government
In the first few years after the civil war, the EU institutions made some attempts to promote *democratic government*. The EU made support for governance reforms a key priority in its support of Angola's peace and reconciliation process. The first country strategy paper signed by the EU and the Angolan government in early 2003 reflects the EU's approach to promote democratic government (Republic of Angola and European Community 2003). The strategy paper highlights that, along with general capacity-building for government institutions and improvements in the transparency and management of public finances, the organisation of parliamentary and presidential elections, improvements to the human rights situation and the rule of law constitute preconditions for the success of Angola's peace process (ibid). Even though the strategy paper mentions the need to empower civil society organisations and their role in holding the government accountable, the focus clearly lies on strengthening government and state institutions (ibid).

According to OECD DAC aid statistics, the EU's financial commitments to support governance reforms indeed increased considerably in the early 2000s. Despite the strong rhetorical emphasis on promoting democratic reforms, the EU committed more aid to support the effectiveness of government institutions (about 74 per cent) than their democratic accountability (about 26 per cent) (Table 5.1).

Table 5.1 EU governance aid commitments to Angola (in USD million and in percent)

Angola	2000–2005	2006–2014
Total governance aid	18.80	72.09
Total aid (all sectors)	603.15	375.04
Governance aid/share in total EU aid	3.1%	19.2%
Output legitimacy	13.95	41.68
Input legitimacy	4.85	30.41
Output legitimacy/share in total governance aid	74.2%	57.8%
Input legitimacy/share in total governance aid	25.8%	42.2%

Source: Author's compilation, based on OECD DAC aid statistics (2016) (Query for EU institutions; 'total governance aid' includes all aid reported under the category '151:I5a: Government & Civil Society-general, Total' to the OECD DAC Creditor Reporting System. 'Output legitimacy' includes public sector and administrative management, public finance management, decentralisation and support to subnational government, anti-corruption organisations and institutions; 'input legitimacy' includes legal and judicial development, democratic participation and civil society, elections, legislature and political parties, media and freedom of information, human rights, women's equality. Data accessible at http://stats.oecd.org; last accessed: 5 October 2016)

Between 2000 and 2005, the EU clearly prioritised the intergovernmental over the transnational channel in its good governance strategy towards Angola.[2] Assistance through the EIDHR to support NGOs was very limited (Table 5.4). The EU directly allocated only small amounts of aid from the EDF to strengthen NGO capacities (about €5 million for 2002–2007) (Republic of Angola and European Community 2003).

The EU's Instruments: Cooperative-Critical

The EU initially pursued a *cooperative-critical* strategy. In addition to political dialogue and governance aid, the EU used strategies of naming and shaming and some material incentives to pressure the Angolan government to accelerate political reforms. The EU made several non-public *démarches* to raise concerns regarding the human rights situation and to address governance issues (Table 5.2). When the EU modified its common position in June 2002, it urged the government to advance democratic reforms, to hold free and fair parliamentary and presidential elections, to allow more spaces for civil society actors and to address the humanitarian crisis. The EU also made critical public statements in the UN and other international fora, asking the Angolan government to hold elections, and criticising its human rights record.

Table 5.2 EU statements and *démarches* related to governance reforms 2000–2012

	2000–2005		2006–2012		Total
	Positive	Critical	Positive	Critical	
EU public statements on governance reforms	4	11	5	–	20
Démarches	–	6	–	2	8

Source: Author's compilation, based on EU annual human rights reports, documents published by the Council of the EU

In 2003, the Angolan President dos Santos sent a letter to the President of the European Commission asking support from the EU to organise an international donor conference to raise international funds for Angola's reconstruction. The EU made his request conditional upon the signing of a framework agreement with the IMF which would have, among other stipulations, required the Angolan government to improve transparency of oil revenues and reduce corruption (Republic of Angola and European Community 2008). The EU did not consider initiating Article 96 negotiations in the first years after the end of the war (PARTICIP et al. 2006).[3]

2000–2005: Angola Started to Very Reluctantly Engage

In response to EU demands to cooperate on the implementation of governance instruments, the Angolan government—albeit very reluctantly—started to engage with the EU.

Angola's Responsiveness: Political and Aid Policy Dialogues
Relatively soon after the end of the civil war, at the end of 2003, the Angolan government agreed to initiate a formal Article 8 political dialogue. Between 2003 and 2005, five meetings took place (Republic of Angola and European Community 2008). However, in contrast to Ethiopia and Rwanda, apparently these meetings did not have a very high political priority for the Angolan government. The Angolan side was represented by the then vice minister of foreign affairs, George Rebelo Chicoti, who became the main interlocutor for the EU. The Angolan government has not opened up this formal dialogue to include representatives from other line ministries, and has been reluctant to discuss issues related to democratic or effective

governance with the EU (much more reluctant than either Ethiopia or Rwanda). Some interviewees, EU documents and information from an independent evaluation suggest that the more the Angolan government gained the impression that the key objective of the dialogue was to discuss issues related to human rights, democratic reforms or the transparency of government finances, the more it lost interest in the dialogue (ECO Consult et al. 2009).

Beyond political dialogue, the Angolan government was indifferent towards the EU's demands to address governance reforms as part of aid policy dialogues. In contrast to Ethiopia and Rwanda, in Angola aid policy dialogues have only been very loosely institutionalised. According to European officials, the government was hesitant to speak about governance reforms within the existing aid policy dialogue formats.

Angola's Responsiveness: Governance Aid and Positive Conditionality
In the early 2000s, the Angolan government started to reluctantly engage with the EU in the implementation of aid targeted at supporting governance reforms. As the following analysis will document, the government was more willing to accept aid geared towards the support of human and administrative capacities of government institutions, than for transparency, the fight against corruption or the democratic quality of the decision-making processes.

The Angolan government signed the EU country strategy paper that put a strong emphasis on good governance, and it agreed to allocate large parts of the EU's aid to support good governance, even though it had a strong preference for infrastructure development. Angola accepted some support for the Ministry of Planning in the process of designing a development strategy for 2005–2006 and a long-term development plan (the 'Visao 2025').[4] It accepted some assistance to improve the capacities of the National Institute for Statistics and the National Assembly. It also agreed to set up projects that promoted decentralisation and governance at the regional level (ECO Consult et al. 2009). Furthermore, the government engaged with the EU in the implementation of aid allocated to support planning and budgeting capacities of ministries responsible for social policies at the national and provincial level (ECO Consult et al. 2009).

Yet, the analysis of joint annual reports on the implementation of EU aid to Angola, interviews with EU officials and independent evaluations of the EU's aid programmes in Angola indicate that apart from these few measures, the government was unwilling to implement good governance programmes.[5] Most of the EU's funds earmarked for governance reforms could therefore not be disbursed. The government was not prepared to sign and implement a programme of about €5 million that the EU had designed to support the election process (European Community and Republic of Angola 2007, 10). The government did not agree with the EU about designing a large programme to support the capacities of the judicial system and to improve access to justice (PARTICIP et al. 2006; European Community and Republic of Angola 2007); it merely agreed to launch a project that supports regional cooperation on justice reform among Portuguese-speaking countries. The government was unwilling to design projects with a view to supporting public financial management and transparency of government funds (PARTICIP et al. 2006; ECO Consult et al. 2009).

The Angolan government was also reluctant to engage with the EU in the implementation of assistance allocated to support the capacities of civil society organisations. The identification and implementation of direct assistance to NGOs encountered difficulties, as programmes financed under the EDF have to be agreed upon by both the EU and the Angolan government (ECO Consult et al. 2009).

We can conclude that, similar to Ethiopia and Rwanda, in Angola the EU also sought to promote *democratic government* in the early 2000s. In its public statements, the country strategy paper, through political dialogue and the allocation of governance aid, the EU expressed the importance it attaches to holding elections, respect for human rights and reform of the justice sector as well as improvements to the transparency of government finances. The EU clearly prioritised the intergovernmental over the transnational channel to support governance reforms and allocated only small amounts of aid to support NGOs. Moreover, again similar to Ethiopia and Rwanda, the EU also adopted a *cooperative-critical* strategy.

In response, the Angolan government hesitantly engaged. Already by the early 2000s, Angola was much more reluctant to respond to the EU's demands than Ethiopia and particularly Rwanda. The government hesitantly agreed to initiate formal political dialogue in the early 2000s, even if meetings subsequently took place irregularly and only at the level of the vice minister of foreign affairs. The government reluctantly started to engage in the implementation of some aid projects geared towards supporting governance reforms. It was indifferent towards the EU and other donors' demands to include a discussion of governance reforms in aid policy dialogues.

The Angolan Government's Survival Strategies

Little Domestic Opposition and Challenge to Regime Survival

The Angolan government faced little challenge from the domestic opposition in the first few years after the end of the civil war. With the MPLA's clear military victory and the death of Jonas Savimbi, the leader of the opposition party UNITA, the MPLA could consolidate its power largely unchallenged. A return to armed conflict was relatively unlikely. The MPLA-led government quickly restored its monopoly on power and extended the reach of the state throughout the country. Only some disputes with separatist movements in the Cabinda province still persist. Moreover, the opposition party UNITA was clearly not in a position to politically challenge the MPLA as it was disorganised internally (Orre 2010).

In light of the physical destruction of the country and the traditionally weak civil society, societal opposition was also weak and unlikely to emerge in the first few years after the war. As one observer put it: '…Angolans [were] exhausted after four decades of conflict and keen on predictability in their lives' (Soares de Oliveira 2011, 293). Within the ruling elite, President dos Santos was largely unchallenged in the early 2000s.

Using State Institutions and the Party for Cooptation

At the end of the civil war, the Angolan leadership had to rebuild its support base and restructure the economy from a war- to a peace-time economy. The leadership established informal state institutions to carefully balance different power centres in order to centralise access to rents and power. Moreover, it used the party as an instrument of cooptation. Both arguments will be further explored in the following sections.

The MPLA plays a major role in Angola as both the main instrument to keep the leadership in power and as a vehicle for cooptation. Rents to coopt regime supporters are channelled through party structures. At the same time, President dos Santos has carefully balanced other informal and formal power houses against the party to prevent it from becoming too powerful. The former chief of the state-owned oil company Sonangol, Manuel Vicente, for instance, has a limited powerbase within the party (Roque 2011) and thus did not constitute a strong rival to President dos Santos.

In the first few years after the war, the Angolan leadership made some efforts to reinforce state institutions at the regional and local level to expand its reach. Developing a civil administration in other urban centres and the rural areas was also a political imperative for the government (Power 2011). However, these measures contributed only slightly to improvements in the effectiveness of the government. If measured according to the WGI, the government's effectiveness only improved slightly in the early 2000s. It remained significantly below the average of sub-Saharan African countries (Fig. 5.2 below), and was clearly worse than Ethiopia and Rwanda.

In addition to formal government structures, the president created new *informal* government structures to centralise resources and balance different factions. Under the auspices of the presidency, a shadow government was responsible for policy formulation and policy implementation in key areas such as security or international relations. Its two main bodies were the Civilian House and Military House (Roque 2011). Within the Military House, the president established the Office of National Reconstruction (GRN) in 2004. One of the main objectives of the GRN was to launch prestigious projects, such as a new airport and railway lines. The GRN quickly became the most important institution for managing infrastructure reconstruction, and thus also for deciding on how the loans extended by the China International Fund should be allocated, which will be discussed more in detail below. These informal state structures allowed the president to reduce the influence of the formal government institutions, that is, the Ministry of Finance (which would have been responsible for the management of credit lines). And it allowed the president to use investments in infrastructure more strategically to reward and coopt regime supporters (Croese 2011; Corkin 2013; Manning 2011, 12).

The Angolan government strongly prioritised investment in the reconstruction of basic infrastructure. Investment in large-scale, physical infrastructure became the priority during the first period of post-war reconstruction between 2002 and the 2008 elections. The devastation of basic infrastructure can hardly be overstated (World Bank 2005). Roads, railways, bridges, electricity and so on were largely destroyed by the war. In Luanda, hardly any investments had been made during the war (Power 2011). Infrastructure investments were clearly much needed.

Yet, at the same time, large investments in infrastructure also constitute a formidable instrument of cooptation. In the absence of budgetary oversight, procurement remained opaque, and companies were selected on the basis of their political connections rather than quality and efficiency (Soares de Oliveira 2011). Quality control also remained limited and some were critical that infrastructure investments have been hugely expensive, but failed to deliver value for money (ibid). According to the World Bank (2011), public expenditure heavily favoured the urban areas (particularly Luanda), instead of the poor and the victims of war.

Managing Arenas of Contestation: Elections
The government has also built up formal democratic institutions after the end of the civil war. The first parliamentary and presidential elections were supposed to take place in 2006. Yet, despite pressure from the EU and other international actors, the government postponed the parliamentary elections several times, before they were finally held in 2008. No date was announced for the first presidential elections. Some observers argue that the government first wanted to make sure that it was in a position to win the elections with a large majority (Hon et al. 2010, xx; Corkin 2013).

Due to the Angolan government's limited efforts in strengthening the effectiveness and democratic quality of decision-making processes, cooperating with the EU on governance reforms was challenging and involved very few benefits. It is thus not surprising that the government had been very hesitant to engage with the EU. Instead, it seems rather surprising that Angola has started to engage with the EU at all. Focusing only on Angola's survival strategies cannot explain why the government, at least reluctantly, cooperated with the EU in the early 2000s. The next sections will therefore analyse both the Angolan government's broader interests in engaging with the EU and the influence of China.

Angola's Economic Dependence on the EU

In the case of Angola, the EU has clearly faced difficulties in establishing itself as an attractive cooperation partner. When Angola approached the EU for support in the reconstruction process, the EU probably missed an opportunity to set incentives for cooperation.

Angola is not aid dependent. The Angolan government relies almost exclusively on resource rents; oil revenues account for almost all government revenues. Development aid as a share of GNI peaked at about 7 per cent in 2004, when donors increased their aid funds to assist Angola's post-conflict reconstruction and rehabilitation (Fig. 5.1). Even though the EU has been one of the largest donors to Angola (Table 5.3), in light of Angola's low dependence on development aid, its interest in EU aid has arguably been quite low, particularly after 2004.

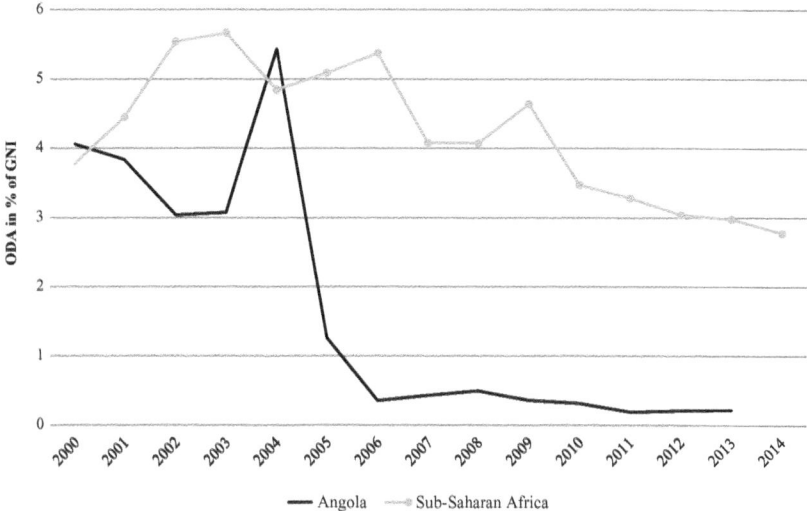

Fig. 5.1 Net ODA as a share of GNI in Angola
Source: Author's compilation, based on World Bank (2016a), World Development Indicators

Table 5.3 EU aid as a share of total DAC donors' aid (in USD million and in per cent)

	2000–2005	2006–2013
DAC aid total	2355 million	1891 million
EU institutions aid total	419 million	362 million
EU share of total DAC aid	18%	19%

Source: Author's compilation, based on OECD Development Assistance Committee CRS Aid statistics (2016)

Despite Angola's generally low aid dependence, at least in the early 2000s, the government had a clear interest in receiving support from the EU. At that time, the EU (as a whole) was still the second-largest destination for Angolan oil after the USA (Fig. 5.3). More importantly, the Angolan government urgently needed financial assistance from international partners for the reconstruction of the country after the end of the civil war (Soares de Oliveira 2011, 299; Corkin 2013, 41). Angola expected that the international community would shoulder parts of the burden of reconstruction, given the involvement of international actors in the war (Corkin 2013, 41). Back then, Angola also had difficulties raising funds in the international capital markets and from Western countries, because negotiations with the Paris Club creditors were not yet concluded and Angola still had USD2 billion in outstanding debts. Furthermore, international oil prices at that time were moderate and Angola's oil production was still comparatively low. In this context, the Angolan government repeatedly asked the international community, and notably the EU, to organise an international donor conference to mobilise international support for the reconstruction process, but without success.

The EU hesitated to actively support a donor conference before negotiations between Angola and the IMF had succeeded. After the war, international NGOs such as Global Witness (2002) published influential reports that suggested that billions of dollars in oil revenues had gone missing. A consensus emerged within the international community that Angola should address the issue of transparency before external financial support could (again) be extended (Soares de Oliveira 2011, 300). Moreover, at that time economic interests of EU member states in Angola were still quite limited. For instance, trade and investment relations with Angola's former colonial power Portugal were negligible. In 2000 Angola was only the tenth export destination for Portuguese goods and services, and Portuguese companies had invested as little as USD40 million (Seabra and Gorjão 2011). As one EU official put it: 'At that time, member states did not yet see the strategic importance of Angola'.[6]

The Angolan government was unwilling to comply with the EU and other international actors' demands to commit to greater transparency in the management of its revenues and to subject itself to IMF conditions.[7] Instead, the EU's attempts to condition support for a donor conference to an agreement between Angola and the IMF was strongly criticised by the Angolan government. Several observers and officials felt that this situation created an atmosphere of alienation between the government and the EU, which also affected relations in the following years.

To summarise, even though the EU has been an important donor to Angola, this does not make it an attractive partner for the Angolan government in light of Angola's very low aid dependency. In the early 2000s, the Angolan government had some interest in engaging with the EU because it was hoping for the EU's support in organising an international donor conference that would provide assistance for its reconstruction efforts. Despite the costs that cooperation on governance reforms entailed, the Angolan government thus decided to at least reluctantly start engaging with the EU.

China: Becoming an Alternative Economic Cooperation Partner

> China needs natural resources and Angola wants development.
> President dos Santos during the visit of Prime Minister Wen Jiabao in Angola in 2006[8]

This short statement nicely captures Angola and China's interests in their relationship. Both sides are primarily interested in economic cooperation. And the relationship is quite interdependent—in contrast to China's relations with most other African countries and similar to the EU's relations with Angola.

Chinese relations with Angola can be characterised as 'a marriage of convenience' (Corkin 2011; Power and Alves 2012). Both sides have a strong and very pragmatic interest in the relationship. For China, Angola has become one of its most important economic cooperation partners in Africa, not only due to the importance of oil exports. At least partly as a result of the oil-for-infrastructure deals, Angola also generates huge business opportunities for Chinese construction, telecommunication and other companies. For the Angolan government, in turn, cooperating with China has significantly bolstered Angola's independence from the EU and other Western actors.

During the civil war, China had mostly supported the UNITA, at times the National Front for the Liberation of Angola (FNLA) and only shortly the MPLA. Until the late 1990s, China's trade, aid and other economic cooperation with Angola was limited, similar to China's relations with other African countries. Only after the turn of the century did China–Angola relations rapidly become more intense. The end of the Angolan civil war in 2002 coincided with the launch of China's 'going out' policy, which paved the way for closer economic and political cooperation with African countries in general and Angola in particular.

In 2003, shortly after the end of the civil war and in the midst of the difficult negotiations between the Angolan government and the IMF, the EU and other traditional partners, the EXIM Bank started negotiating a loan contract with the Angolan government. In March 2004, a USD2 billion loan was signed. As Soares de Oliveira (2011, 301) put it: 'One [cannot] underestimate the extent to which the Chinese credit mattered in 2004, or the symbolic role of the Chinese arrival in the broader transformation of Angolan external relations'.

Due to the timing and the size of the loan as well as its linkage to infrastructure investments and its medium-term effects, it was highly important for both the domestic strategies of the Angolan government and its relations with China, the EU and other partners. First, the agreement with the Chinese EXIM Bank allowed the Angolan government to break off negotiations with the IMF and to stop asking the EU and other donors to organise a donor conference (Traub 2006). The volume of the loan probably exceeded the amount of support that the Angolan government had expected from traditional partners. Second, the EXIM Bank loan had a catalytic effect, because it once again gave the government access to international commercial loans (Corkin 2013, 152; Traub 2006). Third, the Chinese loan was reserved for key public investment projects in the construction and rehabilitation of basic infrastructure, telecommunication and agrobusiness within the framework of the Angolan government's national reconstruction programme. The EXIM Bank loans thus became a major source of funding for the government's public investment programme. Fourth, the timing and the Chinese offer to provide not only a line of credit, but to also *deliver* much-needed infrastructure projects, closely matched the Angolan government's need to launch infrastructure rehabilitation. The Chinese loan was perceived by the Angolan leadership as a quick and convenient answer to the country's basic infrastructure problems. Timely delivery was paramount: most Chinese projects were due to be implemented before the parliamentary elections, 'thus adding prestige and bolstering the MPLA government's credentials of delivery' (Burke et al. 2007, see also Corkin 2013, 154 for a similar argument).

The loans also had considerable advantages for President dos Santos' efforts to bolster his own influence. In 2004, he decided to set up the GRN to manage the Chinese loans and thus to shift responsibility from the Ministry of Finance to informal, 'shadow government' structures directly under his authority. The loans gave the president access to an important flow of resources for cooptation and to secure his power position *vis-à-vis* potential political rivals (Soares de Oliveira 2011, 301; Corkin 2013, 131ff). Marques de Morais (2011b), a civil society activist and outspoken critic of the Angolan government, argues: 'The concentration of power in the presidency has turned Sino-Angolan relations into a new stream for looting'.

Between 2004 and 2006, the EXIM Bank loan financed about 100 contracts in energy, water, transport, agriculture, healthcare and education. At least partly in response to international pressure, information on the specific projects funded under the loan agreement was published on the website of the Angolan Ministry of Finance.[9] The projects were implemented by Chinese, mostly state-owned, companies. The Angolan government negotiated a clause that up to 30 per cent of the value of a project had to be sub-contracted to Angolan companies (Africa-Asia Confidential 2009b).

After 2003, economic cooperation between China and Angola intensified. China rapidly became the second-largest destination for Angola's oil exports (Fig. 5.3). At the same time, Chinese direct investments in Angola remained limited in the early 2000s. Development assistance also played a marginal role in China's relations with Angola, much different from Rwanda and Ethiopia. Angola has received some aid: China sends medical teams to Angola, provides some scholarships for Angolan students to study in China and has funded turnkey infrastructure projects, such as schools and a hospital. Yet, the volume of Chinese aid is not only small compared to its overall economic engagement; according to Chinese officials it is also small compared to the volume of aid that other African countries receive.[10]

Cooperating with China has significantly bolstered the Angolan government's independence from the EU and other Western actors since 2004. China extended important volumes of loans at a crucial point in time when the EU and others sought to condition their assistance on greater transparency of government revenues. China has not only offered important financial flows and has become the second-largest destination for Angolan oil exports, it also delivered inexpensive infrastructure and labour that were crucial for the Angolan government's reconstruction efforts after the civil war and ahead of the 2008 elections.

5.3 The Late 2000s: Angola Largely Indifferent Towards EU Demands to Engage on Governance Reforms Even Though the EU Narrows Its Strategies

Between 2006 and 2014, support for governance reforms has remained a prominent issue on the EU's agenda. However, the Angolan government has been largely indifferent towards EU demands to engage in governance reforms.

EU Good Governance Strategies and Angola's Responsiveness

The EU's Approach: Promoting Effective Government

After 2006, the EU narrowed its good governance strategies to supporting *effective government*. Even though parliamentary elections were postponed, presidential elections had not been held and constitutional reform was still pending, the EU toned down its rhetorical demands for democratic reforms. The subsequent country strategy paper signed by the EU and the Angolan government in 2008 was less outspoken about the need for democratic reforms than the previous one. Instead, the strategy acknowledged that Angola made progress towards democratisation since the end of the civil war, for instance, in preparing for the elections (Republic of Angola and European Community 2008, 14f).

Support to governance reforms became an even more prominent issue in the EU's aid to Angola. The EU made aid to governance reforms the first focal sector of its aid programme. Funding earmarked for governance reforms increased to 20 per cent (€40 million) of the €214 million in aid that the EU planned to spend in Angola between 2008 and 2013 (Republic of Angola and European Community 2008, 47). However, the EU has also modified its definition of good governance, adopting a very narrow understanding of *effective government*. Between 2006 and 2014, about 60 per cent of the EU's governance aid to Angola were allocated for enhancing the effectiveness and efficiency of government institutions rather than the democratic quality of decision-making processes (Table 5.1). Aid allocated with a view to supporting governance reforms should strengthen the human and administrative capacities of the government rather than the accountability of government institutions or the transparency of government finances (Republic of Angola and European Community 2008).

The main activity between 2006 and 2014 that falls into the category of promoting *democratic government* was the EU's support of parliamentary elections. The EU sent an election observer mission to monitor the 2008 elections (European Union 2008). Its final report found that the elections were free and fair and highlighted how peacefully they were conducted. The EU did not send a regular observer mission to the subsequent parliamentary elections that were held in September 2012. Instead, it only dispatched an expert team that was to collect information about the election process for EU internal purposes.

The EU continued to be very reluctant to use the transnational channel. Between 2006 and 2010, EU funding from the EIDHR increased slightly (Table 5.4). Through the EIDHR, the EU aimed at fostering

Table 5.4 EIDHR projects in Angola 2000–2010

	2000–2005	2006–2010	Total
Volume in USD	3,302,701	5,646,841	8,949,542
Number of projects	11	31	42

Source: Author's compilation, based on EU compendia EIDHR projects, various years

freedom of expression and contributing to national reconciliation as well as the election process. An evaluation of the EIDHR projects criticises that funds have predominantly been used for 'promotional' activities (Foley et al. 2010). In contrast, the EU has been reluctant to support interventions that either monitor Angola's human rights record with a view to holding the Angolan government accountable to international human rights norms or that empower the political opposition (ibid).

The EU mainly supported the PAANE programme which was launched in 2007 and entered a second phase in 2010 (European Commission 2010). PAANE strengthens the capacities of NGOs to participate in the decentralisation process (ECO Consult et al. 2009, 156). The project also seeks to both strengthen capacities of CSOs to engage in dialogue with government institutions and to build networks among CSOs, particularly at the local and regional levels. The project's strategy paper points out that as EDF funds depend on an explicit agreement between the EU and the Angolan government, politically more sensitive interventions should be financed through the EIDHR (European Commission 2010, 14).

A final example of the EU's reluctance to promote *democratic governance* is its support for the civil society forum that was held at the end of 2009 in Benguela. Whereas the EU had provided some financial support to the conference, it did not send a high-level delegation to the opening of the conference, in order to avoid conflicts with the Angolan government.[11]

The EU's Instruments: Cooperative Strategy

Between 2006 and 2014, the EU merely pursued a *cooperative* strategy, relying mostly on political dialogue and governance aid. The EU did not use negative incentives to exert pressure on the Angolan government.

The EU made efforts to improve the implementation of its cooperative instruments. Most importantly, it made several attempts to foster a formal

Article 8 political dialogue with the Angolan government (European Union 2010, 2011; Republic of Angola and European Community 2008). In 2009, the EU proposed to launch a Joint Way Forward together with the Angolan government (European Union 2010). The objective of the Joint Way Forward is to strengthen political dialogue and political cooperation between the EU and Angola on issues of 'mutual interest', such as cooperation in energy or peace and security. Yet, the EU has also suggested include dialogue on governance reforms. With Nigeria and Cape Verde, Angola is one of only three African countries to which the EU has proposed upgrading its relationships through a Joint Way Forward in the late 2000s.

By contrast, between 2006 and 2014, the EU clearly refrained from using negative material or non-material incentives to put pressure and openly criticise the Angolan government. Those few public statements that the EU made after 2006 (for instance, after the 2008 parliamentary elections) laud the government for its progress on governance reforms. The EU did not make public statements or declarations to urge the Angolan government to promote democratic reforms (Table 5.2). Nor did it make statements at the UN to comment on the human rights situation. The EU did not comment on the new constitution that the parliament voted into effect in early 2010 and that gives substantially more power to the president. The EU did not comment on a critical IMF (2012) report which argued that several billions of dollars of government funds had gone missing. Critical reports published by Amnesty International, Human Rights Watch or Global Witness also did not prompt the EU to issue critical statements to signal its concern.

Angola Remained Largely Indifferent to Demands for Cooperation from 2006 to 2014

Even though the EU considerably toned down its demands and merely sought to promote *effective government*, the Angolan government has been increasingly indifferent towards the EU's initiatives to cooperate on governance reforms since 2006.

Angola's Responsiveness: Political and Aid Policy Dialogues

In contrast to Ethiopia and particularly Rwanda, Angola has increasingly ignored the EU's requests to intensify formal Article 8 political dialogue. Meetings took place irregularly and have even lost momentum over time.

In 2006 and 2007, meetings took place about three times a year; one meeting was convened in the summer of 2008 (ECO Consult et al. 2009). Between the summers of 2008 and 2012, however, political dialogue did not take place.[12] In those meetings that did happen between 2006 and 2008, only the Angolan vice minister of foreign affairs was present. Whereas the meetings were reportedly held in a cordially atmosphere and allowed for open exchange, discussions did not foster tangible results, and the impact of the dialogue on the position of the government was reported to have been small (ECO Consult et al. 2009). Interviewees suggest that the Angolan government was very hesitant to discuss issues related to governance reforms, which it did not perceive as a dialogue at eye level. Instead, the government has been more interested in discussing regional peace and security issues or the ban on the Angolan airline TAAG flying to the EU.[13]

The Angolan government has also been indifferent towards the EU's demands to engage in political dialogue within the framework of the Joint Way Forward. Interviewees suggest that Angola was initially not very enthusiastic regarding the EU's proposal to launch the Joint Way Forward as an instrument to revitalise political dialogue and to upgrade its relationship with the EU.[14] In 2012, the Angolan government eventually agreed to sign the Joint Way Forward—three years after the EU had launched its initiative and shortly ahead of the parliamentary elections in September 2012.[15] The first high-level dialogue meeting took place immediately following the signing of the document. The first ministerial meeting took place two years later in October 2014; issues of democracy and good governance were also addressed.[16]

Similar to the early 2000s, the government has not been willing to address governance issues as part of its aid policy dialogue with the EU and other donors. In contrast to Ethiopia and Rwanda, Angola has not been actively engaged in the international aid effectiveness agenda. For instance, Angola is one of very few developing countries that have not signed the Paris Declaration in 2005, in which donor and recipient countries agreed on basic principles and standards for development cooperation. Meetings between the government and donors to discuss general issues of aid cooperation take place on a relatively regular basis. However, aid coordination structures between the Angolan government and donors are weak compared to other African (aid-dependent) countries. The government has not agreed to address governance reforms as part of aid policy dialogues.

Angola's Responsiveness: Governance Aid and Positive Conditionality
In contrast to Ethiopia and particularly Rwanda, Angola has further been reluctant to engage with the EU in other instruments that seek to foster cooperation on governance reforms, such as the EU's governance incentive tranche. It has not been willing to draft a governance action plan for the EU, but instead referred the EU to already existing development strategies containing short sections with governance reform objectives. The EU then took the lead and drafted a plan, based on the poverty reduction strategy and the Angolan government's development strategy for 2007–2008 (Republic of Angola and European Community 2008, 40). The objectives and targets identified in the governance action plan were vague and—if at all—process oriented rather than specifying the outcome that should be achieved (Republic of Angola and European Community 2008, 40–42). During the following years, Angola made very limited progress in implementing the governance action plan. An analysis prepared for the EU's midterm review found that until 2009 only nine out of 35 targets had been achieved. The government has clearly been reluctant to use the governance action plan or its national development strategies as a framework for political or aid policy dialogue (Republic of Angola and European Community 2008).

Compared to the period between 2002 and 2005, Angola has been even more reluctant and to some extent indifferent towards EU attempts to engage in the implementation of governance aid. Only reluctantly and after lengthy negotiations did the government sign the country strategy paper and the national indicative programme for the 10th EDF (Republic of Angola and European Community 2008). One EU official suggested that this reluctance can be explained because the government perceived the strategy as being too critical regarding the governance situation in Angola and placed too much emphasis on aiding governance reforms rather than supporting the rebuilding of basic infrastructure.[17]

The analysis of joint annual reports on the implementation of EU aid to Angola, an independent evaluation of EU aid to Angola as well as interviews with officials suggest that the government has been clearly reluctant and often indifferent towards EU demands to implement aid funds earmarked for supporting governance reforms. Whereas it accepted some aid to strengthen the human and administrative capacities of government institutions, it ignored EU attempts to cooperate on the implementation of aid to improve the transparency of government finances or the democratic quality of decision-making processes. Several examples illustrate this assessment.

In line with the objective of the country strategy paper to allocate parts of EU governance aid to justice reform, the EU proposed a programme to improve access to justice but had to wait longtime for a response from the Ministry of Justice (European Community and Republic of Angola 2009). The government did not respond at all to the EU's proposals to allocate some aid to enhance the capacities of the Ministry of Finance. A project to support the human and administrative capacities of the Ministry of Trade took a long time to be negotiated. A programme to support public administration reform was first cancelled by the National Authorising Officer, before the EU and the government eventually reached an agreement. The project that the EU and the Angolan government agreed upon seeks to support the capacities of the Ministry of Planning in managing the implementation of EU aid funds and strengthening donor coordination; it provides assistance to the National Institute of Statistics and promotes regional integration within the South African Development Community (SADC) (European Commission 2010). The project thus has a focus on promoting (a very narrow definition of) effective government. The single most visible activity of the Angolan government to engage with the EU in governance reforms was the 2008 EU election observer mission that the government agreed to (European Union 2008).

We can conclude that, in contrast to Ethiopia and Rwanda, the EU's strategy in Angola shifted from promoting *democratic government* towards promoting a narrow definition of *effective government* that focuses mostly on the capacity-building of government institutions rather than the transparency of government finances. In its support of governance reforms, the EU continued to prioritise the intergovernmental over the transnational channel. After 2006, no instances of the EU using material or non-material negative incentives to put pressure on the Angolan government could be observed.

In contrast to Ethiopia and particularly Rwanda, the Angolan government has been increasingly *indifferent* towards the EU's demands to engage in governance reforms since 2006. It has been indifferent towards the EU's requests to engage in formal political dialogue under Article 8 of the Cotonou Agreement. It took three years to agree to sign the Joint Way Forward; a clear indication of its limited interest in political dialogue. The government has not agreed to engage in aid policy dialogues to discuss governance reforms with the EU. It has been largely indifferent towards the EU's request to draft a governance action plan to become eligible for a governance incentive tranche. It has been unwilling to engage with the EU in the implementation of governance aid; most projects have not been launched or were substantially delayed. The implementation of direct aid to NGOs has also faced difficulties.

The Angolan Government's Survival Strategies

Mounting Opposition from Outside and Within the Ruling Elite
Since the mid-2000s, opposition from outside and within the ruling elite has gradually become more pressing. Particularly since 2009, the Angolan leadership has faced substantially more opposition.

Opposition from beyond the leadership's support coalition has become stronger since the 2008 elections. For the first time since independence in 1975, anti-government demonstrations took place in Luanda in 2011 and 2012 (Croese 2013; Roque 2013). These demonstrations were to some extent influenced by the Arab Spring, and fuelled by the economic crisis in Angola and the limited effects of the government's policies on the lives of ordinary Angolans. Some of the mostly young and urban protesters urged President dos Santos to step down. Most importantly, among them were not only members of the opposition but also some descendants of high-ranking MPLA members (ibid). Some war veterans and other members of the security apparatus also took to the streets to protest about unpaid pensions. Even though demonstrations remained largely peaceful and did not escalate into a full-scale mass movement, they indicated the growing dissatisfaction with the social and economic performance of the regime (Croese 2013; Watch 2012). Popular discontent with the government is not least evident in public opinion polls.[18] According to Gallup polls (2013), only 23 per cent of Angolans had 'confidence in the national government' in 2011, and only 16 per cent showed 'approval of the country's leadership'.

Dissatisfaction also fermented within the MPLA itself. Several high-level figures in the MPLA defected and joined the opposition, thereby weakening the position of the leadership. One indicator for growing discontent within the party was the delay in the process of drafting a new constitution. Even though the 2008 elections won the government a firm majority in parliament, the new constitution was not passed until 2010. Some observers further argue that the delays in publishing the party list for the 2012 elections were a sign of ongoing disputes within the party.[19]

Boosting the Ruling Party as a Vehicle for Cooptation
After 2006, the government continued to use a combination of cooptation and low-intensity coercion to solicit support. The government used funds from oil revenues to maintain support from party members and the military.

The landslide victory for the MPLA in the 2008 elections and the resulting dominance of the parliament allowed the MPLA government to work towards a modification of the constitution. The new constitution which was passed early in 2010, gives the president an even more powerful position than before (Orre 2010, 13).[20] The constitution abolishes direct presidential elections. The candidate at the head of the party list that wins most votes in the general elections automatically becomes president. The new constitution thereby allowed President dos Santos to remain in office without being subject to voters' opinions. One can argue that the constitution formalises de facto power structures and the all-powerful position of the president (Orre 2010).

In response to the growing challenges from within and outside of the elite, the Angolan leadership further expanded the ruling party. Party membership had already increased massively from about 60,000 in 1990 to about four million in 2004 (Soares de Oliveira 2011). Ahead of the 2012 elections, the MPLA was planning to recruit another two million party members (Roque 2011, 5). In a country of about 20 million inhabitants, this is a quite significant figure. Expanding the party membership has created ample opportunities of top-down cooptation. Observers are critical that the MPLA has gained significant influence over the state. Angolans refer to the growing influence of the MPLA on public and private life as 'partidarizacao' or 'party-isation' (Schubert 2010, 659). During the past few years, MPLA-owned companies acquired most of the free press and established new media outlets (Marques de Morais 2010). Moreover, the party created 'special committees' that are involved in all areas of society. These allow for conditioning service delivery and career prospects on loyalty with the party (Roque 2013, 2).

Using Formal and Informal State Institutions for Cooptation Rather than Provision of Public Services
Between 2009 and 2012, the leadership continued to substantially rely on formal as well as informal government structures. The GRN was dismantled in 2010, but its responsibilities in managing the domestic infrastructure investments were not transferred (back) to the Ministry of Finance.

Instead, a new institution within the national oil company Sonangol was set up (Corkin 2013, 131).

Between 2009 and 2012, the Angolan leadership only made subtle efforts to strengthen the effectiveness of formal state institutions. In 2010, the government started to introduce a tax reform to boost non-oil revenues (Anderson 2013). Reform steps were to include an overhaul of the administrative structure and notably preparations for the creation of an integrated revenue authority. Observers contend that the reform is at least partly driven by pressure from the IMF rather than a genuine domestic interest of the Angolan government (Anderson 2013, 2). Moreover, the government has introduced some measures to make public finance more transparent. Observers view these measures as 'window dressing' to comply with IMF conditionality and improve Angola's international standing rather than home-grown reforms in which the government has a genuine interest (Soares de Oliveira 2012). International indices, such as the WGI, suggest that rather than increasing, the effectiveness of the Angolan government has *decreased* between 2009 and 2014 (Fig. 5.2). The Angolan government's effectiveness remains significantly below the sub-Saharan African average and clearly below that of Ethiopia and Rwanda.

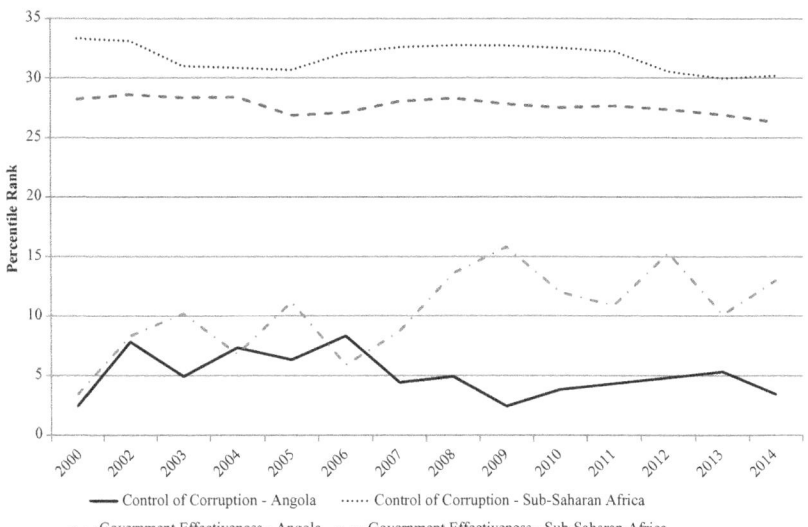

Fig. 5.2 Government effectiveness and control of corruption in Angola
Source: World Bank (2016b), Worldwide Governance Indicators; author's compilation

The Angolan government continues to use state institutions as a means for cooptation by channelling private goods, spoils and perks rather than for providing public goods and improving public services. A closer analysis of spending on infrastructure, the military and social services suggests that the government has a strong interest in using the state to coopt regime opponents and supporters rather than to provide effective services to the broader population.

One case in point is the government's substantial investments in physical infrastructure. Between 2009 and 2012, investments in housing were a government priority (Croese 2011, 16). In the run-up to the 2008 elections, the MPLA had promised that one million affordable houses would be built by 2012 to respond to the needs of a rapidly growing population and to skyrocketing housing prices.[21] The slogan for the election campaign was: 'Angola é um canteiro de obras', which was to say that all of Angola represents a construction site for public works (Marques de Morais 2011a). Total public investments in infrastructure (roads, power, railways and housing) grew by tremendous rates of 14 per cent of GDP or USD4.3 billion per year (World Bank 2011). However, an astonishing USD1.3 billion of the investments or 5 per cent of GDP per year is lost due to 'inefficiencies' (ibid; Soares de Oliveira 2011). With regard to the infrastructure investments, Soares de Oliveira (2011, 295) thus points out that 'many of the policies pursued by the government seem designed to maximise rentierism and minimise oversight'. Examples include prestigious projects such as the rebuilding of Luanda's seaside boardwalk, football stadiums and luxury government buildings (Power 2011).

In contrast to Ethiopia and Rwanda, the Angolan government continues to spend considerable parts of its budget on the military. Even though the government does not face an immediate external security threat[22] and the civil war ended more than a decade ago, the government still spends 17 per cent of its budget (ACTSA 2013), or about 4 per cent of GDP (SIPRI 2013) on the military. Military spending even increased from about USD1.5 billion in 2002 at the end of the war to USD3.8 billion in 2012 (SIPRI 2013). In 2015, Angola was the country with the largest defence budget in sub-Saharan Africa. The government has not demobilised the 120,000 strong army, and army generals were allowed to engage in resource extraction and land grabbing (Power 2011).

Moreover, the government continues to invest relatively little in other types of public goods, such as healthcare and education. Angola's public investments in healthcare as a share of government expenditures continue to be considerably below the average in sub-Saharan Africa and also lower than in Ethiopia and Rwanda, according to the WDI. Moreover, part of the government expenditure in healthcare and education has been spent on scholarships and healthcare subsidies *abroad* for members of the elite rather than on improving services in Angola and for the wider population. Even though Angola has become an upper middle-income country with a per capita GNI as high as USD4800, little progress has been made regarding basic human development during the past decade. Angola ranks near the bottom on the Human Development Index: at position 148 of 186 in 2012 (United Nations Development Programme 2013).

On the other hand, Angola is one of the most corrupt countries in the world. According to the WGI, the level of corruption in Angola has even gone up since the end of the civil war, and particularly since 2006 (Fig. 5.2). The government's discourse on the fight against corruption has become more prominent since 2009 (Marques de Morais 2010), but apparently this has so far not resulted in practical improvements. According to Gallup polls (2013), 87 per cent of the population consider government corruption to be widespread. In its Corruption Perception Index, Transparency International ranked Angola at position 163 of 168 countries in 2015.

The Open Society Initiative for Southern Africa (OSISA) and Global Witness (2011) found that despite improvements in the transparency of government revenues, serious discrepancies between accounts of the Ministry of Finance and Sonangol remain. In 2012, the IMF also reported that an astonishing USD32 billion of Angola's state funds went missing in the past few years. After some discussions with the Angolan government, the IMF reduced the discrepancy by USD27.8 billion and argued that this difference could be explained as 'quasi-fiscal operations' by Sonangol. However, the remaining (and still considerable) gap of USD4.2 billion could not be accounted for by the Angolan government.[23]

Low-intensity Coercion and Managing Arenas of Contestation
The first parliamentary elections were finally held in 2008, after having been postponed several times. As expected, the government gained a large majority with little difficulty. The MPLA secured 191 of 220 seats in the National Assembly and won about 81 per cent of the votes. The main opposition party UNITA got only 10 per cent. The 2008 elections thereby strongly reinforced the position of the MPLA. Even though the playing field ahead of the elections was not level, it substantially

increased the government's domestic (and international) legitimacy (Roque 2009).

In contrast, in light of mounting public dissatisfaction and a stronger opposition, the Angolan leadership faced more severe challenges in 2012. The MPLA gained a mere 71 per cent of the votes. The main opposition party UNITA won about 18 per cent. This reduction in votes for the MPLA suggests that the MPLA was no longer able to fully dominate the electoral arena. Particularly in Luanda, the MPLA's traditional stronghold, UNITA and the newly formed Broad Convergence for the Salvation of Angola—Electoral Coalition (CASA-CE) gained more than 40 per cent, essentially turning the MPLA from an urban-based into a rural-backed party (Croese 2013).

The leadership holds on to power by a mix of legal measures to limit spaces for civil society and critical opposition and informal measures of harassment and coercion as well as cooptation of critical figures. The leadership has established its own 'NGOs'. The most prominent examples are the foundations of the president and his daughter (Power 2011). Civil society actors may find themselves promoted to government or party commissions and receive spoils to silence criticism (Schubert 2010, 666). Members of UNITA are also coopted. Prominent examples include high-level UNITA figures who were appointed as ministers (Croese 2013). The president initiated major reshuffles of the cabinet and other key positions in the economy and the army in 2011.

At the same time, harassment and low-intensity coercion limit the space for civil society, the media and the opposition to engage. During the protests in 2011 and 2012, for instance, Angolan security forces violently suppressed demonstrations (Croese 2013; Watch 2012).

Between 2006 and 2014 cooperating with the EU on governance reforms would have been costly for the Angolan government, in spite of the EU's decision to narrow its good governance strategy. It is thus not surprising that the Angolan government has ignored EU demands for cooperation in the second half of the decade. It faced stronger domestic opposition, particularly since 2009, and it responded by expanding the party and by relying even more strongly on cooptation. Even though the EU has, over time, shifted its good governance strategy towards a narrow understanding of good governance, EU support for governance reforms has not more strongly converged with the Angolan government's preferences. Only EU support for the 2008 elections accrued some benefits for the government as it enhanced external legitimacy. When the domestic opposition was much stronger ahead of the 2012 elections, the government refused to accept EU assistance.

Angola's Economic Dependence on the EU

Since the mid-2000s, the EU has not managed to set incentives that would have outweighed the costs of cooperating on governance reforms. In contrast to the EU's relations with Ethiopia and Rwanda, Angola is clearly not dependent on EU aid. Moreover, the EU institutions face substantial difficulties in offering Angola attractive cooperation packages in other policy fields. Furthermore, EU member states have developed a substantial economic interest in engaging with Angola, which has made it even more difficult to find a coherent European approach.

Between 2006 and 2014, aid accounted for less than 1 per cent of GNI, making Angola one of the least aid-dependent countries in sub-Saharan Africa (Fig. 5.1). Oil prices have boomed since 2005, and Angola has considerably increased its oil production. While oil revenues traditionally constituted a large share of government revenues, resource rents have skyrocketed since 2005. However, Angola's dependence on oil also implied that the dip in oil prices and oil exports during the financial and economic crisis in 2009 had a strong and immediate effect on the Angolan government's revenues. Between 2010 and 2013, oil revenues had again been on the rise. In 2014 oil prices fell sharply for a second time. After Nigeria, Angola is the second-largest oil producer in sub-Saharan Africa.

During the second half of the 2000s, EU member states and European commercial banks as well as other international actors have provided (commercial) lines of credit to Angola (Table 5.5). In the wake of the global financial and economic crises, the Angolan leadership once again reached out more strongly to European and other international actors to secure financial support. In November 2009, negotiations with the IMF finally led to the signing of a standby loan agreement for USD1.4 billion. Earlier that year, President dos Santos also secured funding from several European countries, notably Spain, Portugal and Germany (Table 5.5).

However, the financial and economic crises also demonstrated that the EU institutions play a limited role in Angola's relations with Europe. While EU member states extended lines of credit, what is mostly available as an instrument for bilateral cooperation to the EU institutions are aid funds from the EDF. The EU's proposal to initiate a Joint Way Forward

Table 5.5 Selected credit lines to Angola (in USD)

Country	Volume of flows	Purpose	Years
European			
Portugal	1 billion		
	500 million (COSEC)		2009
Spain	600 million		2007
Belgium	500 million		
Germany	1.7 billion		2009
Non-European			
Canada EXIM	1 billion		2009
Brazil BNDES	5 billion	Finance purchase of Brazilian goods and services	Total credits by 2011
India EXIM	40 million	Railway rehabilitation	2006
	13 million	Purchase of tractors	2010
	15 million	Cotton projects	
	30 million	Industrial park	
Multilaterals			
IMF	1.4 billion	Stand-by agreement	2009
World Bank	360 million	IDA and IBRD	2009–2011

Source: Author's compilation, based on Vines et al. (2009), Corkin (2013), Africa-Asia Confidential (2009b), India EXIM Bank (2013)

has been one attempt to overcome this discrepancy and to identify areas for cooperation 'beyond' a traditional donor recipient relationship that would make the EU an attractive cooperation partner. Yet, its relevance and success remains to be seen.

Since the mid-2000s, the EU's importance as a destination for Angolan oil exports has been on the rise (although nothing in comparison to exports to China) (Fig. 5.3). Yet, oil imports from Angola account for only about 2 per cent of total European oil imports (Helly 2011). Oil imports from Angola are limited to a few EU member states. France, for instance, had imported very little oil from Angola for some time, mostly due to diplomatic disputes over French arms sales to Angola in the 1990s, also known as the 'Angolagate scandal'. However, relations have improved in the mid-2000s after high-level initiatives by the French President Nicolas Sarkozy. As a consequence, oil exports rapidly increased and France now imports between 8 and 15 per cent of its oil from Angola (Helly 2011).

Trade and investment relations with Angola's former colonial power Portugal have gained importance since the mid-2000s. By 2008, Angola

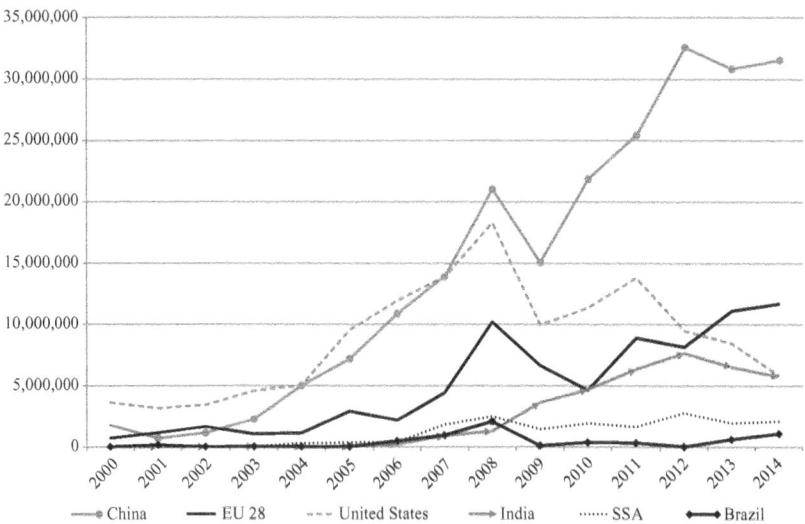

Fig. 5.3 Angolan oil exports to selected partners (in USD thousands)
Source: Author's compilation, based on UNCTAD statistics (2016)

had become the fourth largest destination for Portuguese exports and Portugal's largest trading partner outside the EU. Portuguese investments in Angola have also surged. Not only the size of these figures is notable, but also that relations grew substantially close over a very short period of time (Seabra and Gorjão 2011).

Together with South Africa and Nigeria, Angola is one of the few countries in sub-Saharan Africa that themselves make significant investments abroad. Outward investment flows stood at about USD1 billion in 2010 (African Development Bank et al. 2012). An important share of investments (most of them by the national oil company Sonangol) is targeted at Europe, and notably Portugal. Investments are directed, for instance, towards the Portuguese banking sector and into real estate (Seabra and Gorjão 2011).[24]

The economic and financial crisis in 2008–2009 showed most clearly that Angola's relations with the EU are not characterised by its economic dependence on the EU. The crisis further accelerated changes in the underlying power structures in Angola–EU relations. Even though the crisis hit Angola quite hard due to plummeting oil prices, it hit Portugal even harder. During the crisis, Portugal turned to Angola to attract more investments to cushion the consequences of the crisis, turning former (colonial-based) power relations upside down.[25] Migration flows are one interesting indicator for the changing relationship: due to the economic depression back home, tens of thousands of job-seeking Portuguese moved to Angola in the first few years after the crisis.[26]

To summarise, since the mid-2000s, the EU had very little to no incentive to make the Angolan government address governance issues. The EU institutions mostly relied on the EDF as an instrument to set incentives for cooperation. Only recently has it launched the Joint Way Forward—an attempt to build a strategic partnership 'beyond' aid. Moreover, the EU institutions face difficulties in establishing the EU as an attractive partner and forging a truly European approach in light of some EU member states' strong bilateral cooperation with Angola. Between the mid-2000s and 2012, the Angolan government thus had little interest in engaging with the EU institutions. Cooperating with the EU 'beyond' governance reforms clearly provided no incentives that could have compensated for the costs of engaging in the implementation of good governance instruments.

China: Alternative Economic Cooperation Partner

From the mid-2000s onwards, China has further bolstered its position as a key economic partner for the Angolan government. The volume of credits provided by the China is quite substantial, adding up to at least USD14.5 billion between 2004 and 2012 (Table 5.6), or up to USD21.2 billion until the end of 2014 (Brautigam and Hwang 2016). This is substantially more than Angola has received from any other international actor (Table 5.5). For China, in turn, Angola has become the largest recipient of loans in sub-Saharan Africa according to Chinese officials.

It remains unclear how much money the Hong Kong-based China International Fund (CIF) has given to Angola. The activities of the CIF and the connection between the fund and the Chinese government are highly opaque. Some studies suggest that this fund has advanced at least USD2.9 billion to Angola for infrastructure reconstruction (Levkowitz et al. 2009; Campos and Vines 2008). Many projects initiated by the fund faced problems in the implementation phase and were delayed or ran out of funding. Some of these were then taken over by the EXIM Bank. However, the Chinese government has been careful to distance itself from the fund and to argue that there is no direct link between the activities of

Table 5.6 Chinese loans to Angola 2002–2012 (excluding CIF funds)

Year	Volume and bank	Purpose
March 2004	USD2 billion, EXIM	Infrastructure construction and renovation
July 2007	USD500 million, EXIM	Financing of completion of some of the projects started with the 2004 credit line
September 2007	USD2 billion, EXIM	Financing of projects as part of the government's public infrastructure programme
2009	USD6 billion, EXIM	Infrastructure renovation
2009	USD2.5 billion, ICBC	Infrastructure development
2009 (?)	USD1.5 billion, CDB	Commercial line of credit, not oil-backed, mostly for development of infrastructure and agriculture
2010	USD500 million, CDB	USD 400 million with Ministry of Finance to address food security and improve urban planning; USD100 million SME loan agreement with Angola's Africa Development Bank[a]
2012	USD1.3 billion, CDB	For Sonangol

Total: EXIM Bank: USD10.5 billion; total Chinese financing (all banks): **USD14.5 billion**[b]

Source: Author's compilation, based on Campos and Vines (2008), Corkin (2013)

[a]See China Development Bank press statement, 21 November 2010, CDB will continue to support China-Africa Pragmatic cooperation, online at http://www.cdb.com.cn/english/NewsInfo.asp?NewsId=3479, last access on 3 June 2014

[b]The figure is confirmed by the Chinese ambassador to Angola Zhang Bolun, see *Agence France Press*, 'China lends Angola $15 bn but creates few jobs', 6 March 2011, online at http://www.google.com/hostednews/afp/article/ALeqM5hCrBvXg-npPKNuU_xAnyT4MhL2GA?docId=CNG.b56cef2e1a9915852221926863a725ed.421&hl=en, last access 3 April 2013

the fund and those of the Chinese government (Corkin 2013, 134ff).[27] At the same time, through its joint venture with Sonangol, the CIF functions as an intermediary for Angola's oil exports to China.[28]

During the economic and financial crisis, China remained an important partner for the Angolan government. Dos Santos travelled to China in December 2008 to negotiate a new loan package that was for the first time not to be backed by oil but to be based on a government guarantee.[29] Beyond the EXIM Bank, other Chinese policy banks, such as the China Development Bank and the Industrial and Commercial Bank of China, have started to extend loans to the Angolan government for large-scale infrastructure projects (Table 5.6). Even though the financial and economic crisis required the Angolan government to reach out more strongly to other international actors and to increasingly diversify its external relations, the crisis also reemphasised the importance of China as an economic cooperation partner (see also Corkin 2013, 153).

This continued interest in their mutual relations is also visible in the Angolan government's political outreach to China. In 2010, the Angolan government approached China to initiate a strategic partnership. President dos Santos mentioned the strategic partnership with China in his 'state of the nation' speech in October 2010, sending a clear signal that he attaches great importance to relations with China (Alves 2011, 138f). During the visit of the Chinese vice president (and now president) Xi Jinping to Luanda in November 2010, several areas for cooperation were identified: infrastructure, energy and mining, agriculture, finance and technology.[30]

China continues to support projects that are particularly important to the Angolan leadership. One prominent example is the 'one million houses project'. The Chinese CITIC Group signed a MoU with the GRN for the construction of Chinese-financed social housing near Luanda (in Kilamba Kiaxi municipality) at a cost of USD3.5 billion (Croese 2011, 19; Marques de Morais 2011a). In the 2008 elections, the promise of building affordable houses was deemed crucial for the MPLA's electoral success. The government was thus under pressure to deliver on its promise in order to easily win the 2012 elections as well. However, by 2012, the project was barely half-finished and it became clear that the houses would not be affordable for ordinary Angolans (Croese 2011).

In light of China's rapidly growing engagement with Angola, public dissatisfaction among Angolans regarding the developmental benefits of Chinese loans has been mounting in recent years. In a context where most of the basic infrastructure was destroyed after the long civil war, China's support for national reconstruction is certainly greatly needed. However, Chinese companies have been accused of delivering low-quality infrastructure. The General Hospital in Luanda is a case in point[31]: In June 2010, shortly after it opened, it had to be evacuated because the building was developing dangerous cracks (Marques de Morais 2011a). Similarly, some of the newly paved roads and rehabilitated railways are said to be quickly washed away. Representatives from international companies working together with Chinese state-owned companies argue that in some cases the poor quality results from poor supervision, which would have been the responsibility of the Angolans.[32]

Angolan civil society and other domestic actors have criticised the high number of Chinese workers employed by Chinese companies and the high volume of construction material imported from China.[33] Concerns were raised that China's support for the reconstruction process ultimately creates little economic opportunities for Angolans, but excludes the wider society from the reconstruction process (Croese 2011, 24; Marques de Morais 2011b). During the past few years, incidents of violence and theft against Chinese workers and business people have reportedly become more frequent. According to Zhang Bolun, the Chinese ambassador to Angola, about 50 Chinese state-owned and 400 Chinese private companies were operating in Angola in 2010.[34] The number of Chinese workers staying in Angola was estimated to range somewhere between 60,000 and 70,000.[35]

Sino-Angolan bilateral trade has grown tremendously during the past decade. The rise of China as a major cooperation partner for Angola has thus fundamentally transformed Angola's traditional trade relations. Overall, Sino-Angolan trade remains dominated by Angolan oil exports to China. In 2007, China has overtaken the USA as Angola's most important destination for oil exports (Fig. 5.3). The economic and financial crises and dropping oil prices in 2008 caused a slight dip in the value of Angola's oil exports to China (and other countries). In 2011, Angola was exporting about 40 per cent of its oil to China (EIA 2012). Because China has become the largest oil importer worldwide in 2013 and the US oil imports are likely to further decrease, the importance of China as a destination for Angolan oil exports is likely to grow more in the future.[36] In 2010, China has also overtaken Portugal as the major source of Angola's imports. In contrast to most other African countries, and particularly to Ethiopia and Rwanda, China's trade relations with Angola are much more interdependent—Angola has become the second-largest source of Chinese oil imports, sometimes even surpassing Saudi Arabia (EIA 2012). Angola is China's most important trading partner in Africa, accounting for about half of all African exports to China.

Chinese direct investments in Angola have been mostly concentrated in the oil sector. However, despite these significant investments, Chinese oil companies did not develop a prominent stake in Angola's oil industry between 2000 and 2014.[37] Sinopec secured stakes in the oil block 18, and two of the major producing blocks (15 and 17) through its joint ventures with Sonangol. The entry of Sinopec into the Angolan oil industry was facilitated by the oil-for-infrastructure deals, even though there is no formal, direct link between those transactions (Alves 2011). However, relations quickly soured. After the entry of Sinopec in the Angolan oil sector, the size of the bonuses paid caused relations between Sinopec and Sonangol to harden. Moreover, Chinese support for the refinery in Lobito did not finally materialise, which led to a further deterioration of relations (Alves 2011; 159–166; Africa-Asia Confidential 2009a; Alves 2012, 106ff).[38]

Angola's economic cooperation with other emerging powers has gained prominence in recent years, but with none of these countries are relations as important as with China (Freemantle and Stevens 2011). Cultural and linguistic proximity between Brazil and Angola have facilitated Brazil's investments and trading relations with Angola. Since Brazil has its own vast oil resources, oil imports from Angola have remained limited (Fig. 5.3). However, Brazil's state-owned oil company Petrobras has developed technological expertise in deep water drilling, which is increasingly relevant in Angola. Imports from Brazil are concentrated on agriculture goods and soft commodities because Angola's agricultural production is still limited. Brazil has also extended loans to invest in Angolan agriculture, notably bio-fuels (Table 5.5). Angola's relations with India are concentrated in the oil sector. Angola's oil exports to India have grown in the past few years, particularly since 2009. In 2014 India imported as much oil from Angola as the USA (Fig. 5.3). However, India's oil imports from Angola remain considerably below the amounts of oil imported by China. Moreover, India has not extended loans of any substance (Table 5.5).

Limited Attractiveness of the 'China Model' and Little Cooperation on Survival Strategies
In the Angolan political discourse as well as in public debates in the (state-controlled) media, Chinese political and economic development as a potential model for Angola has not been given a prominent role (see also Corkin 2013; Soares de Oliveira 2015). Instead, due to the colonial heritage and persistently strong economic, political and cultural ties, the Angolan political elite is predominately oriented towards Brazil and Western countries (particularly Portugal). Findings from interviews with Angolan officials and remarks by other observers suggest that while the Angolan elite is generally impressed by China's economic success and political stability, there is little profound engagement and analysis of what the Chinese (economic and political) reform process involves (Soares de Oliveira 2011, 298; Corkin 2013).

The Chinese government has provided little technical assistance to support the Angolan government's human and administrative capacities. The Chinese Ministry of Commerce supports short-term human resource training courses for Angolan government officials. Between 2003 and 2008, 423 Angolan officials have been travelling to China for a week up to a month of short-term training (Alves 2011, 140).

As economic relations between China and Angola intensify, cooperation on legal issues has become more important, particularly since 2010. In response to violence committed against Chinese workers in Angola, the Chinese and Angolan governments have started to cooperate more closely in law enforcement and on human rights issues. In 2011, the Chinese criminal investigation office and the Angolan ministries of home affairs and justice signed a bilateral agreement to cooperate more closely on fighting crime (ANGO Press 2012a). The Chinese embassy in Angola maintains contacts with the Angolan Human Rights Commission (ANGO Press 2012b), and the Angolan audit court has launched an exchange with its Chinese counterpart (ANGO Press 2012d). The Angolan minister for home affairs visited China in 2012. During his visit, he also gathered information on the Chinese prison and police system (ANGO Press 2012e). The Angolan attorney-general has announced a closer working relationship with China.

Party-to-Party Relations

Little cooperation happens between the Angolan and Chinese ruling parties, and party-to-party relations do not seem to have played a prominent role in facilitating economic cooperation. The MPLA and the CCP meet about once a year, either in China or Angola (Fig. 5.4). However, compared to Ethiopia and Rwanda as well as other African countries, the CCP's contacts with the MPLA are quite limited.

This limited relevance of party-to-party contacts is striking in light of the importance of the bilateral economic relations. In other African countries, such as Sudan, where Chinese economic cooperation is also very close, party-to-party relations constitute an integral part and important pillar of bilateral relations. Historical factors may play an important role in explaining the limited engagement. During the Angolan civil war, China has mostly supported the UNITA and at times the FNLA, the other opposition movement. After the end of the civil war, the MPLA remained very sceptical towards the CCP.[39] Limited party-to-party contacts thus seem to be a result of a lack of interest on the Angolan rather than the Chinese side.

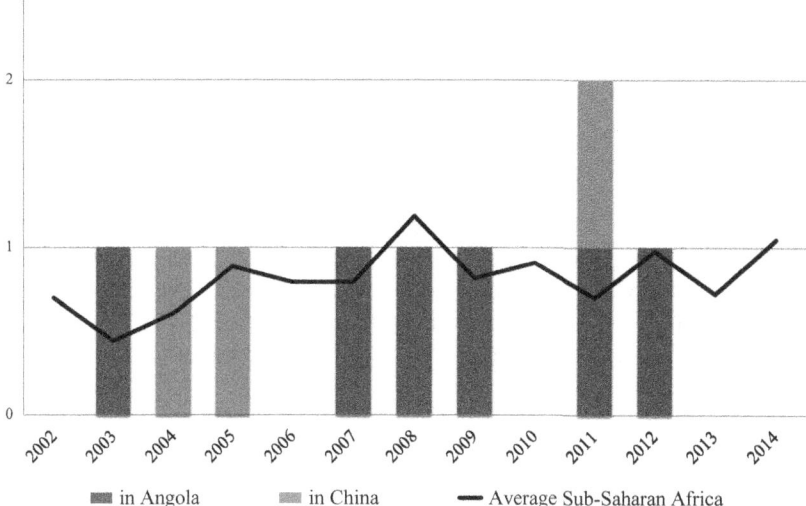

Fig. 5.4 Annual bilateral visits MPLA–CCP
Source: Author's compilation, based on analysis of News Reports, International Department of the Communist Party of Chinese

5.4 Conclusions

In the early 2000s after the end of the civil war, the Angolan government started to reluctantly engage with the EU in governance reforms. However, since the mid-2000s, the government has increasingly been indifferent towards EU demands to cooperate on governance reforms.

Why Did Angola Start to Reluctantly Engage with the EU in Governance Reforms Between 2002 and 2005?

The Angolan government's willingness to reluctantly start engaging with the EU in the aftermath of the civil war can be explained by its interest in cooperation 'beyond' governance reforms rather than an interest in engaging in governance reforms per se.

In the first few years after the end of the civil war, the EU's strategy to promote *effective* and *democratic government* and the EU's adoption of a *cooperative-critical* strategy largely diverged from the preferences of the Angolan government. Cooperation on governance reforms thus generated substantial costs and very few benefits. While the EU and other international actors urged the Angolan government to strengthen formal democratic institutions and hold elections, the government itself had a strong interest in pushing back the election date until the economic reconstruction process had yielded positive outcomes for the wider population. Furthermore, the EU and other international actors' pressure to improve the transparency of government revenues and spending, and to promote the fight against corruption, clearly diverged from the preferences of the ruling elite. After the end of the civil war, the Angolan leadership had to reorganise its strategies to coopt its political support base (i.e. the military). Oil revenues constituted an important instrument in this endeavour.

It thus seems surprising that the Angolan government started to engage with the EU in governance reforms after all. However, in the early 2000s, economic cooperation with the EU implied some benefits for the Angolan government that partly balanced out costs stemming from cooperation on governance reforms. Immediately after the end of the civil war, oil production in Angola as well as international oil prices were relatively low. At that time the EU was the second-largest destination for Angolan oil after the USA. Furthermore, the Angolan government expected that the EU would support it in organising an international donor conference. It anticipated that this conference would mobilise significant volumes of revenue deemed crucial for the reconstruction process and medium-term economic development. At the same time, the Angolan government still had very little access to economic cooperation with China in the early 2000s. China was not yet a major destination for Angolan imports or (oil) exports, and had not yet become an important source of official flows. The relative economic dependence on the EU and expectations regarding future EU support—in the absence of alternative cooperation partners such as China—thus explain why Angola started to, albeit reluctantly, engage with the EU in governance reforms in the early 2000s, in spite of the challenges that this cooperation entails.

Why Has Angola Increasingly Ignored EU Demands to Cooperate Between 2006 and 2014?

Between 2006 and 2014, the EU has significantly narrowed its good governance approach, focusing mostly on *effective government*. Furthermore, the EU refrained from exerting public pressure on the Angolan government and merely adopted a *cooperative* strategy. However, even cooperation based on a very narrow understanding of good governance entailed considerable costs for the Angolan government. It continued to strongly rely on spoils and perks to sustain support from its political support coalition. Global Witness and the IMF criticised the fact that in recent years, billions of dollars in oil revenues were again unaccounted for. In this context, cooperation with the EU—even a narrow definition of good governance limited to effective government institutions—was still costly. The government faced little opposition in the 2008 elections. Yet, it was confronted with public protests and growing discontent before and after the 2012 elections, making cooperation with the EU an even more challenging endeavour.

Moreover, and in contrast to the early 2000s, Angola had little interest in cooperating with the EU beyond governance reforms, which could potentially have compensated for the risks of engaging in governance reforms. The EU's main instrument to engage with Angola is development aid. But with rising oil production and rising international oil prices, development aid accounts for less than 1 per cent of gross national income. The EU has also been relatively marginal as a source of other official flows that the government could have used to further promote the economic reconstruction process. The EU's relative importance as a destination for Angolan exports and a source of imports has generally been very limited since the mid-2000s, even though some EU member states such as Portugal or France were able to intensify their relations with Angola. The EU offered the Angolan government a partnership that was to improve cooperation on energy as well as regional peace and security, and thus promote close relations beyond development aid. Yet, the Angolan government's marked hesitation in signing the so-called Joint Way Forward suggests that it has been relatively unenthusiastic about this partnership.

Since the mid-2000s, China has emerged as one of Angola's most important cooperation partners. China surpassed the USA as the largest destination of Angolan oil exports in 2007. Moreover, the Chinese EXIM Bank and, to a lesser extent the China Development Bank, have extended significant loans that allowed the Angolan government to not only fund its ambitious infrastructure reconstruction programme but to also *deliver* the infrastructure just before the elections in 2008 and 2012. China's offer to provide oil-for-infrastructure loans came at a crucial point in time. The loans not only affected the Angolan government's interest in engaging with the IMF and in complying with IMF conditionality, they also had significant effects on cooperation with the EU in the following years. Beyond this close economic cooperation, China has not offered an alternative to cooperate on governance reforms. However, limited engagement between the Chinese and Angolan ruling parties and limited technical assistance to strengthen government capacities seem to be a result of the Angolan government's limited interest rather than China's unwillingness to extend support.

What If...?

Under what conditions might Angola have been more active and willing to engage with the EU in governance reforms? First of all, if the EU had used a broader approach to promote governance reforms, that would probably not have made Angola more willing to engage. Since even the EU's narrow good governance strategy entailed substantial costs, broadening the EU's governance strategy would have been unlikely to create a stronger interest on the Angolan side. However, the EU's good governance instruments are almost exclusively operationalised in the context of its development policy and the framework of its development aid relations. Thus, one open question is to what extent a broader set of governance instruments (beyond aid) would have allowed for a closer cooperation on governance reforms.

Second, how important is Angola's access to cooperation with China in explaining the government's unwillingness to cooperate with the EU? Or, to put it differently, would Angola have been more willing to cooperate with the EU if China had not emerged as a close cooperation partner? In light of its considerable natural resource deposits, even in the absence of cooperation with China, Angola would probably not have been more interested in receiving EU development aid. However, the EU would by default have been more important as a trading partner and as a source of official flows. The question is whether and how the EU would have used this greater leverage, for instance, in light of the growing economic (and political) interests of some EU member states.

The case of Angola therefore illustrates the limitations of the 'Chinese threat' argument. Even though the Angolan government has received important financial flows from China that have made the government even more independent of other international actors, finance from China (similar to financial support from the EU) is part of a broader set of domestic and international forces that have an impact on the preferences of African governments.

NOTES

1. The ethnic base of the MPLA has traditionally mostly been the Mbundu who represent only about 10 per cent of the Angolan population. Furthermore, the party also has a considerable number of white and *mestiço* members. During the civil war, it was often perceived as mostly representing the urban population.
2. The EU channelled parts of its humanitarian aid through NGOs. Mostly international and some national NGOs have implemented the EU's programmes in health, education or food security, particularly between 2002 and 2004 when the presence of the Angolan government was not assured throughout the country and national NGOs were still very weak (ECO Consult et al. 2009; Republic of Angola and European Community 2008). Since the mid-2000s, NGOs have become less important to implement EU assistance to Angola. Instead, the EU has channelled most of its funds through government structures.
3. The European Parliament and some European NGOs had been asking to launch Article 96 negotiations.
4. Which projects the Angolan government has agreed to implement are analysed based on OECD DAC CRS statistics for aid 'disbursements', the EU Angola joint annual reviews (2002, 2003, 2007) and an independent evaluation (ECO Consult et al. 2009).
5. Interviews with officials from the EU, member states and the Angolan government were conducted in Luanda in November 2009, in Brussels in April 2010 and October 2012 and via phone with the EU delegation in Luanda in December 2012.
6. Interview with EU official in Brussels in April 2010
7. As Traub (2006) summarises his interviews with leading government officials at that time '[Angolan elites] are of the opinion that they have made real strides in tackling inflation, the deficit and exchange rates, while the IMF continued to demand reforms that would be economically risky and politically suicidal'.
8. Quoted in Campos and Vines (2008).
9. The Angolan Ministry of Finance has published information on the first two tranches of the EXIM Bank loans. A list with projects funded by the

first USD2 billion loans is available online at http://www.minfin.gv.ao/docs/dspProjGov.htm, last access on 3 April 2015.
10. Interviews with Chinese officials in Beijing in July 2010 and July 2013.
11. With the closure of the Office of the UN High Commissioner for Human Rights in 2008, the EU became the largest donor to civil society organisations in Angola (Foley et al. 2010).
12. Interviews with EU officials in Luanda in November 2009, in Brussels in April 2010 and October 2010 and with EU officials in Luanda via telephone in December 2012.
13. Ibid.
14. Ibid.
15. The Joint Way Forward document can be accessed at http://eeas.europa.eu/archives/docs/angola/jwf_en.pdf
16. The press statement after the meeting can be found at http://eeas.europa.eu/statements/docs/2014/141017_02_en.pdf
17. Interview with EU official in Brussels, October 2012.
18. Opinion polls have to be taken with great caution in a context where people's chances to express their views are restricted. However, they can still give some indication of public support for the government.
19. See statement by Markus Weimer, quoted in *Business Week*, 'Oil-rich Angola's ruling party split over succession', 9 May 2012, online at http://www.businessweek.com/news/2012-05-08/oil-rich-angola-s-ruling-party-split-over-succession#p2, last access on 3 June 2014.
20. The president is head of state, commander-in-chief of the armed forces and appoints major posts, including the judiciary. As Orre (2010) explains, under the new constitution, it is almost impossible to remove the president.
21. Luanda has a reputation for being one of the most expensive capitals in the world.
22. Relations with the DRC remain tight but not up to the point of a military conflict.
23. See Reuters, 25 January 2012, 'Angola finds most of its missing $32 bln', online at http://www.reuters.com/article/2012/01/25/ozatp-imf-angola-idAFJOE80O00O20120125, last access on 3 June 2014.
24. See www.chinasourceblog.org, last access 5 May 2013.
25. See *New York Times*, 'Fortunes and Tables, Turn for Portugal and Angola', 20 November 2011, online at http://www.nytimes.com/2011/11/20/world/africa/portugals-financial-crisis-leads-it-back-to-angola.html?_r=0, last access on 3 June 2014.
26. See *The Guardian*, 'Portuguese escape austerity and find a new El Dorado in Angola', 16 September 2012, online at http://www.theguardian.com/

world/2012/sep/16/portuguese-exodus-angola-el-dorado, last access on 3 June 2014.
27. See also the discussion between the American and Chinese ambassador in Luanda, released by Wikileaks (2009). *New China Credit Line under Consideration,* online at http://www.wikileaks.org/plusd/cables/09LUANDA51_a.html, last access on 3 June 2013.
28. *The Economist* (2011), China International Fund, The Queensway Syndicate and the Africa trade, online at http://www.economist.com/node/21525847, last access on 3 June 2014.
29. According to information released by Wikileaks (see Note no. 27 above) the Chinese ambassador reported details about dos Santos' visit to China and negotiations on the loan to the US ambassador in Luanda. See also Africa-Asia Confidential (2008).
30. See Xinhua China 'Angola set up strategic partnership' *CCTV* news channel 19 November 2010.
31. Angola and China reached an agreement that the hospital should be rebuilt and a MoU was signed in 2012 (ANGO Press 2012c). Alves (2011, 139) argues that the hospital was an aid project (a grant) and had not been financed through the oil-for-infrastructure loans.
32. Interviews with business representatives in Luanda in November 2009.
33. Angolan companies in the cement and steel sector, for instance, complain that they cannot compete with Chinese companies as much of the material for the construction projects is still imported (Africa-Asia Confidential 2009a).
34. See Macauhub November 2010, online at http://www.macauhub.com.mo/en/2010/11/19/over-50-chinese-state-companies-and-400-private-firms-operate-in-angola/, last access on 10 December 2016.
35. See *Wall Street Journal* 'Hostility towards Workers Cools Angola-China Relationship', 10 August 2010 online at http://www.wsj.com/articles/SB10001424052748704388504575418990791137242, last access on 10 December 2016.
36. See *Financial Times,* 9 October 2013 'The new gas guzzler. China has overtaken the US as the world's top oil importer. FT reporters examine the trends behind a historic shift' online at http://www.ft.com/intl/cms/s/0/01ba1a04-2c24-11e3-acf4-00144feab7de.html#axzz37WngVdLR, last access on 15 July 2014.
37. Sinopec's limited engagement as an operator in Angola's oil industry can partly be explained by its lack of technology and experience in ultra-deep water oil exploration where most of Angola's oil is explored.
38. Also beyond the oil sector, investments have increased in recent years. Some of those Chinese firms that initially come to Angola to implement

infrastructure under the oil-for-infrastructure deals remained in Angola after the completion of the project (Vines and Campos 2010).
39. On both sides, different representatives from the CCP and MPLA take part in the meetings. CCP representatives often have the chance to meet with dos Santos. CCP representatives often take part in national congresses and conferences when they visit Angola.

Open Access This chapter is licensed under the terms of the Creative Commons Attribution 4.0 International License (http://creativecommons.org/licenses/by/4.0/), which permits use, sharing, adaptation, distribution and reproduction in any medium or format, as long as you give appropriate credit to the original author(s) and the source, provide a link to the Creative Commons license and indicate if changes were made.

The images or other third party material in this chapter are included in the chapter's Creative Commons license, unless indicated otherwise in a credit line to the material. If material is not included in the chapter's Creative Commons license and your intended use is not permitted by statutory regulation or exceeds the permitted use, you will need to obtain permission directly from the copyright holder.

CHAPTER 6

Conclusions

Ideological and strategic competition between democracies and autocracies has forcibly re-entered the international arena. Whether and, if so, how the presence of China affects the EU's strategies of supporting governance reforms in Africa is one key aspect in these debates.

This book started off with the empirical observation that the EU's success in using its good governance instruments and making African governments address good governance issues has varied markedly. In the early 2000s, governments in Angola, Ethiopia and Rwanda all began more or less reluctantly engaging with the EU on governance reforms. Since the mid-2000s, when China appeared on the horizon, the Rwandan government has (pro) actively cooperated with the EU. The Ethiopian government has remained reluctant in the face of EU demands to engage. The Angolan government has been largely indifferent towards the EU's requests for cooperation. Against this backdrop, this book has dealt with two main questions. What explains the differences in African governments' willingness to engage with the EU on governance reforms? To what extent does China's presence affect African governments' openness to engage with the EU?

The three case studies have provided explanations for why Angola, Ethiopia and Rwanda's willingness to engage with the EU has changed between 2000 and 2014. This chapter summarises the main findings along the four variables that influence African governments' responsiveness: EU good governance strategies, African government' survival strategies, economic dependence on the EU and access to cooperation with China. The following sections discuss how the variables influence African governments' openness to engage with the EU and how these findings relate to other research on EU good governance policies and authoritarian regimes. This chapter concludes with a brief discussion on the implications for future research and policy-making.

6.1 EU Good Governance Strategies: Not Strategic Enough

The EU has made support for governance reforms a stronger priority in its Africa policy. Comparing the EU's engagement with Angola, Ethiopia and Rwanda demonstrates that the EU has adopted quite different good governance strategies in its relations with individual African countries. The EU's strategies can be analysed along two dimensions (see Chap. 2). The EU may put emphasis on a different content or substance of good governance and use a different channel to support governance reforms. In addition, it can choose different instruments and promote reforms through either a more *conflictive* or a more *cooperative* strategy. The content or substance of what the EU seeks to promote and the instruments the EU uses, both influence African governments' openness to engage on governance reforms.

How has the EU tried to support good governance in Angola, Ethiopia and Rwanda? The EU's strategies were initially strikingly similar. In the early 2000s, the EU adopted a relatively broad good governance approach and promoted *democratic government* in its relations with all three countries. It primarily relied on the intergovernmental channel and aimed at strengthening not only the effectiveness and transparency of decision-making processes, but also their democratic quality. The EU also used a very similar *cooperative-critical* strategy *vis-à-vis* all three countries. In all of them, it mainly relied on cooperative instruments such as political dialogue and good governance aid to promote reforms, but combined these cooperative instruments with material incentives and public shaming to pressure the three governments into introducing reforms (Table 6.1).

Since mid-2000s, the EU's good governance strategies towards the three countries have varied markedly. In Angola, the EU has narrowed its understanding of good governance, addressing mainly the capacities of

CONCLUSIONS 195

Table 6.1 EU approaches to promote governance reforms between 2000 and 2014

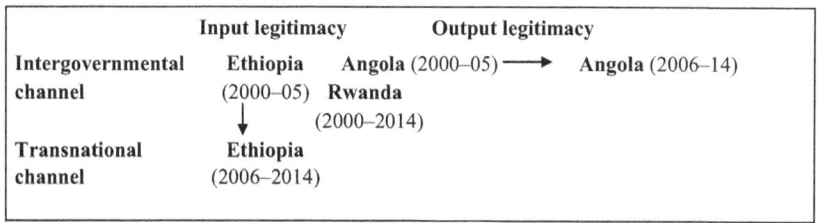

Source: Author's compilation

government institutions. The EU's approach has thus been increasingly limited to promoting *effective government*. Moreover, the EU has clearly refrained from using critical public statements (shaming) or material incentives to put pressure on the Angolan government. It has shifted towards a *cooperative* strategy, relying mainly on dialogue and governance aid.

In Ethiopia, the EU has broadened its good governance approach slightly towards *democratic governance*. The EU provided more support to non-state actors to empower them *vis-à-vis* the government and continued attempts to promote not only the effectiveness, but also the democratic quality, of decision-making processes. After the 2005 election crisis, the EU used cooperative instruments, such as political dialogue and governance aid, and continued to pressure the Ethiopian government through critical public statements and material incentives. Even though the EU has not used aid funds as leverage, since the mid-2000s it has been more critical *vis-à-vis* the Ethiopian government than towards Angola or Rwanda.

In Rwanda, relatively little change in the EU's approach can be observed over time. Since 2005, the EU has continued to support not only the capacities of government institutions and the transparency of political processes, but also the democratic quality of decision-making processes, promoting *democratic government*. In Rwanda, the EU has not relied on cooperative instruments alone. Instead, it has even *rewarded* the Rwandan government by increasing development aid and using aid modalities such as direct budget support, signalling the government that the governance situation is seen positively. The EU changed its strategy only in 2012, when it put pressure on Rwanda to stop supporting rebel groups in the eastern provinces of the DRC by withholding and shifting direct budget-support funds to other aid modalities (Fig. 6.1).

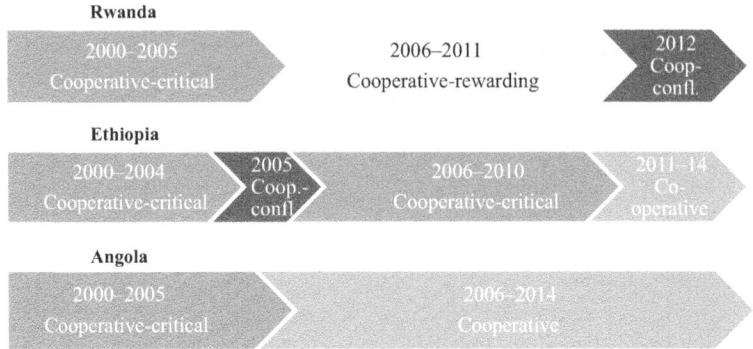

Fig. 6.1 EU instruments to support governance reforms 2000–2014
Source: Author's compilation

Changes in the EU's policies towards Angola, Ethiopia and Rwanda over time cannot easily explain variances in the responsiveness of African governments. The EU initially adopted very similar strategies. In response, all three African governments have reluctantly started to engage. However, despite striking similarities in the EU's good governance strategies, in the early 2000s some differences could already be observed in the responsiveness of the three governments. Rwanda was slightly more forthcoming in engaging with the EU than Ethiopia. Angola was more hesitant in cooperating with the EU than Ethiopia. If the EU's strategies were the key factor that would explain African governments' responsiveness, one would have expected to find stronger similarities there in the early 2000s.

Modifications *over time* in both the EU's good governance strategies and African governments' responsiveness further suggest that the EU's strategies are not the key factor to explain why African governments are willing to engage. In Rwanda, changes in the EU's strategies over time seem to have some explanatory power in accounting for changes in the government's responsiveness. While the EU continued to promote democratic government between 2000 and 2014, since the mid-2000s it has shifted its instruments towards a *cooperative-rewarding* strategy. One can argue that the EU has thereby increased the benefits and reduced the costs for the Rwandan government, making it easier for Rwanda to engage.

The cases of Angola and Ethiopia, however, exemplify that the EU's good governance strategies have a limited influence on African governments' responsiveness. In Ethiopia, the EU has not only continued to use *cooperative-critical* instruments since the 2005 election crisis, it has also broadened its approach in promoting governance reforms, making it more difficult for the Ethiopian government to engage. Even since the election crisis, the Ethiopian government has continued to at least reluctantly engage with the EU; it has decided not to completely ignore EU demands for cooperation on governance reforms.

In Angola, the EU has narrowed its approach over time and has increasingly refrained from exerting pressure, clearly reducing the costs for the Angolan government to engage. However, even though the EU has made it 'easier' for Angola to cooperate, the government has not become more responsive towards the EU. Instead, since 2006 it has largely ignored EU demands for cooperation on governance reforms. Changes in the EU's strategy thus had no effect on the responsiveness of the Angolan government.

Finally, during a short period of time in Ethiopia (during the 2005 election crisis) and Rwanda (in 2012), the EU used a relatively broad approach and *cooperative-conflictive instruments* to exert considerable pressure on both governments (notably budget-support suspensions). Nevertheless, despite similarities in the EU's strategy towards Ethiopia in 2005 and Rwanda in 2012, the Ethiopian government was indifferent towards the EU's demands for engagement during that period, whereas the Rwandan government has continued to actively cooperate with the EU.

The findings suggest that the EU's good governance strategies as such have limited explanatory power in accounting for the differences in African governments' responsiveness. This has been seen most clearly in the case of Angola. Even though the EU has narrowed its strategy over time, the government has become increasingly indifferent to engagement with the EU. This result is interesting in view of the fact that scholars investigating why the EU uses a certain type of instrument or strategy to promote governance reforms in third countries often start by assuming that coherent and consistent EU good governance policies are a necessary condition for the effectiveness of the EU's strategies (Jünemann and Knodt 2007; Börzel and Risse 2009; Kotzian et al. 2011; Wetzel and Orbie 2011; Del Biondo 2015). However, the empirics here illustrate that the specific strategy that the EU adopts predicts the success of the EU's policies less clearly than often assumed. Instead, much more attention needs to be paid to the 'receiving end' of the EU's engagement and to understanding the basic preferences and interests of governments in authoritarian regimes in engaging with the EU on governance reforms. The EU's strategies thus need to be analysed in conjunction with the survival strategies of African governments, their dependence on the EU and access to cooperation with other external actors, such as China.

6.2 Quite Diverse: African Dominant Party Systems' Survival Strategies

When African governments decide whether to engage with the EU on governance reforms, they assess the costs and benefits that cooperation with the EU entails in light of their domestic survival strategies. The analysis demonstrates that the domestic survival strategies of governments in African authoritarian regimes are the key factor that influences the willingness of these governments to cooperate with the EU.

The Survival Strategies of Dominant Party Regimes: Angola, Ethiopia and Rwanda

Governments in African dominant party regimes employ different strategies for increasing their chances of remaining in power. They can decide to invest in the party or the state to strengthen public goods provision or coopt regime opponents and supporters. They may use coercion to open or close political spaces. They may more or less successfully manage arenas of contestation, such as elections, to strengthen their domestic and international legitimacy and signal their firm grip on power to regime opponents. Strong state institutions or strong ruling parties are key for governments in dominant party systems to effectively manage arenas of contestation and use coercion to open or close political spaces. The specific strategies that governments choose are influenced first of all by structural factors, such as access to natural resources (like oil) or how the regime came to power. They are further shaped by situational factors, such as the type of threats from the opposition that governments face during a specific period.

Angola: Using the Party and the State for Cooptation

Angola is a dominant party system in which the leadership has developed an extensive patronage network. The Angolan leadership can rely on vast revenues from oil exports that are relatively easy to extract and that require little cooperation from the party or the population. The leadership therefore has made relatively little efforts to strengthen the effectiveness of government institutions or invest in the institutionalisation of party structures. Instead, it uses formal and informal state institutions as well as the ruling party to provide spoils and perks to regime supporters and to coopt regime opponents. The leadership has at times even taken deliberate steps to weaken state institutions to reduce the chances of independent centres of power emerging. In addition to cooptation mechanisms, the government relies on low-intensity coercion to prevent and respond to challenges from the opposition.

In the first few years after the end of the civil war, the Angolan leadership experienced a period of relative stability with very few challenges from within the ruling elite or from the opposition outside the ruling party. Since the 2008 elections, however, dissatisfaction within the MPLA as well as in the broader population has been growing. Compared with the 2008 elections, the government thus faced more difficulties in winning the 2012 (and 2017) elections. In response to mounting dissatisfaction, the leadership invested even more in expanding the ruling party and using the party as an instrument of cooptation. With the drop in oil prices that started in 2014, the government's financial means for sustaining the extensive patronage system are arguably fading away with unclear implications for the medium- to longer-term stability of the regime.

Rwanda: Using Effective State Institutions for Public Goods Provision and Coercion
Unlike Angola, Rwanda is a dominant party system in which the leadership has heavily invested in the effectiveness of government institutions to improve public goods provision. Since the mid-2000s, the Rwandan leadership has been more active in this regard not only compared with Angola but also compared with Ethiopia and other African dominant party systems. At the same time, the Rwandan leadership has relied on low-intensity coercion to prevent challenges to regime survival and it has been successful in managing arenas of contestation.

The Rwandan government faced challenges from within the ruling elite ahead of the 2003 elections. Since the mid-2000s, it has enjoyed a period of relative domestic stability with little challenges from political opponents. Some members of the ruling elite (notably the military and security forces) have defected, but made little attempts to develop a political alternative.

Academic literature and policy debates on Rwanda are highly polarised. Scholars either criticise the authoritarian, repressive political regime (for example Reyntjens 2013) or they highlight Rwanda's great progress in terms of poverty reduction and economic growth (for example Booth and Golooba-Mutebi 2012). Here it is argued that political repression and public goods provision constitute two sides of the same coin. Rwanda is an example of those very few authoritarian, dominant party systems that invest in effective state institutions to improve public goods provision, while at the same time closing spaces for the media, civil society and opposition parties.

The Rwandan regime has emerged in a very specific context and under very specific structural conditions. Rwanda has scarce domestic resources and a very small territory. The ruling party originates from a military movement that had to fight against the *génocidaires* with little international (financial or other material) support. It relies on a small political (still) ethnic-based support group. It is therefore no coincidence that it is in Rwanda that a strong authoritarian state with a rational-legal and meritocratic bureaucracy has developed and that these state institutions are not only used for controlling the political arena but also for public goods provision.

Ethiopia Somewhere 'In-Between': Party Expansion and Effective State, Public Goods, Cooptation and Coercion
Ethiopia is a dominant party system in which the government has also invested in the effectiveness of state institutions. Yet in light of strong challenges from the domestic opposition, the government modified its survival strategies in the mid-2000s, putting more emphasis on party expansion, cooptation and coercion.

In the early 2000s, the Ethiopian leadership adopted a strategy similar to that which the Rwandan government has used since 2006. In response to the split in the TPLF central committee in 2001, the Ethiopian government started to heavily invest in the effectiveness of government institutions with a view to improving public goods provision. At the same time, the government used low-intensity coercion to prevent an opposition from emerging. However, ahead of the 2005 elections, the Ethiopian leadership opened political spaces because it thought that it would be in a secure position. When the opposition made considerable gains in the elections and thereby threatened regime survival, the Ethiopian leadership fundamentally altered its survival strategies. It started to invest more strongly in expanding the ruling party. In parallel, state institutions were increasingly also used as instruments for cooptation.

Some of the structural conditions that impact the governments' survival strategies are quite similar in Ethiopia and Rwanda: both have very limited access to revenues from natural resources and both parties came to power through a violent struggle during which they had little support from the international community. Instead, differences in Ethiopia's and Rwanda's survival strategies since the mid-2000s are caused by varying challenges to regime stability and threats from political opponents. In this regard, Ethiopian and Rwanda nicely illustrate how the domestic political game between the ruler and political opponents from inside or outside the ruling coalition is a key factor in the domestic politics of authoritarian regimes as well as their external relations.

Dominant Party Regimes' Survival Strategies Meet EU Good Governance Strategies

Comparing Angola, Ethiopia and Rwanda at first confirms the widely held assumption that cooperation on governance reforms can generate substantial costs for authoritarian governments. In some countries, such as Angola, cooperation does indeed cause difficulties and brings almost no benefits for the government. However, in other dominant party regimes, such as Ethiopia and Rwanda, cooperation can produce costs *and* benefits for the government.

Angola: Mainly Costs in Engaging on Good Governance Reforms with the EU

In resource-rich, dominant party regimes like Angola that distribute spoils and perks to remain in power, cooperation on governance reforms challenges regime survival. The Angolan leadership has made few attempts to invest in formal state institutions, but relies to an important extent on *informal* state institutions and the party. In this context, cooperating with the EU, even on a narrow understanding of *effective government* that 'only' involves reforms related to transparency, public financial management, tax reform or the fight against corruption, would be risky. Despite the shift in the EU's good governance strategy and the EU's decision to narrow its approach to *effective government* and to not use conflictive instruments, cooperation has mostly incurred costs for the government. While the Angolan leadership at least partly governed through *informal* state structures and the party, the EU mostly engages with *formal* state structures.

On the other hand, cooperation on *democratic government* would have been challenging for the Angolan government and hardly happened. The government was quite secure in its position ahead of the 2008 elections; in fact, it postponed the election date several times until it was expecting an easy victory. EU support for the elections therefore accrued some benefits in the form of external legitimacy and improvements in international reputation. Ahead of the 2012 elections, however, the Angolan government was under greater domestic pressure due to stronger public opposition and dissatisfaction within the MPLA. In this context, cooperation with the EU on the elections would have potentially been costly, and therefore did not occur.

Ethiopia and Rwanda: Costs and Benefits to Engage with the EU
Comparing Angola with Ethiopia and Rwanda demonstrates that in dominant party regimes where governments have a strong genuine interest in building effective states, at least part of the EU's good governance strategies converges with the preferences of the governments.

Ethiopia and Rwanda both clearly have a stronger interest than Angola in building capable states that generate domestic (tax) revenues and provide public goods to a broader segment of society. In this context, EU support for *effective government* institutions aligns with the preferences of the government for state modernisation. However, the comparison of Ethiopia and Rwanda shows that the size of these benefits still varies over time. In Rwanda, cooperating with the EU on building an effective state was more attractive after 2005 than in the early 2000s. When the government launched several reform programmes to strengthen the civil service, increase taxes, improve public financial management systems and reduce corruption, the government's preferences strongly converged with the EU's offer to support the effectiveness of government institutions.

In the case of Ethiopia, those elements of the EU's approach that were geared towards strengthening the *effectiveness* of government institutions converged more strongly with the government's preferences in the early 2000s than after the 2005 election crisis. In response to the split within the TPLF central committee in 2001, the Ethiopian leadership launched a major reform programme to enhance the effectiveness of state institutions. The EU and other donors' support for this programme was thus very welcomed by the Ethiopian government. After the 2005 election crisis, building effective government institutions remained important for the Ethiopian leadership. However, state institutions and public goods provision were also increasingly used as mechanisms for cooptation, for instance, by expanding state employment.

At the same time, the Ethiopian leadership invested heavily in expanding the reach of the party and conditioned access to basic social services (at least to some degree) to party membership. When international NGOs accused the Ethiopian government of using aid funds as an instrument of cooptation, the EU and other donors came under considerable pressure. Investing in the party as an instrument of cooptation thus caused friction in EU–Ethiopia relations. In other words, the case of Ethiopia between 2005 and 2010 illustrates that even though the EU does not directly engage with the ruling party as part of its good governance strategies, the Ethiopian leadership's decision to strengthen the reach of the party can still induce considerable tension for bilateral relations.

Furthermore, comparing Ethiopia and Rwanda reveals that in African dominant party regimes, EU attempts to promote both *democratic government* and *democratic governance* can induce various costs and some (few) benefits. These costs and benefits vary depending on the threat from the opposition that the government faces and the survival strategies it uses. Between 2000 and 2004, the EU's strategies coincided with a period of instability in both Ethiopia and Rwanda. However, both governments' response strategies varied. Whereas Rwanda closed political spaces to secure its election victory, Ethiopia—at least slightly—opened up. Cooperation on *democratic government* was thus very risky for Rwanda and easier for Ethiopia. After 2005, the EU's demands to engage in governance reforms were made during a time of regime stability in the case of Rwanda and regime instability in the case of Ethiopia. While both governments used similar strategies of low-intensity coercion, EU demands to engage in democratic government (and governance) have therefore inflicted substantial costs for the government in Ethiopia, but not in Rwanda. For instance, as the Rwandan government was quite sure of winning the 2008 and 2010 parliamentary and presidential elections, it could engage with the EU. The Ethiopian government, instead, only agreed to cooperate during the 2010 elections, once it was sure to win by a substantial majority.

Several conclusions emerge from this analysis. Cooperation on governance reforms can be risky—but also beneficial—for governments in African dominant party regimes. Academic work on authoritarianism often assumes that the implementation of good governance instruments mostly produces costs (Wright 2009; Cornell 2012; Escribà-Folch and Wright 2015; see also Andrews 2013). By contrast, this book has shown that support for governance reforms may also converge with the preferences of governments in dominant party systems. This phenomenon was most clearly illustrated in the case of Rwanda. This is an important point because it demonstrates that more attention needs to be paid to (negative) unintended effects of the EU and other external actors' good governance policies.

By modifying its strategy, the EU can increase the incentives and disincentives for African governments to engage. However, the EU has not always been strategic in adjusting its good governance policies to the local dynamics and the domestic political game between the ruler and opponents. Analysing the EU's good governance policies together with the survival strategies of African authoritarian regimes suggests that the EU often has not used the most appropriate strategy to support reforms. The EU at times exerts pressure and promotes a broad understanding of good governance when African governments have very little leeway to engage with the EU (for example, in the case of Ethiopia in the years following the 2005 election crisis). More importantly, the EU at times fails to use windows of opportunity to promote reforms when African governments have enough room to manoeuvre and engage with the EU (for example, in the case of Rwanda after 2005 when the government faced very little domestic political opposition). The EU, thereby, not only misses an opportunity to support the basic conditions that may contribute to democratic change in the medium- to longer-term perspective, but it also risks endorsing the regime in place.

The survival strategies have considerable explanatory power in accounting for differences across the three countries. However, they do not fully explain the variation in the three governments' openness for engaging with the EU on governance reforms. The interaction of the EU's strategies and African governments' survival strategies elucidates why Ethiopia is less willing to engage with the EU than Rwanda. Yet, by focussing merely on these two factors, one would expect that Ethiopia would not engage at all with the EU on governance reforms after 2005, given the high risks of cooperation. Focussing on the survival strategies also cannot explain why Rwanda only reluctantly cooperated in the early 2000s, but then shifted its strategy towards proactive engagement after 2005. Moreover, it does not explain why Angola reluctantly engaged with the EU in the early 2000s, despite the low benefits and high costs that cooperation entailed at that time.

6.3 Economic Dependence: Less Important Than Thought

African governments take their decisions whether to engage in governance reforms first of all by assessing the costs and benefits that this cooperation entails in light of their survival strategies. The incentives of cooperating with the EU on governance reforms are then further mitigated by African governments' broader interests in cooperating with the EU. The cases analysed here demonstrate that African countries' economic dependence on the EU can tip the scale; it can increase or reduce the incentives for African governments to engage with the EU. However, economic dependence is not an alternative explanation to African governments' survival strategies. The empirics in this book do not suggest that African countries' dependence on the EU is irrelevant. Yet, the relevance of that dependence hinges on African governments' survival strategies.

In the early 2000s, Ethiopia and Rwanda were both quite dependent on the EU, whereas Angola's dependence was relatively low (Fig. 6.2). Rwanda was slightly more dependent on the EU than

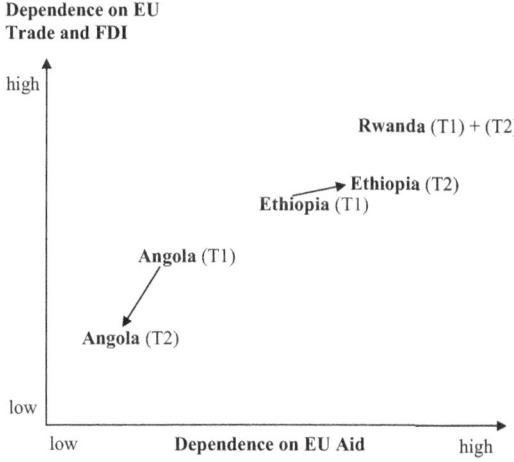

Fig. 6.2 Economic dependence of Angola, Ethiopia and Rwanda on the EU between 2000 and 2014
Source: Author's compilation; 'T' stands for 'time period', for Rwanda T1: 2000–2005, T2: 2006–2014; Ethiopia T1: 2000–2005, T2: 2006–2014; Angola T1: 2002–2004; T2: 2005–2014

Ethiopia. Aid as a share of GNI peaked at almost 20 per cent in Ethiopia in 2003, and at almost 25 per cent in Rwanda in 2004. The Ethiopian and Rwandan governments both actively embraced the emerging international aid effectiveness agenda to maximise access to international development aid flows. Furthermore, the EU was among their largest trading partners and an important source of direct investments for Ethiopia as well as Rwanda at that time. Yet, for both governments trade (and investments) still generated fewer revenues than aid. Moreover, as the EU has largely operationalised its good governance instruments in the area of aid, it has limited leverage to use dependence on trade and investments to set direct incentives for cooperating on governance reforms.

In the early 2000s, Rwanda's dependence on the EU thus set incentives for the government to reluctantly start engaging in governance reforms, even though this type of activity was risky at that time. For Ethiopia, cooperation on governance reforms was also difficult in the early 2000s, as it was for Rwanda. In this regard, Ethiopia's slightly lower dependence on the EU compared with Rwanda explains why, in the early 2000s, Ethiopia was slightly more reluctant to engage than Rwanda was.

For Angola, economic cooperation with the EU in the early 2000s provided some benefits and at least partly balanced out costs that cooperation on governance reforms entailed. Unlike Ethiopia and Rwanda, Angola was clearly not dependent on aid at that time. However, even though aid as a share of GNI was quite low (only 4 per cent), the government reached out to the EU (and other Western donors) for support. After the end of the civil war, it urgently needed financial assistance for the reconstruction process. Angola turned to the EU, when the IMF and other Western actors were not willing to extend support.[1] Moreover, in the early 2000s, the EU still had a comparatively large stake in trade with Angola; oil exports to the EU came second after the USA. This moderate dependence on the EU explains why the Angolan government started to at least reluctantly engage in the implementation of governance instruments in the early 2000s.

Since the mid-2000s, Rwanda has remained strongly dependent on the EU. The EU kept its position as a key donor to Rwanda. The modalities by which the EU provided aid (budget support) and the sectors to which it directed aid (social services and infrastructure) have matched the Rwandan government's preferences. The EU also continued to be the most important destination for Rwandan exports (until 2012) and source of direct investments. In light of the shift in EU good governance strategies towards a *rewarding* strategy and the low costs stemming from cooperation on governance reforms between 2006 and 2014, high dependence on the EU can thus explain why the government not only actively but *proactively* engaged with the EU. Only with the EU and other donors' usage of negative conditionality and their shift from budget support to sector budget support in the summer of 2012, have Rwanda's interests in engaging with the EU begun decreasing.

Ethiopia's dependence on the EU slightly increased in the mid-2000s. After the 2005 elections, output legitimacy became even more important to regime stability. The EU and other donors' support for social services and infrastructure development therefore became even more relevant for the Ethiopian government after 2005. Moreover, the EU remained an important destination for Ethiopia's exports, which slightly increased after 2005. In light of the high risks that cooperation on governance reforms entailed after the 2005 elections, Ethiopia's high level of EU dependence explains why the government did not ignore EU demands for cooperation on governance reforms, but at least reluctantly engaged.

In the case of Angola, dependence on the EU further decreased since 2005. The share of aid to GNI dropped below 1 per cent. Even though the EU is one of the largest donors to Angola, development aid clearly provides no incentive that could balance out the costs that cooperation on governance reforms would entail for the Angolan government. Moreover, the EU's relative importance as a destination for Angolan exports or as a source of loans has diminished rapidly. The EU has made some attempts to develop a more comprehensive partnership with Angola to offer incentives for cooperation beyond aid. The EU's proposal to initiate a 'Joint Way Forward' was meant to open new avenues for cooperation beyond the framework of the Cotonou Partnership Agreement, for instance on energy and regional peace and security. Even though it is still early to judge the outcome, the Angolan government's strong hesitation in signing the Joint Way Forward indicates the government's limited interest in this type of partnership.

Comparing the economic dependence of Angola, Ethiopia and Rwanda on the EU suggests that aid dependence is an important factor that influences African governments' willingness to engage with the EU. Some have argued that governments mainly cooperate on governance reforms to assure continued aid flows, but with little genuine interest in the particular reforms (Andrews 2013). This raises the question of how important the three countries' dependence on the EU is compared with their survival strategies in explaining their willingness to engage in governance reforms.

Findings from the case of Angola appear ambiguous. The EU has narrowed its good governance approach and has become less critical towards the Angolan government. Changes in the Angolan government's survival strategies over time have not made it more difficult to engage with the EU. At the same time, the government's dependence on the EU decreased further. It is thus difficult to draw conclusions from the case of Angola regarding the relative importance of the government's survival strategies compared with the government's dependence on the EU.

The examples of Ethiopia and Rwanda, however, show compellingly that African countries' dependence on the EU cannot fully explain their strategies, but needs to be considered in conjunction with and against the background of their own survival strategies. Ethiopia has become more dependent on the EU over time, but the government continued to only reluctantly engage with the EU on governance reforms between 2006 and 2014. If the government's aid dependence had been the main factor in explaining its willingness to engage, one would have expected the Ethiopian government to become more open to cooperation over time. Rwanda's level of dependence on EU aid, on the other hand, remained similar between the early 2000s and 2014. However, the Rwandan government still decided to proactively engage with the EU after 2006. If Rwanda's willingness to engage had been primarily driven by its dependence on the EU, one would have expected Rwanda's openness to cooperation to remain similar over time.

We can draw three main conclusions from this part of the analysis. First, in cases of strong aid dependency, the EU can use aid as an incentive to compensate for some of the costs that cooperating on governance reforms involves. This was observed most clearly in Ethiopia between 2005 and 2010. Even though cooperation on governance reforms was risky for the Ethiopian government, it engaged with the EU—at least reluctantly. The importance of the EU as a donor to Ethiopia, the EU's aid modalities and the choice of sectors to which it has targeted its aid arguably have made the EU's overall cooperation package attractive enough for the Ethiopian government to hesitantly accept cooperation on governance reforms. Even if Ethiopia only 'reluctantly' engaged, this can be viewed as a success given the substantial challenges that cooperation on governance reforms entailed for the Ethiopian government in the post-2005 election period.

Second, the EU's good governance policies face strong limitations in countries where cooperation on governance reforms is costly for the target government and where aid dependence is low. This is most obvious in the case of Angola. The EU is basically left with no financial incentives to convince the government to address governance issues. Moreover, it has little means to set (material) incentives 'beyond' development aid to convince the Angolan government to engage on governance reforms.

Third, African countries' dependence on the EU is a factor that can 'tip the balance' and set additional incentives for cooperation. However, African countries' dependence on the EU is not an *alternative* explanation to account for African governments' willingness to cooperate on governance reforms. Instead, it needs to be analysed in conjunction with African governments' survival strategies and the EU's good governance strategies to account for different levels of responsiveness.

6.4 Does China Matter? Yes, But Less Than Expected

Finally, the analysis of China's engagement with Angola, Ethiopia and Rwanda confounds the widely held belief in policy and academic debates that China made it more difficult for the EU to support governance reforms in Africa between 2000 and 2014. Even though China has emerged as an alternative partner in Ethiopia and to some extent Angola, this has had limited effects on the Ethiopian and Angolan governments' willingness to engage with the EU on governance reforms.

Comparing Angola, Ethiopia and Rwanda reveals that African governments' access to cooperation with China has varied substantially between 2000 and 2014, not only over time but also across the three countries. Depending on China's economic and political interests in engaging with African countries, the opportunities presented to African governments differ considerably. The following sub-section will examine to what extent China's economic cooperation with African countries has reduced African governments' dependence on the EU and to what extent China engages with African countries on their survival strategies. It will then delve into the question of whether China's engagement in Africa has affected African governments' willingness to cooperate with the EU on governance reforms.

China: Reducing African Countries' Economic Dependence on the EU in Some Cases

In the early 2000s, when the EU started to put governance reforms more prominently onto the agenda in its relations with African governments, African countries had little access to economic cooperation with China. Angola, Ethiopia and Rwanda were no exception in this regard. For all three countries, levels of bilateral trade with China, access to Chinese development aid and other official flows, as well as direct investments from China were quite low at the turn of the millennium. However, China's accession to the World Trade Organization (WTO), the Chinese government's launch of the 'going out' policy and its growing needs for energy resources created a number of (mostly economic) incentives for China to strengthen its engagement with African countries.

Since the mid-2000s, China's economic relations with Angola, Ethiopia and Rwanda have intensified substantially. For all three countries, a specific point in time can be identified when relations started to become more important. In the case of Angola, that was in 2004 when China and Angola signed the first oil-for-infrastructure deal, and for Ethiopia it was in early 2006 with the first master loan facility; and shortly after the Ethiopian government's dispute with the EU and other international actors. China–Rwanda relations deepened with the third meeting of the Forum for China-Africa Cooperation that took place in Beijing in October 2006. However, due to China's specific economic and political interests in engaging with the three countries, the countries' access to aid, official flows, trade and investments from China have differed considerably since the mid-2000s.

In the case of Angola, China has rapidly become a major economic cooperation partner, further reducing the country's vulnerability to EU pressure. After 2004, China quickly emerged as Angola's second-largest trading partner; in 2007, China overtook the USA as the largest destination for Angolan oil exports. China has become by far the largest source of official flows to Angola. Angola has become the most important recipient of Chinese loans in Africa. Chinese loans not only allowed the Angolan government to fund its ambitious infrastructure reconstruction programme but also to *deliver* the infrastructure in time for the parliamentary elections in 2008 and in 2012, respectively.

The example of Angola, therefore, illustrates the pivotal role of resource interests as a driving force for closer economic cooperation between China and African countries. Angola has emerged as the second-largest (at times largest) source of Chinese oil imports, also indicating the importance of Angola to China. China's relations with Angola (not unlike the EU's relations with Angola) are thus clearly interdependent. However, the case of Angola also highlights that China's engagement and interests in Africa are not *limited* to resource interests. From the Chinese perspective, Angola has become an important market for Chinese (mostly state-owned) construction companies. Moreover—and again not too different from the EU—Chinese officials view Angola as an important political and security actor within the wider region.

In the case of Ethiopia, China has also become a major source of official flows, an important destination for Ethiopia's exports and a relatively important source of direct investments. China has become almost as important an economic partner for Ethiopia as the EU. China's engagement with Ethiopia thus considerably reduces Ethiopia's vulnerability to EU pressure. The EXIM Bank supports large infrastructure projects; trade with China has opened new export markets and contributed to the diversification of Ethiopia's trade, and in doing so has generated important additional profits for the government. China has granted aid to support some high-profile government projects such as a railway, infrastructure development in Addis Ababa and a prestigious expressway.

As Ethiopia has exported few natural resources, the amount of Chinese official flows to Ethiopia seems surprising at first glance. But Ethiopia's position on the Horn of Africa, the size of its (potential) market and its influence in African regional debates make the country an attractive partner for China. Hosting the African Union and thus representatives from all African countries, the visibility of China's support in Addis Ababa has an immediate multiplier effect throughout the continent.[2] According to Chinese and Ethiopian officials, the Ethiopian government has been one of the driving forces behind the FOCAC meetings on the African side (Taylor 2011). Chinese officials (like their European counterparts) view Ethiopia as a pole of relative stability within the Horn of Africa.

In contrast to Angola and Ethiopia, Rwanda has relatively little access to economic cooperation with China. China's economic cooperation with Rwanda is small compared with its trade, official flows and investments in and with Angola and (to a lesser extent) Ethiopia. More importantly, from the perspective of the Rwandan government, China has not (yet) emerged as an economic cooperation partner that is as important as the EU or

Rwanda's other traditional partners. China's development aid to Rwanda has increased since 2006. However, China remains a relatively small to medium-sized donor when compared with the EU and other OECD DAC donors. Unlike Ethiopia and Angola, Chinese policy banks do not (yet) provide commercial or preferential loans for infrastructure development to Rwanda. In 2011, China overtook the EU as the most important destination for Rwandan exports, but Rwanda still mostly exports its traditional commodities to China and has not (yet) been able to use cooperation with China to diversify its exports (unlike Ethiopia). Even though China gave some assistance to Rwanda in 2012 during a period when the EU and other donors used budget-support funds to exert pressure on the Rwandan government, China's support only slightly reduced Rwanda's vulnerability to EU pressure.

What explains the stark difference in China's engagement with Rwanda and Ethiopia, since both have little access to natural resources? China has fewer economic (and political) interests in engaging with Rwanda than it does with Ethiopia. As a landlocked country with a very densely crowded, but relatively small population, large Chinese state-owned companies have less incentive to invest in Rwanda. Even though regional economic integration has improved in recent years, cross-border trade remains costly, and Rwanda thus has difficulty positioning itself as a hub of the region. However, despite limited economic interests that China has in Rwanda, it is a medium-sized recipient of Chinese aid and receives more aid than what would be expected given the size of the country and its volumes of bilateral trade. This relative importance as an aid recipient can probably be explained by Rwanda's political weight in Africa and President Kagame's strong voice in international debates. Moreover, the Rwandan government is perceived to be quite active in reaching out to China to make sure that all the available aid funds are used.

To sum up, between 2005 and 2014, China's economic engagement with the three countries considerably reduced Ethiopia's and Angola's vulnerability to EU pressure. China has emerged as a major economic partner for Rwanda but has not (yet) become as important as the EU.

China as an Alternative Partner for Engaging with African Governments on Their Survival Strategies

In addition to reducing African governments' dependence on the EU, China may also provide alternative support for African governments' survival strategies. In the three countries analysed here, China's assistance for African governments' survival strategies differs considerably. Only in the case of Ethiopia are party-to-party relations very close, and China has supported government measures to strengthen the effectiveness of state institutions and the usage of low-intensity coercion. China's engagement with Angola and Rwanda, instead, is limited to economic cooperation.

Party-to-Party Relations
In contrast with the EU's Africa policy, party-to-party contacts constitute an important pillar of Sino-African relations.[3] Zhong Weiyun (2012), vice-director of the Africa Bureau of the International Department of the Central Committee of the CCP, explains the interest of the CCP and African ruling parties in bilateral relations:

> African political parties, especially those ruling parties, hope to learn the experience of the CPC in party building and country construction. Many parties explicitly say that they want the CPC to train their senior leaders. The CPC has also carried out research into the experiences of African ruling parties that have a long history in order to improve its own party building in the new era. [...] [African ruling parties] take part in workshops of different types and topics, including party building, economic development, poverty reduction, young people and women. The CPC also sends experts to some African countries on their request to brief them about China and the experience of the CPC.

Information on the relations between the CCP and ruling parties in individual African countries is generally difficult to obtain. Findings from a press review and interviews with Chinese and African officials suggest that the CCP has emerged as a prominent cooperation partner only in the case of the EPRDF. In the case of the Angolan MPLA, party-to-party contacts have remained very limited. For the RPF, exchange is more intense than with the MPLA, but more limited than with the EPRDF.

Contacts between the EPRDF and the CCP also appear to be quite close if analysed within the broader regional context. If measured in terms of the number of bilateral visits, the EPRDF is among the five most important African cooperation partners for the CCP (Fig. 6.3). The CCP has similarly frequent exchanges only with the ruling parties in South Africa, Sudan, Zimbabwe and Namibia. For the CCP, the intensity of

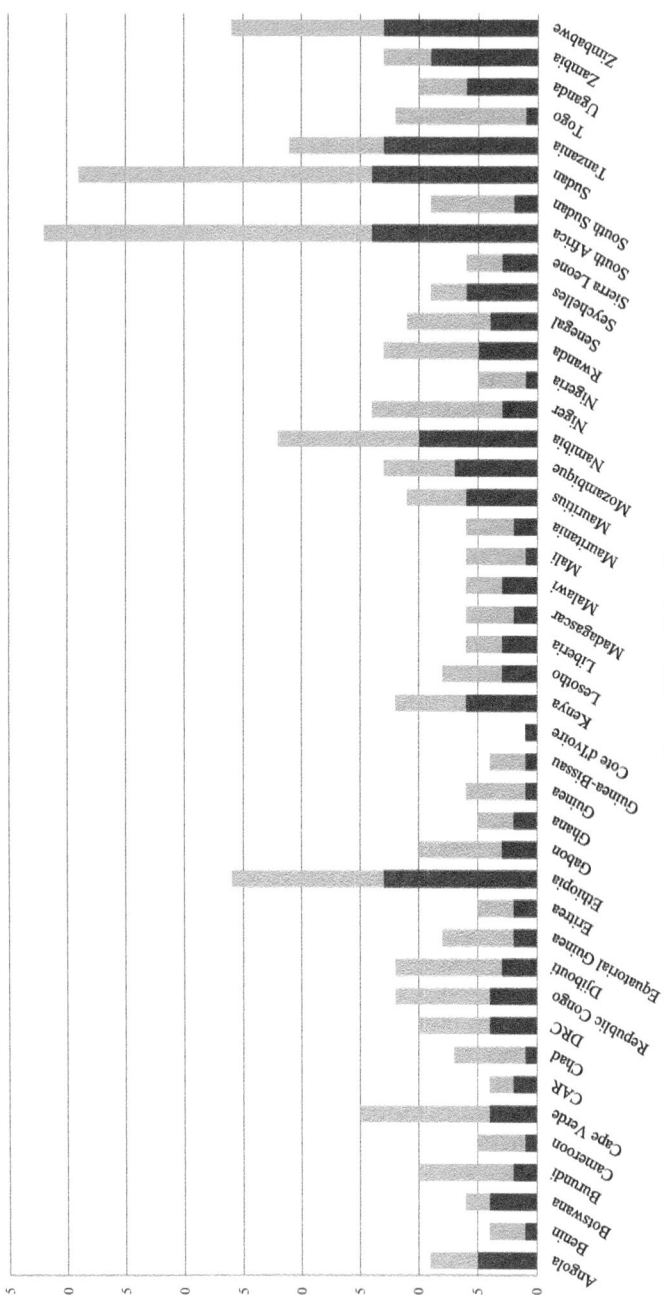

Fig. 6.3 Number of bilateral visits between the Chinese Communist Party and African ruling parties (2002–2014)
Source: Author's compilation, based on systematic analysis of news items on visits between cadres from the CCP and African parties from the website of the CCP

party-to-party links with Rwanda figures in the medium range. Party-to-party links with Angola figure at the lowest end of CCP contacts with any African party.

What explains these differences? Several tentative explanations may account for the variance that should be further tested and nuanced in future research. First, a cursory cross-country review suggests that historic relations and similar ideology play an important role. The CCP has the closest relations with some of those parties that it already supported during their liberation struggle, such as ruling parties in Zimbabwe and Namibia. In this regard, history also seems to play a role in the limited contacts between the MPLA and the CCP, as China supported the rival party UNITA during the civil war. Second, party-to-party contacts are closer in cases where African ruling parties have a strong interest in strengthening party institutions. For instance, as the EPRDF has been much more active than the MPLA in investing in inner-party reforms and expanding its status as a ruling party, it seems to have a stronger genuine interest in party-to-party exchanges with the CCP. On the other hand, limited contacts between the CCP and the MPLA (or the ruling party in Nigeria) seem to be an indication that economic interests are not a prominent factor to explain close party-to-party links. The CCP maintains relations with parties in almost all countries, including relatively small ones like Benin, Burundi, Lesotho and Sierra Leone, where China has limited economic interests (Fig. 6.3).

Other Forms of Support for African Governments' Survival Strategies
In addition to engaging with the ruling party, the Chinese government could also support the effectiveness of government institutions or assist African governments' strategies of using coercion and managing arenas of contestation. Comparing Angola, Ethiopia and Rwanda illustrates that only in the case of Ethiopia has a close cooperation between ruling parties emerged and some technical support for the capacities of government institutions been provided. China's engagement with African countries thus varies widely, not only in terms of economic engagement but also with regard to how China engages with African governments on their survival strategies.

In Ethiopia, China has supported the government's measures to strengthen state institutions and its usage of low-intensity coercion (Chap. 4). Information from interviews with Ethiopian and Chinese officials and a press review suggest that Ethiopia received technical assistance for its state media and some (albeit limited) support for justice sector reform.[4] Ethiopia has also sent considerably greater numbers of government officials to China for training than Rwanda or Angola.

In Angola, China has apparently given very little technical assistance to support the capacities of state institutions. Interviews, a press review and available secondary literature on China–Angola relations do not give any indication that, in addition to financing and constructing large infrastructure projects, China has provided substantial technical support to strengthen the administrative or human capacities of government institutions. Growing economic interdependencies between Angola and China have sparked public protests in Angola against the high number of Chinese workers and companies, and Chinese businessmen have been attacked. In order to address these negative side-effects of growing interdependencies, some exchange in the area of human rights and justice reform has taken place (Chap. 5).

Finally, in the case of Rwanda, China has provided even less technical assistance to support the human or administrative capacities of government institutions than in Angola (Chap. 3).

China: What Effects does it have on Cooperating with the EU on Governance Reforms?

Analysing China's engagement with Angola, Ethiopia and Rwanda in light of the EU's demands to cooperate on governance reforms, the three governments' survival strategies and their dependence on the EU suggest that China's engagement has limited effects on African governments' willingness to cooperate with the EU on governance reforms. Table 6.2 summarises the main findings from the analysis on China's cooperation with the three countries.

Rwanda

Since the mid-2000s when China became a more important cooperation partner, the EU's good governance strategies have largely converged with the Rwandan government's preferences. One would thus expect any effect China has on the Rwandan government's willingness to engage with the EU on governance reforms to be limited. Moreover, for Rwanda, China has become neither a substantial alternative partner for economic cooperation, nor a partner for cooperating on the government's survival strategies. China only very recently has emerged as a more important economic cooperation partner. Even though China started to cooperate more closely in 2012, at a point in time when the EU put considerably more pressure

Table 6.2 Engaging with China—effect on the three governments' willingness to cooperate on governance reforms

		Does cooperation with China reduce economic dependence on the EU?	
		Yes	No
China engaging in survival strategies?	Yes	Strong effect Ethiopia: since 2005	Medium effect
	No	Medium effect Angola: since 2004 Rwanda: since 2012 (?)	No effect Ethiopia: 2000–2005 Angola: 2000–2004 Rwanda: 2000–2012

Source: Author's compilation

on Rwanda, official flows provided by China did not significantly reduce Rwanda's dependence on the EU. The effect of China's engagement in the Rwandan government's decision to engage with the EU on governance reforms has therefore been weak.

Angola
Assessing the impact of China's engagement with Angola on the Angolan government's willingness to cooperate with the EU on governance reforms is more challenging. Cooperating with the EU on governance reforms mainly incurred costs for the Angolan government. Moreover, for Angola, China has clearly emerged as an alternative cooperation partner, particularly in terms of economic cooperation. However, even in the absence of China as an alternative cooperation partner, the Angolan government's dependence on the EU would have been limited. The Angolan government might not have been completely indifferent towards the EU's demands to engage on governance reforms after 2005, but it is unlikely that in the absence of China it would have been much more forthcoming in cooperating with the EU.

Ethiopia: A 'Crucial Case'?
Of the three countries, Ethiopia represents a 'crucial case' (Gerring 2007, 231). If the arguments set up in the theoretical framework hold, then Ethiopia is a case where we would expect China's engagement to have affected the government's willingness to cooperate with the EU on governance reforms (Table 6.2). In the case of Ethiopia, all facts central to the

confirmation of the argument that China negatively affects EU good governance support seem to be present. Not only is Ethiopia an example where China has become an alternative cooperation partner, but it is also a case where, since the mid-2000s, cooperating with the EU was very difficult for the government. The Ethiopian regime was facing significant challenges from the opposition during the 2005 election crisis, making cooperation an endeavour with potentially disruptive effects for regime survival. Between 2006 and 2010, the EU broadened its good governance approach towards *democratic governance* and used a *cooperative-critical* strategy, making it riskier for the government to engage. At the same time, Ethiopia was largely dependent on EU aid and (to a lesser extent) on trade and investments.

In this specific context, one would expect that Ethiopia would refuse to cooperate with the EU on governance reforms, when China emerged as an alternative cooperation partner. However, Ethiopia has continued to at least reluctantly engage with the EU. The Ethiopian case thereby challenges the argument that China's engagement with African countries has substantially influenced African governments' willingness to cooperate with the EU on governance reforms. It suggests that access to cooperation with China has had limited effects on African governments' willingness to engage on governance reforms.

We can thus gain several insights regarding the relevance of China. First, the case studies indicate that in some countries China has indeed already become an alternative cooperation partner for African governments, not only in terms of economic cooperation, but also as a partner to cooperate on African governments' survival strategies. For Ethiopia, economic cooperation with China is as important as its cooperation with the EU; for Angola, China is even more important as an economic cooperation partner in terms of official flows, trade and investments; for Rwanda, China has only very recently become a considerable alternative partner. Only in the case of Ethiopia has China offered the government support for its survival strategies and closely engaged with the ruling party.

In addition, the analysis strongly suggests that between 2000 and 2014 China's cooperation with African countries did not negatively affect the EU's good governance strategies. The study thus refutes assumptions widely held in policy and public debates that the rise of China has made it more difficult for the EU to make African governments address governance issues. If measured in terms of African governments' openness for cooperating on governance reforms, the emergence of China has so far had little effect. Ethiopia in particular is a crucial case where one would expect that the government's strategy towards the EU would have changed when China became an alternative partner. However, this proposition could not be confirmed empirically. Instead, economic engagement with China is part of a broader set of domestic and international factors that impact on the preferences of African governments.

Finally, this finding ultimately implies that the EU's strategy to support governance reforms through a cooperative approach, in which the EU seeks to establish active cooperation with African governments on governance reforms, has made the EU's strategies less sensitive or vulnerable to the influence of China. The EU managed to establish at least some cooperation with governments in African dominant party regimes, where the EU's strategies converged with the preferences of the government (Rwanda post-2005), or where the EU's strategies diverged from the preferences of the government, but where the EU could set financial incentives for cooperation (Ethiopia post-2005). At the same time, we have seen that the EU is often not very strategic in adapting its good governance policies to the country context. In particular, the EU has not used windows of opportunity to promote reforms when African governments have faced little domestic pressure from opponents and have some leeway to engage (Rwanda post-2005). Instead of worrying about China, the EU should tap into the full potential of its own strategies.

6.5 Some Avenues for Future Work

Results from this analysis open several avenues for future work. Some relate to the debate on authoritarianism and the effectiveness of good governance support in authoritarian regimes. Others relate more specifically to the interaction between China's rise and (the EU's) good governance support.

A first issue for further investigation refers to the domestic politics of authoritarian regimes. While dominant party systems are the most prominent type of authoritarian regime today (Hadenius and Teorell 2007; Magaloni and Kricheli 2010), they do not constitute a homogeneous group. The survival strategies of governments in dominant party systems differ widely, as we have seen for the cases of Angola, Ethiopia and Rwanda. Governments may choose to invest in building effective states or to expand party structures, they may use coercion to open or close political spaces, and they need to manage arenas of contestation. Moreover, the willingness of governments to engage with external actors in governance reforms varies considerably. Given this great variety within the group of party-based regimes, future research should invest in developing a new typology of authoritarian, dominant party systems, focussing on the role of the ruling party, the level of institutionalisation of the ruling party and its relation to the state and society. This typology would allow for better understanding the variety of dominant party regimes and explaining differences in their economic and social performance, conditions under which these regimes may or may not democratise, and differences in the external influence of the EU, China and others.

A second issue for future work relates to the domestic political game between the ruler and political opponents from inside or outside the ruling coalition. This domestic game appears to be a crucial factor in the domestic politics of authoritarian regimes as well as their external relations. The domestic dynamic between the government and political opponents not only influences authoritarian governments' survival strategies but also shapes governments' interests in engaging with the EU, China or other external actors. This domestic political dynamic is not only relevant with regard to the willingness of African governments to engage on governance reforms. It also matters for the EU and China's engagement with authoritarian regimes in other policy fields. Experts on authoritarianism seek to understand the performance of authoritarian regimes regarding ecological sustainability (Wurster 2013; Pridham 1991), trade openness (Hankla and Kuthy 2011), the risk of civil conflict (Fjelde 2010) and the protection of foreign investments (Gehlbach and Keefer 2011). While they take the variety of authoritarianism as a starting point, they rarely investigate and compare the domestic incentives that are specific to authoritarian, dominant party systems. Findings of this book on the similarities and differences of dominant party systems and the domestic interaction between the ruler and opponents are thus also relevant beyond research on the effectiveness of (the EU's) good governance support in authoritarian regimes.

Another point for exploration refers to the tendency in the literature on EU good governance strategies to focus on exceptional situations where authoritarian regimes use high-intensity coercion as a measure of last resort to secure regime survival and where the EU and other donors use sanctions (Portela 2010; Del Biondo 2015; von Soest and Wahman 2015) or budget-support suspensions (Faust et al. 2012; Molenaers et al. 2015) to respond to imminent political crises. Consider situations like the 2005 election crisis in Ethiopia. Analysing this crisis through the lens of the domestic logic of political survival corroborates arguments that expectations on what external actors can achieve in these exceptional situations must be modest. However, this book has also pointed out that governments in dominant party systems usually rely on low-intensity coercion to gradually open or close political spaces. Future research should therefore pay more attention to periods of relative domestic political stability, when authoritarian governments rely on low-intensity coercion. In such situations, donors may have considerably more leeway to decide which strategy to use, as they face little pressure from public opinion and their own domestic constituencies to revert to sanctions or budget support suspensions. We have seen that during periods when governments in dominant party regimes face little pressure from domestic opponents, they are more likely to accept governance aid, engage in dialogue and allow civil society, the media or opposition parties more freedom, which may contribute to democratic reforms in the medium- to long-term.

Finally, in addition to focusing more on periods of relative domestic political stability, the specific role of the ruling party and its external relations requires further investigation. It is widely acknowledged that political parties have important influence on regime durability, political reform and economic prosperity (Smith 2005; Magaloni 2006; Brownlee 2007; Gehlbach and Keefer 2011; Bueno de Mesquita et al. 2003). Empirics in this book have exemplified the different functions ruling parties can play in authoritarian dominant party systems, and how party structures may fuse with state institutions and maintain close linkages with the business sector. Yet, literature on authoritarianism, on external party support as part of Western democracy promotion, or on China–Africa relations, has so far largely neglected the international relations of authoritarian parties as well as the CCP's relations to other parties. The CCP's engagement with African political parties can be quite close (as documented here for the case of Ethiopia). A cursory review on the CCP's contacts with parties across sub-Saharan African countries has indicated that there is great variance with regard to the intensity of party-to-party relations. The factors influencing party-to-party cooperation, the effects of party-to-party engagement and the interaction effects of the CCP's and European engagement with African parties (for example through some EU member states' political foundations) would thus be relevant for future work.

6.6 Policy Implications: Facing a Fork in the Road?

The basic parameters that have shaped African government's responsiveness towards the EU since the late 1990s are currently undergoing fundamental changes, suggesting that the EU's good governance strategies are now at a crossroad. Support for governance reforms is still on the EU's agenda. Yet, the security and migration agenda increasingly dominates EU external relations. There is a growing uncertainty among European policy-makers whether supporting governance reforms is the right thing to do. Moreover, domestic challenges in Europe, such as growing populism and illiberal domestic reforms in some EU member states, the Brexit or the EU's response to the refugee and migration crisis, question the EU's credibility and legitimacy to support reforms elsewhere. Even though the EU gradually strengthened good governance support between 2000 and 2014, there is no guarantee that this trend will continue in the future. Three developments suggest that the EU will face more challenges to implementing its agenda in the coming years: changes in the field of international development policy, the stabilisation of (dominant party) authoritarian contexts and China's evolving African policy.

First, the field of development policy, which has substantially influenced the EU's good governance policies in Africa, is undergoing significant changes (Klingebiel and Ashoff 2014). The international aid effectiveness agenda has passed its peak (Chandy and Kharas 2011; Mawdsley et al. 2014) and the 'decade of generosity', during which aid budgets successively grew, seems to have come to an end. Instead, with the increases in refugee and migration flows, aid budgets have come under pressure to support short-term measures to prevent refugees and migrants from moving to Europe and to cover the refugee costs in Europe rather than to promote long-term sustainable development.

These changes in the area of development policy have important direct implications for the EU's policies to support governance reforms in African countries. Shifts in aid modalities (for instance the decline in direct budget support) and changes in donor-government aid dialogues at country level as a consequence of the unravelling international aid effectiveness agenda make it more difficult for the EU to use these fora to bring governance reforms onto the agenda of its relations with African governments. Moreover, setting material incentives for African governments to cooperate on governance reforms becomes more challenging, if aid is concentrated on countries where migrants originate or transit, and if aid is used for short-term crisis prevention and migration management. If the EU gives priority to using aid funds to leverage cooperation on migration management, it cannot credibly leverage for cooperation on governance reforms at the same time.

Second, the question of how to find the most appropriate strategy to engage with dominant party regimes will remain a key challenge for the EU in the near future. One-third of all countries in the world are authoritarian dominant party systems (Magaloni and Kricheli 2010, 125). The façade of nominally democratic institutions is making it quite difficult for the EU (and for other actors) to find an appropriate approach to supporting governance reforms. The same type of intervention (for instance, support for elections or the judicial system) may diverge from the preferences of the government under some circumstances, while it may match them in others. The analysis presented here gives reasons for policy-makers to pay more attention to the incentives of authoritarian governments to set up formal democratic institutions to enhance their position in power rather than to view these institutions as natural stepping stones towards a more democratic system.

The EU needs to design its good governance strategies in such a way that incentives are set for African governments to engage with the EU. Otherwise, if governments do not engage at all, the EU cannot make any impact. The problem is, if the EU's good governance strategies fully converge with the preferences of the government and the EU does not use windows of opportunity to press for greater political openness, it risks endorsing the regime rather than encouraging reform. Thus, finding the right balance between aligning with the preferences of African governments and pressuring for governance reforms is a delicate issue.

Third, China is likely to become *more* rather than *less* relevant as a cooperation partner for African governments. China's 'footprint' in Africa will increase further. Over the past few years, China has been as important an economic cooperation partner as the EU only in a few African countries (such as Angola and Ethiopia). However, the example of Rwanda shows that China is likely to become more relevant for those African countries that have few natural resources and a limited (geo-)strategic and political importance. In conjunction with shifting priorities and strategies in the field of development policy due to the rise of the migration agenda, the EU will also face more difficulties in remaining an attractive partner in these countries and thus a partner who can credibly ask African governments to engage in governance reforms.

The more China invests in Africa and the more economic relations intensify, the more one can expect that the Chinese government will have an interest in government stability, regime stability and effective policy-making processes. While China has continued to lend rhetorical support for its non-interference policy, its implementation has become more differentiated in response to the specific context in African countries (Verhoeven 2014; Aidoo and Hess 2015). This has also been visible in the cases analysed here. Even if China does not develop similar instruments as the EU to support the effectiveness of government institutions, there might be more convergence in the EU and China's preferences at least for stable and *effective* institutions.

At the same time, divergences in the EU and China's strategies will remain with regard to supporting the inclusiveness and democratic quality of decision-making processes. We have seen that China's rise in Africa did not undermine the EU's efforts to engage with African governments on governance reforms between 2000 and 2014. China's presence is one of the several factors that impact African governments' preferences and incentive structures to introduce political reforms and to engage with the EU in such reforms. More relevant than China's presence is whether the EU itself is tapping the full potential of its strategies. With a cooperative approach that aims at establishing an active engagement with African governments in governance reforms, the EU is potentially well-situated to support reforms even in light of the rise of China. However, the EU should be more strategic in exploring opportunities for supporting political reforms.

Which Way Forward?

Academic research and findings from this book give evidence that EU's good governance support can work, if it is not overly ambitious, well-targeted to the local context and consistently applied. However, conclusions from the analysis presented here point to the need for the EU to take the domestic power game in African countries more strongly into account and to further adapt its strategies to local political dynamics. In other words, one size clearly does not fit all. Such a clear differentiation would need to happen at several levels.

The EU needs to strengthen and further develop instruments to support governance reforms 'beyond' the field of development policy. Other policy fields such as trade, energy, fisheries or climate policy increase in importance, opening additional areas to set incentives for and to engage in governance reforms. The case of Angola has been a particularly revealing example of the limited reach of the EU's bilateral aid instruments in supporting governance reforms. In light of the close integration of the Angolan elite in international financial markets and the tremendous flight of capital, EU support for draining tax havens, for instance, can have a direct effect on domestic political reforms and would thus need to be considered as part of the EU's policy for supporting governance reforms in certain countries.

In addition, the EU needs to more strongly differentiate its strategies for engaging with different regime types. The EU should not only distinguish between democratic and authoritarian but also distinguish between different types of authoritarian regimes, and notably between different dominant party systems. The EU can adapt its strategies when engaging with different countries, as this study has shown. Yet, ultimately, the EU still draws from the same toolbox when engaging with African countries regardless of their regime type. In light of the growing diversification of domestic contexts and political realities in African countries, the EU will need to make more efforts to diversify this 'toolbox'.

The changes within the EU and in EU development policy, the consolidation of dominant party regimes and the rise of China produce considerable adaptation pressure for EU good governance strategies. However, unlike events such as the Arab Spring or the crisis in the Ukraine, this adaptation pressure rises *gradually* rather than *imminently*, making incremental rather than fundamental changes to the EU's policies a likely scenario.

NOTES

1. Angola's rate of oil production and international oil prices were still relatively low at that time.
2. China's decision to grant the new African Union headquarters is probably the most visible sign in this regard.
3. According to Zhong Weiyun (2012), the CCP started to establish relations with African communist parties and national liberation movements in the 1950s. In the 1970s, the CCP expanded its cooperation to non-communist African parties. Zhong argues that the political openings in Africa in the early

1990s had a negative impact for the CCP's relations with African ruling parties because some parties were swept away and the new incumbents had little knowledge and sometimes little interest in closer party-to-party links. With the turn of the century and China's growing economic cooperation with African countries, party relations again gained prominence. Zhong's article 'Inter-Party relations promote Sino-African Strategic Partnership' is published online at http://www.china.org.cn/opinion/2012-08/28/content_26353120_3.htm, last accessed 5 October 2013.
4. China provided technical assistance for the Ethiopian News Agency, the Ministry of Information and the state-owned radio station. These actors receive very little to no support from the EU or other Western donors (see Chap. 4).

Open Access This chapter is licensed under the terms of the Creative Commons Attribution 4.0 International License (http://creativecommons.org/licenses/by/4.0/), which permits use, sharing, adaptation, distribution and reproduction in any medium or format, as long as you give appropriate credit to the original author(s) and the source, provide a link to the Creative Commons license and indicate if changes were made.

The images or other third party material in this chapter are included in the chapter's Creative Commons license, unless indicated otherwise in a credit line to the material. If material is not included in the chapter's Creative Commons license and your intended use is not permitted by statutory regulation or exceeds the permitted use, you will need to obtain permission directly from the copyright holder.

References

Aalen, Lovise, and Kjetil Tronvoll. 2009. The End of Democracy? Curtailing Political and Civil Rights in Ethiopia. *Review of African Political Economy* 36 (120): 193–207.

Abbink, Jon. 2006. Discomfiture of Democracy? The 2005 Election Crisis in Ethiopia and Its Aftermath. *African Affairs* 105 (419): 173–199.

———. 2009. The Ethiopian Second Republic and the Fragile "Social Contract". *Africa Spectrum* 44 (2): 3–28.

Acemoglu, Daron, and James A. Robinson. 2012. *Why Nations Fail: The Origins of Power, Prosperity and Poverty*. New York: Crown Business.

ACTSA. 2013. *Angola Monitor, Issue 2/13*. London: Action for Southern Africa.

AfDB, OECD and UNDP. 2016. *African Economic Outlook 2016: Sustainable Cities and Structural Transformation*. Paris: African Development Bank Group, Organization for Economic Co-operation and Development, United Nations Development Programme.

Africa-Asia Confidential. 2008. No Oil Guarantees: New Chinese Investment in Angola Has a Note of Risk Attached. *Africa-Asia Confidential* 1 (7).

———. 2009a. Best Friends Again. *Africa-Asia Confidential* 2 (4).

———. 2009b. Oil Votes and Beijing. *Africa-Asia Confidential* 2 (7).

African Development Bank, Organization for Economic Co-operation and Development, United Nations Development Programme, and United Nations Economic Commission for Africa. 2011. *African Economic Outlook. Special Theme: Africa and Its Emerging Partners*. Paris.

———. 2012. *African Economic Outlook 2012: Promoting Youth Employment*. Paris.

Aidoo, Richard, and Steve Hess. 2015. Non-Interference 2.0: China's Evolving Foreign Policy Towards a Changing Africa. *Journal of Current Chinese Affairs* 44 (1): 107–139.

Alden, Chris. 2007. *China in Africa*. London: Zed Books Ltd.

Alden, Chris, Daniel Large, and Ricardo Soares de Oliveira, eds. 2008. *China Returns to Africa: A Rising Power and a Continent Embrace*. London: Hurst & Company.

Altenburg, Tilman. 2010. *Industrial Policy in Ethiopia*, DIE Discussion Paper 2/2010. Bonn: Deutsches Institut für Entwicklungspolitik / German Development Institute (DIE).

Alves, Ana Cristina. 2011. *China's Oil Diplomacy: Comparing Chinese Economic Statecraft in Angola and Brazil*. Unpublished PhD Thesis, The London School of Economics and Political Science (LSE).

———. 2012. Taming the Dragon: Sinopec's Interests in Angola. In *China and Angola. A Marriage of Convenience?* ed. Ana Cristina Alves and Marcus Power, 105–123. Cape Town: Pamazuka Press.

Amnesty International. 2010. *Safer to Stay Silent. The Chilling Effects of Rwanda's Laws on 'Genocide Ideology' and 'Sectarianism'*. London: Amnesty International Publications.

———. 2012. *Rwanda Shrouded in Secrecy. Illegal Detention and Torture by Military Intelligence*. London: Amnesty International Publications.

Anderson, Emily Jean. 2013. *Will Tax Reform Drive Equitable Development in Oil-Dependent Angola?* Policy Briefing 70: Global Powers and Africa Programme. Johannesburg: South Africa Institute for International Affairs (SAIIA).

Andrews, Matt. 2013. *The Limits of Institutional Reform in Development: Changing Rules for Realistic Solutions*. Cambridge: Cambridge University Press.

ANGO Press. 2012a. *Angola, China Boost Co-operation in Fight Against Crime*. http://www.portalangop.co.ao/angola/en_us/noticias/politica/2012/7/31/Angola-China-boost-operation-fight-against-crime,17db70f5-5e73-41b9-8fee-7626100e65c8.html. Accessed 5 June 2015.

———. 2012b. *Angola, China Record Excellent Cooperation in Human Rights Field*. http://www.portalangop.co.ao/angola/en_us/noticias/politica/2012/2/12/Angola-China-record-excellent-cooperation-human-rights-field,cda779df-0853-4627-9647-02a6b4b4c3ab.html. Accessed 5 June 2015.

———. 2012c. *Angola, China Sign Memorandum for New General Hospital of Luanda*. http://www.portalangop.co.ao/angola/en_us/noticias/saude/2012/3/16/Angola-China-sign-memorandum-for-new-General-Hospital-Luanda,ea71cc03-64c9-4062-afec-d0ee306f2563.html. Accessed 5 June 2015.

———. 2012d. *Audit Court Chief Highlights China's Fraternity and Confidence*. http://www.portalangop.co.ao/motix/en_us/noticias/politica/2012/5/24/Audit-Court-chief-highlights-China-fraternity-and-confidence,d1b78c06-503c-4f2c-ae84-9314f9fad5f7.html. Accessed 5 June 2015.

———. 2012e. *Home Minister Checks Functioning of Police Stations in Shenyang*. http://www.portalangop.co.ao/motix/en_us/noticias/politica/2012/3/17/Home-minister-checks-functioning-police-stations-Shenyang,db4f91cb-f9d2-4d6a-93f8-df041501e928.html. Accessed 5 June 2015.

Ansoms, A. 2009. Re-engineering Rural Society: The Visions and Ambitions of the Rwandan Elite. *African Affairs* 108 (431): 289–309.

Ansoms, An, and Donatella Rostagno. 2012. Rwanda's Vision 2020 Halfway Through: What the Eye Does Not See. *Review of African Political Economy* 39 (133): 427–450.

Arriola, Leonardo R. 2008. Ethnicity, Economic Conditions and Opposition Support: Evidence from Ethiopia's 2005 Elections. *Northeast African Studies* 10 (1): 115–144.

Bader, Julia. 2015a. *China's Foreign Relations and the Survival of Autocracies*. London/New York: Routledge.

———. 2015b. Propping Up Dictators? Economic Cooperation from China and Its Impact on Authoritarian Persistence in Party and Non-party Regimes. *European Journal of Political Research* 54 (4): 655–672.

Bader, Julia, and Jörg Faust. 2014. Foreign Aid, Democratization and Automatic Survival. *International Studies Review* 16 (4): 575–595.

Bader, Julia, Jörn Grävingholt, and Antje Kästner. 2010. Would Autocracies Promote Autocracy? A Political Economy Perspective on Regime-Type Export in Regional Neighbourhoods. *Contemporary Politics* 16 (1): 81–100.

BBC. 2006. Ethiopian Finance Minister Holds Talks in China on Economic Cooperation. *BBC Monitoring International Reports, Asia Pacific*, January 11.

———. 2011. *Ethiopia 'Using Aid as Weapon of Oppression'*. http://news.bbc.co.uk/2/hi/programmes/newsnight/9556288.stm. Accessed 5 Oct. 2016.

Bergthaller, Martina, and Karin Küblböck. 2009. *Budgethilfe in Äthiopien*, Working Paper 25. Vienna: Österreichische Forschungsstiftung für Internationale Entwicklung.

Beswick, Danielle. 2010. Managing Dissent in a Post-genocide Environment: The Challenge of Political Space in Rwanda. *Development and Change* 41 (2): 225–251.

Blair, Tony, and Howard G. Buffett. 2013. *Stand with Rwanda. Now Is Not the Time to Cut Aid to Kigali*. http://www.foreignpolicy.com/articles/2013/02/21/_stand_with_rwanda_aid:un_report. Accessed 5 Oct. 2016.

Blanchard, Jean-Marc F., and Norrin M. Ripsman. 2013. *Economic Statecraft and Foreign Policy, Sanctions, Incentives, and Target State Calculations*. London/New York: Routledge.

Booth, D., and F. Golooba-Mutebi. 2012. Developmental Patrimonialism? The Case of Rwanda. *African Affairs* 111 (444): 379–403.

Borchgrevink, Axel. 2008. Limits to Donor Influence: Ethiopia, Aid and Conditionality. *Forum for Development Studies* 35 (2): 195–220.

Börzel, Tanja A., and Thomas Risse. 2009. Venus Approaching Mars? The European Union's Approaches to Democracy Promotion. In *Democracy Promotion in the US and the EU Compared*, ed. Amichai Magen, Thomas Risse, and Michael McFaul, 34–60. Houndmills: Palgrave Macmillan.
———. 2012. When Europeanization Meets Diffusion. Exploring New Territory. *West European Politics* 35 (1): 192–207.
Börzel, Tanja A., Yasemin Pamuk, and Andreas Stahn. 2008a. *Good Governance in the European Union*, Working Paper on European Integration No. 7. Berlin.
———. 2008b. *The European Union and the Promotion of Good Governance in Its Near Abroad. One Size Fits All?*, SFB-Governance Working Paper Series No 18. Berlin.
Bratton, Michael, and Nicolas Van de Walle. 1997. *Democratic Experiments in Africa. Regime Transitions in Comparative Perspectives*. Cambridge: Cambridge University Press.
Brautigam, Deborah. 2009. *The Dagon's Gift. The Real Story of China in Africa*. Oxford: Oxford University Press.
———. 2011. "Aid with Chinese Characteristics": Chinese Foreign Aid and Development Finance Meet the OECD-DAC System. *Journal of International Development* 23 (5): 752–764.
———. 2015. *Will Africa Feed China?* New York: Oxford University Press.
Brautigam, Deborah, and Jyhjong Hwang. 2016. *Eastern Promises: New Data on Chinese Loans in Africa, 2000 to 2014*, CARI Working Paper #4 China Africa Research Initiative Johns Hopkins University School of Advanced International Studies. Washington, DC: CARI.
Brown, Stephen. 2005. Foreign Aid and Democracy Promotion: Lessons from Africa. *The European Journal of Development Research* 17 (2): 179–198.
———. 2010. The Rule of Law and the Hidden Politics of Transnational Justice in Rwanda. In *Peacebuilding and Rule of Law in Africa. Just Peace?* ed. Chandra Lekha Sriram, Olga Martin-Ortega, and Johanna Herman. London: Routledge.
Brownlee, Jason. 2007. *Authoritarianism in an Age of Democratization*. Cambridge: Cambridge University Press.
Brüne, Stefan. 2007. Testfall Äthiopien: Die neue Afrikastrategie der Europäischen Union. In *Externe Demokratieförderung durch die Europäische Union*, ed. Annette Jünemann and Michèle Knodt, 53–70. Baden-Baden: Nomos.
Bueno de Mesquita, Bruce, and Alastair Smith. 2010. The Pernicious Consequences of UN Security. *Journal of Conflict Resolution* 54 (4): 667–686.
Bueno de Mesquita, Bruce, Alastair Smith, Randolph M. Siverson, and James D. Morrow. 2003. *The Logic of Political Survival*. Cambridge/London: The MIT Press.
Burke, Christopher, Lucy Corkin, and Nastasya Tay. 2007. *China's Engagement of Africa: Preliminary Scoping of African Case Studies. Angola, Ethiopia, Gabon, Uganda, South Africa, Zambia*. Stellenbosch: Centre for Chinese Studies Stellenbosch University.

Burnell, Peter, ed. 2000. *Democracy Assistance: International Co-operation for Democratization.* London: Frank Cass.
———. 2010. *Is There a New Autocracy Promotion?* Working Paper 96. Madrid: Fundación para las Relaciones Internacionales y el Diálogo Exterior (FRIDE).
Burnell, Peter, and Peter Calvert. 2005. Promoting Democracy Abroad. *Democratization* 12 (4): 433–438.
Burnell, Peter, and Oliver Schlumberger. 2010. Promoting Democracy—Promoting Autocracy? International Politics and National Political Regimes. *Contemporary Politics* 16 (1): 1–15.
Campos, Indira, and Alex Vines. 2008. Angola and China. A Pragmatic Partnership. Working Paper Presented at a CSIS Conference, "Prospects for Improving US-China-Africa Cooperation," 5 December 2007.
Carbone, Maurizio. 2010. The European Union, Good Governance and Aid Co-ordination. *Third World Quarterly* 31 (1): 13–29.
———. 2011. The European Union and China's Rise in Africa: Competing Visions, External Coherence, and Trilateral Cooperation. *Journal of Contemporary African Studies* 29 (2): 203–221.
Carothers, Thomas. 1999. *Aiding Democracy Abroad: The Learning Curve.* Washington, DC: Carnegie Endowment for International Peace.
Carothers, Thomas, and Saskia Brechenmacher. 2014. *Closing Space: Democracy and Human Rights Support Under Fire.* Washington, DC: Carnegie Endowment for International Peace.
Chandy, Laurence, and Homi Kharas. 2011. Why Can't We Just Get Along? The Practical Limits to International Development Cooperation. *Journal of International Development* 23 (5): 739–751.
Checkel, Jeffrey. 2000. *Compliance and Conditionality,* ARENA Working Paper 00/18. Oslo: ARENA Centre for European Studies University of Oslo.
Cheeseman, Nic. 2015. *Democracy in Africa. Successes, Failures, and the Struggle for Political Reform, New Approaches to African History.* New York: Cambridge University Press.
Clapham, Christopher. 2009. Post-war Ethiopia: The Trajectories of Crisis. *Review of African Political Economy* 36 (120): 181–192.
Conrad, Courtenay R. 2011. Constrained Concessions: Beneficent Dictatorial Responses to the Domestic Political Opposition1. *International Studies Quarterly* 55 (4): 1167–1187.
Conzelmann, Thomas. 2003. Auf der Suche nach einem Phänomen: Was bedeutet Good Governance in der europäischen Entwicklungspolitik? *Nord-Süd aktuell* 17 (3): 468–477.
Cooke, Jennifer G. 2011. *Rwanda: Assessing Risks to Stability,* A Report of the CSIS Africa Program. Washington, DC: Center for Strategic & International Studies.

Corkin, Lucy. 2011. *China and Angola: Strategic Partnership or Marriage of Convenience?* Angola Brief. Bergen: Chr. Michelsen Institute (CMI) and Centro de Estudos e Investigacao Científica (CEIC).

———. 2013. *Uncovering African Agency: Angola's Management of China's Credit Lines.* New ed. Surrey/Burlington: Ashgate Publishing Limited.

Cornell, Agnes. 2012. Does Regime Type Matter for the Impact of Democracy Aid on Democracy? *Democratization* 20 (4): 642–667.

Crawford, Gordon. 2001. *Foreign Aid and Political Reform: A Comparative Analysis of Democracy Assistance and Political Conditionality*, International Political Economy Series. New York: Palgrave Macmillan.

Croese, Sylvia. 2011. 1 Million Houses?: Angola's National Reconstruction and Chinese and Brazilian Engagement. In *Strengthening the Civil Society Perspective Series II: China and Other Emerging Powers in Africa*, ed. Emerging Powers in Africa Initiative and Fahamu. Nairobi: Fahamu.

———. 2013. *Angola: Chronicle of an Unfulfilled Promise: A Hundred Days After the Elections*, International Policy Analysis. Berlin: Friedrich Ebert Stiftung.

Croissant, Aurel, and Stefan Wurster. 2013. Performance and Persistence of Autocracies in Comparison: Introducing Issues and Perspectives. *Contemporary Politics* 19 (1): 1–18.

DAG. 2005a. *Annual Report 2004.* Addis Ababa: Development Assistance Group - Ethiopia.

———. 2005b. *DAG Pooled Fund: Annual Report 2004.* Addis Ababa: Development Assistance Group—Ethiopia.

———. 2006. *Annual Report 2005.* Addis Ababa: Development Assistance Group—Ethiopia.

———. 2009. *Annual Report 2008.* Addis Ababa: Development Assistance Group—Ethiopia.

———. 2010. *Annual Report 2009.* Addis Ababa: Development Assistance Group—Ethiopia.

———. 2011. *Annual Report 2010.* Addis Ababa: Development Assistance Group—Ethiopia.

———. 2012. *Annual Report 2011.* Addis Ababa: Development Assistance Group—Ethiopia.

Davenport, Christian. 2007. State Repression and Political Order. *Annual Review of Political Science* 10: 1–23.

Del Biondo, Karen. 2011. EU Aid Conditionality in ACP Countries: Explaining Inconsistency in EU Sanctions Practice. *Journal of Contemporary European Research* 7 (3): 380–395.

———. 2015. Donor Interests or Developmental Performance? Explaining Sanctions in EU Democracy Promotion in Sub-Saharan Africa. *World Development* 75 (11): 74–84.

Di John, Jonathan. 2010. The Political Economy of Taxation and Resource Mobilization in Sub-Saharan Africa. In *The Political Economy of Africa*, ed. Vishnu Padayachee, 110–131. Abingdon/New York: Routledge.

Dietrich, Simone, and Joseph Wright. 2012. *Foreign Aid and Democratic Development in Africa*, WIDER Working Paper 2012/20. Helsinki: UNU World Institute for Development Economics Research.

Dimitrova, Antoaneta, and Rilka Dragneva. 2009. Constraining External Governance: Interdependence with Russia and the CIS as Limits to the EU's Rule Transfer in the Ukraine. *Journal of European Public Policy* 16 (6): 853–872.

Dolzer, Rudolf. 2004. Good Governance: Neues transnationales Leitbild der Staatlichkeit? *Zeitschrift für ausländisches öffentliches Recht und Völkerrecht* 64: 535–546.

Doner, Richard F., Bryan K. Ritchie, and Dan Slater. 2005. Systemic Vulnerability and the Origins of Developmental States: Northeast and Southeast Asia in Comparative Perspective. *International Organization* 59 (2): 327–361.

Dunning, Thad. 2004. Conditioning the Effects of Aid: Cold War Politics, Donor Credibility, and Democracy in Africa. *International Organization* 58 (2): 409–423.

ECO Consult, AGEG, APRI, Euronet, IRAM, and NCG. 2009. Country Level Evaluation Angola. Final Report. Volume 1: Main Report. In *Evaluation Carried Out on Behalf of the European Commission by a Consortium Composed of ECO Consult and Others*.

ECO Consult, AGEG, APRI, Euronet, IRAM, and NCG. 2012. Evaluation of the Commission of the European Union's Co-operation with Ethiopia. Country Level Evaluation. Final Report Vol. 1: Main Report. In *Evaluation Carried Out on Behalf of the Commission of the European Union. EVA 2007/geo-acp*.

EIA. 2012. *China Analysis*, EIA Report 2012. Washington, DC: U.S. Energy Information Administration.

EIU. 2011. *Country Report Rwanda—November 2011*. London: Economist Intelligence Unit.

———. 2012. *Country Report Ethiopia—June 2012*. London: Economist Intelligence Unit.

———. 2013. *Country Report Rwanda—March 2013*. London: Economist Intelligence Unit.

Escribà-Folch, Abel. 2012. Authoritarian Responses to Foreign Pressure: Spending, Repression, and Sanctions. *Comparative European Politics* 45 (6): 683–713.

Escribà-Folch, Abel, and Joseph Wright. 2015. *Foreign Pressure and the Politics of Autocratic Survival, Oxford Studies in Democratization*. Oxford: Oxford University Press.

Ethiopia and European Community. 2002. *Country Strategy Paper and Indicative Programme for the Period 2002–2007*. Brussels.
———. 2007. *Country Strategy Paper and National Indicative Programme for the Period 2008–2013*. Lisbon.
———. 2008. *Country Strategy Paper and National Indicative Programme for the Period 2008–2013*. Lisbon.
Ethiopian Economic Association. 2009. *A Survey of the Economic and Trade Relationships Between China, India and Ethiopia*, Draft Study Report for Friedrich-Ebert-Stiftung. Addis Ababa: Ethiopian Economic Association.
Euréval, and PRODEV. 2006. Evaluation de la Coopération de la Commission Europeénne avec le Rwanda. Evaluation de niveau pays. Rapport final. Volume 1—Appréciation d'ensemble. In *Evaluation pour la Commission européenne*, ed. Jacques Toulemonde. Brussels: PRODEV EGEval II—Euréval.
European Commission. 1995–2012. EIDHR. http://www.eidhr.eu/home. Accessed 5 Oct. 2016.
———. 2009a. Commission Decision of 18 December 2009 on the Annual Action Programme 2009 in Favour of Rwanda to Be Financed from the 10th European Development Fund. In *PE/2009/9821 C(2009) 10201*. Brussels.
———. 2009b. Commission Decision of 21 December 2009 on the Annual Action Programme 2009 in Favour of Ethiopia to Be Financed from the 10th European Development Fund. In *PE/2009/9714 C(2009) 10211*. Brussels.
———. 2010. Commission Decision of 15/12/2010 on the Annual Action Programme 2010 in Favour of Angola, to Be Financed from the 10th European Development Fund. In *C(2010) 8954 final*. Brussels.
———. 2011. *Increasing the Impact of EU Development Policy: An Agenda for Change*. Brussels.
European Commission, and Ethiopia. 2002. *Joint Annual Report 2002*. Addis Ababa.
———. 2004. *Joint Annual Report 2003*. Addis Ababa.
———. 2009. *Draft Joint Annual Report 2008*. Brussels.
European Commission, and Rwanda. 2003. *Joint Annual Report 2002*. Brussels.
———. 2005. *Joint Annual Report 2004*. Brussels.
———. 2007. *Joint Annual Report 2006*. Brussels.
———. 2008. *Joint Annual Report 2007*. Brussels.
European Community, and Republic of Angola. 2007. *Joint Annual Report 2007*. Brussels & Luanda.
———. 2009. *Joint Annual Report 2009*. Brussels.
European Parliament. 2008. Report on China's Policy and Its Effects on Africa. In *2007/2255(INI)*: Committee on Development, Rapporteur: Ana Maria Gomes, 28 March 2008.
European Union. 2002. *Council Common Position on Rwanda and Repealing Common Position 2001/799/CFSP*. Brussels.

———. 2004a. Declaration by the Presidency on Behalf of the European Union on the Statement of the Rwandan Government to the Parliamentary Report on Genocidal Ideology, 6 October 2004. In *13110/04 (Presse 285)*. Brussels.
———. 2004b. *Ethiopia—2004 Mid-Term Review Conclusions*. Brussels.
———. 2004c. *Mid-Term Review for the Republic of Rwanda: Conclusions*. Brussels.
———. 2005. *The European Consensus on Development*. Signed by the Council and the Representatives of the Governments of the Member States. Brussels.
———. 2008a. *Angola Final Report Parliamentary Elections 5 September 2008*. Brussels: European Union Election Observation Mission.
———. 2008b. *Election Observation Mission Rwanda, Final Report on the Legislative Elections, 15–18 September*. Brussels: European Union Election Observation Mission.
———. 2010a. Declaration by the High Representative Catherine Ashton on Behalf of the European Union on the Publication of the Final Report of the EU Election Observation Mission to Ethiopia 2010. In *15964/10, PRESSE 295*. Brussels: European Union.
———. 2010b. Human Rights and Democracy in the World: Report on EU Action—July 2008 to December 2009. In *EU Annual Report on Human Rights and Democracy in the World*. Brussels.
———. 2011. *EU Annual Report on Human Rights and Democracy in the World in 2010*. Brussels.
———. 2012. *Ethio-China Relations: Aid, Trade and Investments (Unpublished Study)*. Addis Ababa.
Faust, Jörg. 2004. Good Governance, Transformationsprobleme und Entwicklungszusammenarbeit - eine Collective-Choice-Perspektive. *Nord-Süd aktuell* 18 (3): 486–498.
———. 2007. Autocracies and Economic Development: Theory and Evidence from 20th Century Mexico. *Historical Social Research* 32 (4): 305–329.
Faust, Jörg, Stefan Leiderer, and Johannes Schmitt. 2012. Financing Poverty Alleviation vs. Promoting Democracy? Multi-Donor Budget Support in Zambia. *Democratization* 19 (3): 438–464.
Financial Times. 2007. Ethiopia Looks East to Slip Reins of Western Orthodoxy. http://www.ft.com/intl/cms/s/0/cb811a48-b586-11db-a5a5-0000779e2340.html#axzz39FdhWqVq. Accessed 5 June 2015.
Fjelde, Hanne. 2010. Generals, Dictators and Kings: Authoritarian Regimes and Civil Conflict 1973–2004. *Conflict Management and Peace Science* 27 (3): 195–218.
Foley, Conor, Bert Fret, and Clément Lorvao. 2010. Capitalisation Study of the EIDHR Programme in Angola, Project Financed by the European Union. In *The European's Union Lot No.7 Programme*.

Fourie, Elsje. 2012. *New Maps for Africa? Contextualising the 'Chinese Model' Within Ethiopian and Kenyan Paradigms of Development*. Unpublished PhD Thesis, University of Trento.

Fraser, Alastair, and Lindsay Whitfield. 2009. Understanding Contemporary Aid Relationships. In *The Politics of Aid. African Strategies for Dealing with Donors*, ed. Lindsay Whitfield, 74–107. Oxford: Oxford University Press.

Freemantle, Simon, and Jeremy Stevens. 2011. BRIC Dominant in Angola's Economic Awakening. *Africa: Insight and Strategy—Economics BRIC and Africa*. Pretoria: Standard Bank.

Freyburg, Tina, Sandra Lavenex, Frank Schimmelfennig, Tatiana Skripka, and Anne Wetzel. 2011. Democracy Promotion Through Functional Cooperation? The Case of the European Neighbourhood Policy. *Democratization* 18 (4): 1026–1054.

Furtado, Xavier, and W. James Smith. 2009. Ethiopia: Retaining Sovereignty in Aid Relations. In *The Politics of Aid. African Strategies for Dealing with Donors*, ed. Lindsay Whitfield, 131–155. Oxford: Oxford University Press.

Fuster, Thomas. 1998. *Die "Good Governance" Diskussion der Jahre 1989 bis 1994. Ein Beitrag zur jüngeren Geschichte der Entwicklungspolitik unter spezieller Berücksichtigung der Weltbank und des DAC*. Bern: Haupt.

Gallup. 2013. *Home*. http://www.gallup.com/home.aspx?ref=logo. Accessed 5 Oct. 2016.

Gandhi, Jennifer. 2008. *Political Institutions Under Dictatorship*. Cambridge/New York: Cambridge University Press.

Gandhi, Jennifer, and Adam Przeworski. 2007. Authoritarian Institutions and the Survival of Autocrats. *Comparative Political Studies* 40 (11): 1279–1301.

Geda, A., and A. Meskel. 2009. Impact of China-Africa Investment Relations: Case Study Ethiopia. *Final Draft Prepared for the AERC Collaborative Research on the Impact of China on Africa*. Mombasa.

Geddes, Barbara. 2003. *Paradigms and Sand Castles: Theory Building and Research Design in Comparative Politics*. Ann Arbor: University of Michigan Press.

———. 2006. *Why Parties and Elections in Authoritarian Regimes?* Paper Prepared for Presentation at the Annual Meeting of the American Political Science Association 2005, Washington, DC.

Gehlbach, Scott, and Philip Keefer. 2011. Investment Without Democracy: Ruling-Party Institutionalization and Credible Commitment in Autocracies. *Journal of Comparative Economics* 39 (2): 123–139.

Gerring, John. 2007. *Case Study Research. Principles and Practices*. Cambridge: Cambridge University Press.

Gerschewski, Johannes. 2013. The Three Pillars of Stability: Legitimation, Repression, and Co-optation in Autocratic Regimes. *Democratization* 20 (1): 13–38.

Global Witness. 2002. *Tous les hommes des Présidents. L'histoire accablante du pétrole et des affaires bancaires dans la guerre privatisée de l'Angola*. http://www.globalwitness.org/library/all-presidents-men. Accessed 5 Apr.

Goldsmith, A. 2001. Foreign Aid and Statehood in Africa. *International Organization* 55 (1): 123–148.

Government of Ethiopia. 2006. *Ethiopia: Building on Progress: A Plan for Accelerated and Sustained Development to End Poverty (PASDEP)*, 2005/06-2009/10. Addis Ababa: Ministry of Finance and Economic Development (MoFED).

Government of Ethiopia, and United Nations Development Programme. 2007. *Multi-Donor Support for the Democratic Institutions Programme, Programming Document*. Addis Ababa.

Government of Rwanda. 2006. *Rwanda Aid Policy*. http://www.minecofin.gov.rw/fileadmin/documents/Aid_Policy.pdf. Accessed 5 Oct. 2016.

Government of the Republic of Rwanda, and European Commission. 2002. *Country Strategy Paper for Rwanda 2002–2007*. Brussels.

———. 2007. *Country Strategy Paper for Rwanda 2008–2013*. Lisbon.

Government of the Republic of Rwanda, and World Bank. 2008. Rwanda: Joint Governance Assessment Report. In *JGA Report, Final Approved Version*. Kigali.

Greenhill, Romilly, Annalisa Prizzon, and Andrew Rogerson. 2013. *The Age of Choice: Developing Countries in the New Aid Landscape: A Synthesis Report*, Working Paper 364. London: Overseas Development Institute (ODI).

Grimm, Sven, and Christine Hackenesch. 2017. China in Africa: What Challenges for a Reforming European Union Development Policy? Illustrations from Country Cases. *Development Policy Review* 35 (4): 549–566.

Grimm, Sonja, and Julia Leininger. 2012. Not All Good Things Go Together: Conflicting Objectives in Democracy Promotion. *Democratization* 19 (3): 391–414.

Grimm, Sven, Heike Höß, Katharina Knappe, Marion Siebold, Johannes Sperrfechter, and Isabel Vogler. 2010. *Coordinating China and DAC Development Partners: Challenges for the Aid Architecture in Rwanda*, DIE Studies 56. Bonn: Deutsches Institut für Entwicklungspolitik/German Development Institute (DIE).

Grimm, Sven, Rachel Rank, Matthew McDonald, and Elizabeth Schickerling. 2011. *Transparency of Chinese Aid*. http://www.ccs.org.za/wp-content/uploads/2011/09/Transparency-of-Chinese-Aid_final.pdf. Accessed 9 Jan. 2016.

Gu, Xiaojie. 2008. "China Never Imposes Its Will on Ethiopia by Way of Its Assistance" Interview of Walta Info with Gu Xiaojie, Chinese Ambassador to Ethiopia. http://www.waltainfo.com/index.php?option=com_content&task=view&id=2110&Itemid=96. Accessed 12 Jan. 2016.

Hackenesch, Christine. 2016. *Good Governance in EU External Relations: What Role for Development Policy in a Changing International Context?* Study for the European Parliament, Directorate-General for External Policies. Brussels: European Parliament.

Hadenius, Axel, and Jan Teorell. 2006. *Authoritarian Regimes: Stability, Change, and Pathways to Democracy, 1972–2003*, Working Paper 331. Notre Dame: The Helen Kellogg Institute for International Studies.

———. 2007. Pathways from Authoritarianism. *Journal of Democracy* 18 (1): 143–157.

Halper, Stefan. 2010. *The Beijing Consensus. How China's Authoritarian Model Will Dominate the Twenty-First Century*. New York: Basic Books.

Hankla, Charles R., and Daniel Kuthy. 2011. *Economic Liberalism in Illiberal Regimes: Authoritarian Variation and the Political Economy of Trade*. Annual Conference of the International Studies Association, Montreal.

Hausman, David. 2011. *Rebuilding the Civil Society After War: Rwanda After Genocide, 1998–2009*, Reports: Innovations for Successful Society. Princeton: Princeton University.

Hawkins, Darren et al. 2010. *Codebook for Assembling Data on China's Development Finance*. http://www.aiddata.org/research/china. Accessed 10 Mar. 2016.

Hayman, Rachel. 2006. *The Complexity of Aid: Government Strategies, Donor Agendas and the Coordination of Development Assistance in Rwanda 1994–2004*, Unpublished PhD Thesis. Edinburgh: University of Edinburgh.

———. 2008. *Evaluating International Influences on Democratic Development (Volume 2: Post-conflict Countries)*, Evaluation Report—External Democracy Promotion in Post-conflict Zones: Evidence from Case Studies. Berlin: Freie Universität Berlin.

———. 2009. From Rome to Accra Via Kigali: 'Aid Effectiveness' in Rwanda. *Development Policy Review* 27 (5): 581–599.

———. 2011. Funding Fraud? Donors and Democracy in Rwanda. In *Remaking Rwanda. State Building and Human Rights After Mass Violence*, ed. Scott Strauß and Lars Waldorf, 118–131. Madison: The University of Wisconsin Press.

Helly, Damien. 2011. Europe and Angola: The Case for Deeper Engagement. In *Analysis, 22 September, 2011*. Paris: European Union Institute for Security Studies.

Herdegen, Matthias. 2007. Der Beitrag des modernen Völkerrechts zu Good Governance. In *Good Governance Gute Regierungsführung im 21. Jahrhundert*, ed. Rudolf Dolzer, Matthias Herdegen, and Bernhard Vogel, 107–127. Freiburg: Herder Verlag.

Hon, Tracy, Johanna Jansson, Garth Shelton, Liu Halfang, Christopher Burke, and Carine Kiala. 2010. *Evaluating China's FOCAC Commitments to Africa and Mapping the Way Ahead*. New York: Centre for Chinese Studies and Rockefeller Foundation.

Huening, Lars-Christopher. 2013. Making Use of the Past: The Rwandaphone Question and the 'Balkanisation of the Congo'. *Review of African Political Economy* 40 (135): 13–31.

Humphrey, John, and Dirk Messner. 2008. *Poor and Powerful—The Rise of China and India and the Implications for Europe*, DIE Discussion Paper 13/2008. Bonn: Deutsches Institut für Entwicklungspolitik/German Development Institute (DIE).
Huntington, Samuel. 1969. *Political Order in Changing Societies.* New Haven: Yale University Press.
IMF. 2012. *Angola 2012 Article IV Consultations and Post Program Monitoring*, IMF Country Report No. 12/215. Washington, DC: International Monetary Fund.
———. 2013. Rwanda: 2012 Article IV Consultation and Fifth Review Under the Policy Support Instrument and Request for Modification of Assessment Criteria—Staff Report; Staff Supplement; Public Information Notice and Press Release on the Executive Board Discussion; and Statement by the Executive Director for Rwanda. International Monetary Fund Country Report No. 13/77.
India EXIM Bank. 2013. *Annual Report 2012–2013.* http://www.eximbankindia.com/ar1213.pdf. Accessed 5 July 2015.
Information, Ministry of. 2002. *The Federal Democratic Republic of Ethiopia Foreign Affairs and National Security Policy and Strategy*, ed. Press and Audiovisual Department. Addis Ababa.
Information Office of the State Council. 2011. *Chinese White Paper on Foreign Aid.* Beijing: Information Office of the State Council.
Ingelaere, Bert. 2010. Peasants, Power and Ethnicity: Bottom-Up Perspective on Rwanda's Political Transition. *African Affairs* 109 (435): 273–292.
———. 2011. The Ruler's Drum and the People's Shout: Accountability and Representation Rwanda's Hills. In *Remaking Rwanda. State Building and Human Rights After Mass Violence*, ed. Scott Strauß and Lars Waldorf, 67–78. Madison: The University of Wisconsin Press.
International Crisis Group. 2009. *Congo: A Comprehensive Strategy to Disarm the FDLR*, Africa Report No.151. Brussels.
IRIN. 2013. *ETHIOPIA: Government Denies Food Aid "Manipulated" for Political Gain.* http://www.irinnews.org/Report/89382/ETHIOPIA-Government-denies-food-aid-manipulated-for-political-gain. Accessed 5 Oct. 2016.
Iyer, Deepa. 2012. *Improving Coordination and Prioritization: Streamlining Rwanda's National Leadership Retreat, 2008–2011*, Reports: Innovations for Successful Societies. Princeton: Princeton University.
JGA Steering Committee. 2011. *Joint Governance Assessment (JGA) Review 2008/2009.* Kigali: Rwanda Governance Advisory Council.
Jünemann, Annette, and Michele Knodt, eds. 2007. *Externe Demokratieförderung durch die Europäische Union——European External Democracy Promotion.* Baden-Baden: Nomos.

Kalyvitis, Sarantis, and Irene Vlachaki. 2010. Democratic Aid and the Democratization of Recipients. *Contemporary Economic Policy* 28 (2): 188–218.
Kaufmann, Daniel, Aart Kraay, and Pablo Zoido-Lobatón. 1999. *Governance Matters, Policy Research Working Paper 2196*. Washington, DC: World Bank.
Keefer, Philip. 2007. Governance and Economic Growth in China and India. In *Dancing with Giants: China, India, and the Global Economy*, ed. Alan L. Winters and Shahid Yusuf, 211–242. Singapore: World Bank Publications.
Kemmerzell, Jörg. 2010. Stabilitäts- und Reproduktionsbedingungen autoritärer Systeme in Sub-Sahara Afrika. In *Autoritarismus Reloaded: neuere Ansätze und Erkenntnisse der Autokratieforschung*, ed. Holger Albrecht and Rolf Frankenberger, 331–350. Baden-Baden: Nomos.
Keohane, Robert O. 1984. *After Hegemony. Cooperation and Discord in the World Political Economy*. Princeton: Princeton University Press.
Keohane, Robert O., and Joseph S. Nye. 1987. Power and Interdependence Revisited. *International Organization* 41 (4): 725–753.
Killick, Tony. 1997. Principals, Agents, and the Failings of Conditionality. *Journal of International Development* 9 (4): 483–495.
Kimonyo, Jean-Paul, Noël Twagiramungu, and Christopher Kayumba. 2004. *Supporting the Post Genocide Transition in Rwanda. The Role of the International Community*, Working Paper 32. The Hague: Netherlands Institute of International Relations.
Kitano, Naohiro, and Yukinori Harada. 2015. Estimating China's Foreign Aid 2001–2013. *Journal of International Development* 28 (7): 1050–1074.
Klingebiel, Stephan. 2011. Schriftliche Stellungsmaßnahme zum Thema "Budgethilfen" im Rahmen der öffentlichen Anhörung des Deutschen Bundestages. In *Ausschuss für Wirtschaftliche Zusammenarbeit und Entwicklung*. Berlin.
Klingebiel, Stephan, and Guido Ashoff. 2014. Transformation of a Policy Area. Development Policy Is in a Systematic Crisis and Faces the Challenge of a More Complex System Environment. In *Entwicklungstheorien: Weltgesellschaftliche Transformationen, entwicklungspolitische Herausforderungen, theoretische Innovationen, PVS Sonderheft*, ed. Franziska Müller, Elena Sondermann, Ingrid Wehr, Cord Jakobeit, and Aram Ziai, 166–199. Baden-Baden: Nomos.
Klingebiel, Stephan, and Timo Mahn. 2011. Auf der Überholspur. *E+Z* 52 (6).
Kohler-Koch, Beate, and Berthold Rittberger. 2006. Review Article: The 'Governance Turn' in EU Studies. *Journal of Common Market Studies Annual Review* 44: 27–49.
Köllner, Patrick, and Steffen Kailitz. 2013. Comparing Autocracies: Theoretical Issues and Empirical Analyses. *Democratization* 20 (1): 1–12.
Kopstein, Jeffrey. 2005. The Transatlantic Divide over Democracy Promotion. *The Washington Quarterly* 29 (2): 85–98.
Kotzian, Peter, Michéle Knodt, and Sigita Urdze. 2011. Instruments of the EU's External Democracy Promotion. *Journal of Common Market Studies* 49 (5): 995–1018.

Kuziemko, Ilyana, and Eric Werker. 2006. How Much Is a Seat on the Security Council Worth? Foreign Aid and Bribery at the United Nations. *Journal of Political Economy* 114 (5): 905–930.

Lavenex, Sandra, and Frank Schimmelfennig. 2009. EU Rules Beyond EU Borders: Theorizing External Governance in European Politics. *Journal of European Public Policy* 16 (6): 791–812.

Lefort, Réne. 2007. Powers –Mengist—and Peasants in Rural Ethiopia: The May 2005 Elections. *Journal of Modern African Studies* 45 (2): 253–273.

———. 2010. Powers—Mengist—and Peasants in Rural Ethiopia: The Post-2005 Interlude. *Journal of Modern African Studies* 48 (3): 435–460.

Leftwich, Adrian. 1994. Governance, the State and the Politics of Development. *Development and Change* 25 (2): 363–386.

Leininger, Julia. 2010. 'Bringing the Outside in': Illustrations from Haiti and Mali for the Reconceptualization of Democracy Promotion. *Contemporary Politics* 16 (1): 63–80.

Lektzian, David, and Mark Souva. 2007. An Institutional Theory of Sanctions Onset and Success. *Journal of Conflict Resolution* 51 (6): 848–871.

Levitsky, Steven, and Lucan A. Way. 2010. *Competitive Authoritarianism: Hybrid Regimes After the Cold War*. Cambridge: Cambridge University Press.

Levkowitz, Lee, Marta McLellan Ross, and J.R. Warner. 2009. The 88 Queensway Group. A Case Study in Chinese Investors' Operations in Angola and Beyond. In *U.S.-China Economic & Security Review Commission*.

Lindberg, Staffan I. 2009. The Power of Elections in Africa Revisited. In *Democratization by Elections: A New Mode of Transition?* ed. Staffan I. Lindberg, 25–46. Baltimore: John Hopkins University Press.

Longman, Timothy. 2004. Obstacles to Peacebuilding in Rwanda. In *Durable Peace: Challenges for Peacebuilding in Africa*, ed. Taisier M. Ali and Robert O. Matthews. Toronto: University of Toronto Press.

———. 2011. Limitations to Political Reforms: The Undemocratic Nature of Transition in Rwanda. In *Remaking Rwanda. State Building and Human Rights After Mass Violence*, ed. Scott Strauß and Lars Waldorf, 25–47. Madison: University of Madison Press.

Lynch, Gabrielle, and Gordon Crawford. 2011. Democratization in Africa 1990–2010: An Assessment. *Democratization* 18 (2): 275–310.

Lyons, Terrence. 2011. *Ethiopia: Assessing Risks to Stability*, A Report of the CSIS Africa Program. Washington, DC: Center for Strategic & International Studies.

Magaloni, Beatriz. 2006. *Voting for Autocracy: Hegemonic Party Survival and Its Demise in Mexico*. Cambridge: Cambridge University Press.

Magaloni, Beatriz, and Ruth Kricheli. 2010. Political Order and One-Party Rule. *Annual Review of Political Science* 13: 123–143.

Magaloni, Beatriz, Jonathan Chu, and Eric Min. 2013. Autocracies of the World, 1950–2012 (Version 1.0). Dataset, Stanford University.

Magen, Amichai, and Michael McFaul. 2009. Introduction: American and European Strategies to Promote Democracy—Shared Values, Common Challenges, Divergent Tools? In *Promoting Democracy and the Rule of Law. American and European Strategies*, ed. Amichai Magen, Thomas Risse, and Michael McFaul, 2–33. Houndmills: Palgrave Macmillan.

Magen, Amichai, and Leonardo Morlino. 2009. Methods of Influence, Layers of Impact, Cycles of Change. A Framework for Analysis. In *International Actors, Democratization and the Rule of Law. Anchoring Democracy?* ed. Leonardo Morlino and Amichai Magen, 26–52. London/New York: Routledge.

Manning, Carrie. 2011. *Countries at the Crossroads 2011: Angola*, Country Report. Washington, DC: Freedom House.

Marques de Morais, Rafael. 2010. *MPLA Ltd.: The Business Interests of Angola's Ruling Elite*. http://www.pambazuka.org/en/category/features/62194/print. Accessed 5 Oct. 2016.

———. 2011a. *The Ill-Gotten Gains Behind Angola's Kilamba Housing Development*, 12 October 2011. http://www.pambazuka.org/en/category/features/77070/print. Accessed 10 Apr. 2016.

———. 2011b. The New Imperialism: China in Angola. *World Affairs Journal*: (March/April) 67–74. http://www.worldaffairsjournal.org/article/new-imperialism-china-angola

Marysse, Stefaan, An Ansoms, and Danny Cassimon. 2006. *The Aid 'Darlings' and 'Orphans' of the Great Lakes Region in Africa*, Discussion Paper. Antwerpen: Institute of Development Policy and Management.

———. 2007. The Aid 'Darlings' and 'Orphans' of the Great Lakes Region in Africa. *The European Journal of Development Research* 19 (3): 433–458.

Mawdsley, Emma, Laura Savage, and Sung-Mi Kim. 2014. A 'Post-aid World'? Paradigm Shift in Foreign Aid and Development Cooperation at the 2011 Busan High Level Forum. *The Geographical Journal* 180 (1): 27–38.

McGreal, Chris. 2007. Chinese Aid to Africa May Do More Harm than Good, Warns Benn. *The Guardian*, February 8.

Melnykovska, Inna, Hedwig Plamper, and Rainer Schweickert. 2012. Do Russia and China Promote Autocracy in Central Asia? *Asia Europe Journal* 10 (1): 75–89.

Men, Jing, and Benjamin Barton. 2011. China and the EU in Africa: Changing Concepts and Changing Policies. In *China and the European Union in Africa: Partners or Competitors?* ed. Jing Men and Benjamin Barton, 1–23. Franham: Ashgate.

Milner, Helen. 1992. Review Article: International Theories of Cooperation Among Nations: Strengths and Weaknesses. *World Politics* 44 (3): 466–496.

Ministry of Commerce People's Republic of China. 2010. *Statistical Yearbook*. http://english.mofcom.gov.cn/article/statistic/. Accessed 5 Mar 2013.

Ministry of Finance and Economic Development. 2013. *Bulletin No. 10 (2008/09–2011/12 and 31/12/2012)*, ed. Debt Management Directorate. Addis Ababa: Ministry of Finance and Economic Development, Federal Democratic Republic of Ethiopia.

Ministry of Foreign Affairs. 2010. *Statement of the Ministry of Foreign Affairs of the Federal Republic of Ethiopia on the Report of the European Union Election Observer Mission (EU EOM)*. Addis Ababa: Federal Democratic Republic of Ethiopia.

Molenaers, Nadia. 2012. The Great Divide? Donor Perceptions of Budget Support, Eligibility and Policy Dialogue. *Third World Quarterly* 33 (5): 791–806.

Molenaers, Nadia, and Leen Nijs. 2009. From the Theory of Aid Effectiveness to the Practice: The European Commission's Governance Incentive Tranche. *Development Policy Review* 27 (5): 561–580.

Molenaers, N., A. Gagiano, L. Smets, and S. Dellepiane. 2015. What Determines the Suspension of Budget Support? *World Development* 75: 62–73.

Moore, Mick. 1995. Promoting Good Governance by Supporting Institutional Development? *IDS Bulletin* 26 (3): 89–96.

Moustafa, Tamir, and Tom Ginsburg. 2008. Introduction: The Functions of Courts in Authoritarian Politics. In *Rule by Law: The Politics of Courts in Authoritarian Regimes*, ed. Tamir Moustafa and Tom Ginsburg, 1–22. Cambridge: Cambridge University Press.

MWH, ODI, and ECDPM. 2004. *Evaluation of the European Commission's Country Strategy for Ethiopia*. Volume I: Final Report, ed. MWH. Brussels: Overseas Development Institute and European Centre for Development Policy Management.

New Times. 2010. Rwanda Ruling Party, Chinese Communist Party Sign Deal to Boost Ties. *New Times*, March 30.

———. 2012. China Pledges $25 Million Grant to Rwanda, Kigali. New Times, September 12.

OECD. 2011. OECD. Stat Extracts. Organisation for Economic Co-operation and Development. http://stats.oecd.org. Accessed 5 Oct.

OECD DAC. 2016. *Creditor Reporting System (CRS)*. http://stats.oecd.org/Index.aspx. Accessed 5 Oct.

Olsen, Gorm Rye. 1998. Europe and the Promotion of Democracy in Post Cold War Africa: How Serious Is Europe and for What Reason? *African Affairs* 97: 343–367.

Oomen, Barbara. 2005. Donor-Driven Justice and Its Discontents: The Case of Rwanda. *Development and Change* 36 (5): 887–910.

Orre, Aslak. 2010. *Who's to Challenge the Party State in Angola? Political Space and Opposition in Parties and Society*. Election Processes, Liberation Movements and Democratic Change in Africa, Maputo, 8–11 April 2010.

OSISA, and Global Witness. 2011. *Oil Revenues in Angola: Much More Information but Not Enough Transparency*. London.
Ottaway, Marina. 2003. *Democracy Challenged: The Rise of Semi-Authoritarianism*. Washington, DC: Carnegie Endowment for International Peace.
PARTICIP, CIDEAL, Channel Research, and South Research. 2006. *Thematic Evaluation for the European Commission Assistance to Third Countries Supporting Good Governance*. Country note for Angola. Brussels.
Pender, John. 2007. Country Ownership: The Evasion of Donor Accountability. In *Politics Without Sovereignty. A Critique of Contemporary International Relations*, ed. Christopher J. Bickerton, Philip Cunliffe, and Alexander Gourevitch, 112–130. Abingdon/New York: University College London Press.
Peterson, Stephen. 2010. Reforming Public Financial Management in Africa. In *Research Working Paper Series RWP10-048*, ed. HKS Faculty. Cambridge: John F. Kennedy School of Government, Harvard University.
Portela, Clara. 2010. *European Union Sanctions and Foreign Policy: When and Why Do They Work?* Abingdon/New York: Routledge.
Power, Marcus. 2011. Angola 2025: The Future of the "World's Richest Poor Country" as Seen Through a Chinese Rear-View Mirror. *Antipode* 44 (3): 993–1014.
Power, Marcus, and Ana Cristina Alves. 2012. *China and Angola: A Marriage of Convenience?* Cape Town: Pamazuka Press.
Prichard, Wilson R.S. 2010. *Taxation, Responsiveness and Accountability in Sub-Saharan Africa*. Unpublished PhD Thesis. Institute of Development Studies, University of Sussex.
Pridham, Geoffrey. 1991. International Influences and Democratic Transition: Problems of Theory and Practice in Linkage Politics. In *Encouraging Democracy: The International Context of Regime Transition in Southern Europe*, ed. Geoffrey Pridham, 18–48. New York: St Martin's Press.
Prunier, Gerard. 1997. *The Rwanda Crisis: History of Genocide*. New York: Columbia University Press.
———. 2009. *Africa's World War: Congo, the Rwandan Genocide, and the Making of a Continental Catastrophe*. Oxford/New York: Oxford University Press.
Puddington, Arch. 2008. Freedom in Retreat: Is the Tide Turning? Findings of Freedom in the World 2008. *Freedom House*. http://www.freedomhouse.org/report/freedom-world-2008/essay-freedom-retreat. Accessed 5 Oct. 2016.
Putnam, Robert D. 1988. Diplomacy and Domestic Politics. *International Organization* 42 (3): 427–460.
Rahmato, Dessalegn, and Meheret Ayenew. 2004. *Democracy Assistance to Post-conflict Ethiopia. Building Local Institutions?* Working Paper 27. The Hague/Addis Ababa: Netherlands Institute of International Relations.

Reilly, James, and Wu Na. 2007. China's Corporate Engagement in Africa. In *Africa in China's Global Strategy*, ed. Marcel Kitissou, 132–155. London: Adonis & Abbey Publishers Ltd.
Remmer, Karen L. 2004. Does Foreign Aid Promote the Expansion of Government? *American Journal of Political Science* 48 (1): 77–92.
Republic of Angola, and European Community. 2003. *Country Strategy Paper and National Indicative Programme for the Period 2002–2007*. Luanda.
———. 2008. *Country Strategy Paper and National Indicative Programme for the Period 2008–2013*. Luanda.
Reuter, Ora John, and Jennifer Gandhi. 2011. Economic Performance and Elite Defection from Hegemonic Parties. *British Journal of Political Science* 41 (1): 83–110.
Reyntjens, Filip. 2004. Rwanda, Ten Years on: From Genocide to Dictatorship. *African Affairs* 103 (411): 177–210.
———. 2009. *The Great African War: Congo and Regional Geopolitics, 1996–2006*. Cambridge: Cambridge University Press.
———. 2010. Constructing the Truth, Dealing with Dissent, Domesticating the World: Governance in Post-Genocide Rwanda. *African Affairs* 110 (438): 1–34.
———. 2013. *Political Governance in Post-Genocide Rwanda*. Cambridge: Cambridge University Press.
Risse, Thomas, and Nelli Babayan. 2015. Democracy Promotion and the Challenges of Illiberal Regional Powers: Introduction to the Special Issue. *Democratization* 22 (3): 381–399.
Robinson, Richard, and Wil Hout. 2009. Where to Now? The Ende of 'Good Governance' a Policy Agenda. In *Governance and the Depoliticisation of Development*, ed. Wil Hout and Richard Robinson, 197–199. Abingdon/New York: Routledge.
Rolfing, Ingo. 2012. *Case Studies and Causal Inference. An Integrated Framework*. New York: Palgrave Macmillan.
Roque, Paula Cristina. 2008. *Angolan Legislative Elections: Analysing the MPLA's Triumph*, Situation Report. Pretoria: Institute for Security Studies.
———. 2009. Angola's Façade Democracy. *Journal of Democracy* 20 (4): 137–150.
———. 2011. *Angola: Parallel Governments, Oil and Neopatrimonial System Reproduction*, Situation Report. Pretoria: Institute for Security Studies.
———. 2013. *Angola's Second Postwar Elections: The Alchemy of Change*, Situation Report. Pretoria: Institute for Security Studies.
Ross, Michael. 1999. The Political Economy of the Resource Curse. *World Politics* 51 (2): 297–322.
Samset, Ingrid. 2011. Building a Repressive Peace: The Case of Post-Genocide Rwanda. *Journal of Intervention and Statebuilding* 5 (3): 265–283.

Sanderson, Henry, and Michael Forseythe. 2013. *China's Superbank: Debt, Oil and Influence—How China Development Bank Is Rewriting the Rules of Finance.* Singapore: John Wiley & Sons Singapore Pte. Ltd.

Santiso, Carlos. 2003. Sisyphus in the Castle: Improving European Union Strategies for Democracy Promotion and Governance Conditionality. *The European Journal of Development Research* 15 (1): 1–28.

Sarkin, Jeremy. 2001. The Tension Between Justice and Reconciliation in Rwanda: Politics, Human Rights, Due Process and the Role of the Gacaca Courts in Dealing with the Genocide. *Journal of African Law* 45 (2): 143–172.

Scharpf, Fritz W. 1999. *Governing Europe. Effective and Legitimate?* Oxford: Oxford University Press.

Schedler, Andreas. 2009. *The New Institutionalism in the Study of Authoritarian Regimes.* Mexico City: Centro de Investigación y Docencia Económicas (CIDE).

Schimmelfennig, Frank. 2007. Europeanization Beyond Europe. *Living Reviews in European Governance* 2 (1): 4–22.

Schimmelfennig, Frank, and Ulrich Sedelmeier. 2005. Introduction: Conceptualising the Europeanization of Central and Eastern Europe. In *The Europeanization of Central and Eastern Europe*, ed. Frank Schimmelfennig and Ulrich Sedelmeier. Ithaca: Cornell University Press.

Schmidt, Petra. 2005. *Budgethilfe in der Entwicklungszusammenarbeit der EU*, DIE Studies 10. Bonn: Deutsches Institut für Entwicklungspolitik/German Development Institute (DIE).

Schubert, Jon. 2010. Democratisation and the Consolidation of Political Authority in Post-war Angola. *Journal of Southern African Studies* 36 (3): 657–672.

Seabra, Pedro, and Paulo Gorjão. 2011. *Intertwined Paths: Portugal and Rising Angola*, Occasional Paper No 89. Johannesburg: South African Institute of International Affairs.

Silva-Leander, Sebastian. 2008. On the Danger and Necessity of Democratisation: Trade-offs Between Short-Term Stability and Long-Term Peace in Post-Genocide Rwanda. *Third World Quarterly* 29 (8): 1601–1620.

Simpser, Alberto, and Daniela Donno. 2012. Can International Election Monitoring Harm Governance? *The Journal of Politics* 74 (2): 501–513.

SIPRI. 2013. *Military Expenditure Database.* http://www.sipri.org/research/armaments/milex/milex_database. Accessed 5 Oct. 2016.

Smith, Benjamin. 2005. Life of the Party. *World Politics* 57 (3): 421–451.

Soares de Oliveira, Ricardo. 2011. Illiberal Peacebuilding in Angola. *The Journal of Modern African Studies* 49 (2): 287–314.

———. 2012. Guest Column: Transparency Reforms Yield Little Change. *Financial Times*, July 18.

———. 2015. *Magnificent and Beggar Land: Angola Since the Civil War.* London: Hurst Publishers.

Sogge, David. 2009. *Angola, "Failed" Yet "Successful"*, Working Paper. Madrid: FRIDE.

Stroh, Alexander. 2008. *Ruanda: Keine Zeit für Demokratie? Parlamentswahlen und andere Prioritäten*, GIGA Focus No 11. Hamburg: German Institute of Global and Area Studies.
Svolik, Milan W. 2012. *The Politics of Authoritarian Rule*. Cambridge: Cambridge University Press.
Tadesse, Kirubel. 2012. *China Loans 600 Million Dollars to Ethiopia Over Five Months*. http://www.capitalethiopia.com/index.php?option=com_content&view=article&id=262:china-loans-600-million-dollars-to-ethiopia-over-five-months&catid=54:news&Itemid=27. Accessed 5 Oct. 2016.
Tadesse, Medhane, and John Young. 2003. TPLF: Reform or Decline? *Review of African Political Economy* 30 (97): 389–403.
Taylor, Ian. 2010. *China's New Role in Africa*. London: Lynne Rienner Publishers.
———. 2011. *The Forum on China-Africa Cooperation (FOCAC)*. Oxford: Routledge.
Tetlock, Philip E., and Aaron Belkin. 1996. *Counterfactual Thought Experiments in World Politics: Logical, Methodological, and Psychological Perspectives*. Princeton: Princeton University Press.
The Howard G. Buffett Foundation. 2013. *Assessing the 2012 UN Group of Experts Report on the DRC. An Analysis of Methodology, Cooperation and Implications*. http://www.thehowardgbuffettfoundation.org/wp-content/uploads/pdfs/HGBF-UNReport-3-26P.pdf. Accessed 29 May 2016.
The New Times. 2014. Rwanda: Africa Doesn't Need Tied Aid, Says Chinese Official. *The New Times*, March 22. http://allafrica.com/stories/201403240479.html?mkt_tok=3RkMMJWWfF9wsRonsqvKe%2B%2FhmjTEU5z17u8qW6e3hokz2EFye%2BLIHETpodcMTcNqNL3YDBceEJhqyQJxPr3DJNUN0ddxRhbkDQ%3D%3D&viewall=1.
Tilly, Charles. 2007. *Democracy*. Cambridge: Cambridge University Press.
Tolstrup, Jakob. 2013. *Russia vs. the EU: The Competition for Influence in Post-Soviet States*. Boulder: Lynne Rienner Publishers.
Traub, James. 2006. China's African Adventure. *The New York Times*, November 19. http://www.nytimes.com/2006/11/19/magazine/19china.html?pagewanted=all&_r=1&. Accessed 5 Oct. 2016.
Tronvoll, Kjetil. 2009. Ambiguous Elections: The Influence of Non-electoral Politics in Ethiopian Democratisation. *Journal of Modern African Studies* 47 (3): 449–474.
———. 2010. The Ethiopian 2010 Federal and Regional Elections: Re-establishing the One-Party State. *African Affairs* 110 (438): 121–136.
Ulfelder, Jay. 2005. Contentious Collective Action and the Breakdown of Authoritarian Regimes. *International Political Science Review* 26 (3): 311–334.
UN Group of Experts. 2012. *Letter Dated 12 October 2012 from the Group of Experts on the Democratic Republic of the Congo Addressed to the Chair of the United Nations Security Council Committee Established Pursuant to Resolution 1533 (2004) Concerning the Democratic Republic of the Congo*. http://www.un.org/ga/search/view_doc.asp?symbol=S/2012/843. Accessed 5 Oct. 2016.

UNCTAD. 2016. *UNCTAD Statistics.* United Nations Conference on Trade and Development. http://unctad.org/en/Pages/Statistics.aspx. Accessed 5 Oct.
United Nations. 2013. *United Nations Commodity Trade Statistics Database.* http://comtrade.un.org/. Accessed 5 Oct. 2016.
United Nations Commodity Trade Statistics Database. 2010. *UN Comtrade.* http://comtrade.un.org/. Accessed 5 Oct. 2016.
United Nations Development Programme. 2013. *The Rise of the South: Human Progress in a Diverse World*, Human Development Report 2013. New York: United Nations.
Vachudova, Milada A. 2005. *Europe Undivided: Democracy, Leverage and Integration After Communism.* Oxford: Oxford University Press.
van Hüllen, Vera. 2012. Europeanization Through Cooperation? EU Democracy Promotion in Morocco and Tunisia. *West European Politics* 35 (1): 117–134.
———. 2015. *EU Democracy Promotion and the Arab Spring: International Cooperation and Authoritarianism.* Basingstoke: Palgrave Macmillan.
Vanderhill, Rachel. 2012. *Promoting Authoritarianism Abroad.* Boulder: Lynne Rienner Publishers.
Vaughan, Sarah. 2011. Revolutionary Democratic State-Building: Party, State and People in the EPRDF's Ethiopia. *Journal of Eastern African Studies* 5 (4): 619–640.
Vaughan, Sarah, and Mesfin Gebremichael. 2011. *Rethinking Business and Politics in Ethiopia. The Role of EFFORT, the Endowment Fund for the Rehabilitation of Tigray*, Africa Power and Politics Programme Research Report, No. 2, August 2011. London: Overseas Development Institute (ODI).
Verhoeven, Harry. 2014. Is Beijing's Non-interference Policy History? How Africa Is Changing China. *The Washington Quarterly* 37 (2): 55–70.
Vines, Alex, and Indira Campos. 2010. China and India in Angola. In *The Rise of China and India in Africa. Challenges, Opportunities and Critical Interventions*, ed. Fantu Cheru and Cyril Obi. London/New York: Zed Books.
Vines, Alex, Lillian Wong, Markus Weimer, and Indira Campos. 2009. *Thirst for African Oil: Asian National Oil Companies in Nigeria and Angola*, A Chatham House Report. London: Royal Institute of International Affairs.
von der Heijden, Hendrik. 2007. *Accelerating Development in Ethiopia. Suggested Road Map for Scaling Up External Financing and Aid.* Addis Ababa: Delegation of the European Commission.
von Soest, Christian. 2015. Democracy Prevention: The International Collaboration of Authoritarian Regimes. *European Journal of Political Research* 54 (4): 623–638.
von Soest, Christian, and Michael Wahman. 2015. Are Democratic Sanctions Really Counterproductive? *Democratization* 22 (6): 957–980.
Warkotsch, Alexander. 2008. Non-compliance and Instrumental Variation in EU Democracy Promotion. *Journal of European Public Policy* 15 (2): 227–245.

Watch, Human Rights. 2010. *Development Without Freedom. How Aid Underwrites Repression in Ethiopia.* New York.

———. 2012. Angola: Protesters Detained, Disappeared, Pre-election Environment Marred by Crackdown, 5 July 2012. *Human Rights Watch News.* http://www.hrw.org/news/2012/07/05/angola-protesters-detained-disappeared. Accessed 5 Oct. 2016.

Waugh, Colin M. 2004. *Paul Kagame and Rwanda: Power, Genocide and the Rwandan Patriotic Front.* Jefferson/North Carolina/London: McFarland & Company.

Wetzel, Anne, and Jan Orbie. 2011. Promoting Embedded Democracy? Researching the Substance of EU Democracy Promotion. *European Foreign Affairs Review* 16 (5): 565–588.

Whitfield, Lindsay. 2009. Aid and Power: A Comparative Analysis of Country Studies. In *The Politics of Aid*, ed. Lindsay Whitfield and Alastair Fraser. Oxford: Oxford University Press.

Whitfield, Lindsay, and Alastair Fraser. 2009. Negotiating Aid. In *The Politics of Aid. African Strategies for Dealing with Donors*, ed. Lindsay Whitfield, 27–44. Oxford: Oxford University Press.

Wintrobe, Ronald. 2001. How to Understand, and Deal with Dictatorship: An Economist's View. *Economics of Governance* 2 (1): 35–58.

Wissenbach, Uwe. 2011. Conclusion: China and the EU in Africa: Partners or Competitors? In *China and the European Union in Africa Partners or Competitors?* ed. Jing Men and Benjamin Barton, 269–272. Farnham: Ashgate.

World Bank. 2005. *Private Solutions for Infrastructures in Angola: A Country Framework Report.* Washington, DC.

———. 2011. *Angola's Infrastructure: A Continental Perspective. Africa Infrastructure Country Diagnostic*, Country Report. Washington, DC.

———. 2016a. *World Development Indicators.* http://data.worldbank.org/datacatalog/world-development-indicators. Accessed 5 Oct. 2016.

———. 2016b. *Worldwide Governance Indicators.* http://info.worldbank.org/governance/wgi/index.aspx#home. Accessed 5 Oct. 2016.

Wright, Joseph. 2009. How Foreign Aid Can Foster Democratization in Authoritarian Regimes. *American Journal of Political Science* 53 (3): 552–571.

Wurster, Stefan. 2013. Comparing Ecological Sustainability in Autocracies and Democracies. *Contemporary Politics* 19 (1): 76–93.

Young, Crawford. 2004. The End of the Post-colonial State in Africa? Reflections on Changing African Political Dynamics. *African Affairs* 103 (410): 23–49.

Zhao, Suisheng. 2010. The China Model: Can It Replace the Western Model of Modernization? *Journal of Contemporary China* 19 (65): 419–436.

Zimelis, Andris. 2011. Conditionality and the EU-ACP Partnership. A Misguided Approach to Development. *Australian Journal of Political Science* 46 (3): 389–406.

INDEX

A
African governments' response strategies, 24
African governments' responsiveness to EU strategies, 16, 17
Agenda for Change, 4
Ahmad, Sufyan, 117
Aid conditionality, 27
Aid effectiveness agenda, 75, 102
Aid modalities, 42, 64, 76, 83, 117
Angola
  aid as share of GNI, 158, 176, 207
  China as alternative economic cooperation partner, 179–184, 210
  China becoming an alternative economic partner, 161
  China model, 183–184
  Chinese loans to Angola, 179
  Chinese workers in, 182, 184
  civil war, 149, 150
  cooperation beyond governance reforms, 188, 207
  cooperation with China, 188
  corruption, 153, 172, 174
  cost-benefit calculations, 149, 186, 201
  counterfactual conjectures, 187–189
  credit lines, 177
  economic dependence on the EU, 158–161, 176–179, 205–207
  EIDHR projects, 165
  elections, 157, 169–171, 175, 199
  EU aid as a share of total DAC donors' aid, 158
  EU demands-reluctance and indifference towards, 168
  EU good governance strategies, 151, 194, 196, 201, 208
  EU governance aid, 152, 154–155
  EU public statements, 152, 166
  EU strategy paper, 151, 154, 164
  financial transparency issues, 160
  government's effectiveness, 157, 172
  government's responsiveness, 153–154, 164, 208
  human rights issues, 152, 184

Angola (*cont.*)
  IMF conditionality, 172, 188
  IMF negotiations, 176
  infrastructure projects, 157, 162, 163, 173, 181
  international donor conference request, 153, 160
  natural resources, 188
  net ODA as a share of GNI, 159
  oil exports, 161, 163, 176–178, 182, 187
  oil-for-infrastructure deals, 161, 210
  oil revenues, 153, 158, 160, 176, 199
  oil sector investment, 182
  peace dividend, 150, 156
  political and aid policy dialogues, 153–154
  political outreach to China, 181
  and Portugal, 160
  positive conditionality, 154–155
  public financial management, 155
  public goods provision, 173
  public opinion of government, 170, 173
  public protests, 170, 175
  statements and démarches, 153
  survival strategies, 156–158, 170–176, 198
  tax reform, 172
  Wen Jiabao, 161
  Xi Jingping visit, 181
Angolagate Scandal, 177
Angolan Human Rights Commission, 184
Angolanisation policy, 15
Angolan Ministry of Finance, 163, 171, 174
Arrion, Michel, 65
Authoritarian dominant party regimes, 14–18

B
Bizimungu, ex-president of Rwanda, 57
Börzel, T. A., 24, 26
Broad Convergence for the Salvation of Angola-Electoral Coalition (CASA-CE), 175

C
Cabinda province separatists, 156
CCP, *see* Communist Party of China
Charities and Societies Agency, 126
Chicoti, George Rebelo Pinto, 153
China
  African countries cooperation with, 44–45, 47, 86
  African countries economic dependence on the EU, 210
  aid and official flows, 44
  aid budget, 9
  as alternative partner to African governments, 213
  Angola-alternative economic partner, 161–163, 179, 210
  Angola-as cooperation partner, 188
  Angola-Chinese workers in, 182, 184
  Angola-loans to, 179
  Angola-oil-for-infrastructure deals, 161, 210
  Angola-political outreach, 181
  economic cooperation with, 62, 79–80
  Ethiopia-aid, loans, and official flows, 117–118, 130, 137, 142, 210
  Ethiopia-cooperation partner to, 130–137
  Ethiopia-geographical importance, 212

Ethiopia-investment stocks, 113, 129
Ethiopia-limited engagement with, 112–113
Ethiopia-material assistance, 135
foreign policy, 12, 45
going out policy, 161, 210
importance to Africa, 9
Memorandum of Understanding with EPRDF, 136
Rwanda-policy change towards, 85–86
Rwanda relationship with, 62
Rwands-economic cooperation with, 61
technical assistance, 46, 81, 135, 184
China Africa Development Fund (CADFund), 81, 138
China Development Bank, 86, 130–132, 180, 187
China EXIM Bank, 86
China International Fund (CIF), 157, 179
Chinese banks, 9
Chinese EXIM Bank
 loans to Angola, 161, 162, 179, 180, 187
 loans to Ethiopia, 130, 132, 210
 loans to Rwanda, 78
Chinese Ministry of Commerce (MOFCOM), 80
Chinese threat argument, 188
Christian Relief and Development Association (CRDA), 126
Civil administration, 157
Civilian House (Angola), 157
Civil service reform, 107
Civil society actors
 Angola, 130
 Ethiopia, 102
 Rwanda, 52
Civil society forum (Angola), 165
Civil Society Fund (Ethiopia), 118, 119, 123
Civil society organisations
 Angola, 155
 Ethiopia, 103, 106, 119, 123, 126, 135
 Rwanda, 53, 58, 68
Clarke, Tim, 115
Coalition for Unity and Democracy (Ethiopia), 114
Coercion, 126–127, 140
 Angola, 171, 174
 Ethiopia, 133
 high or low-intensity, 35–36, 40
 Rwanda, 49, 58, 74, 89
Commercial Bank of Ethiopia, 133
Commission on Human Rights (Rwanda), 57
Communist Party of China (CCP)
 and African ruling parties, 46, 213
 bilateral relations with African countries, 213
 cooperating on governance reforms, 203
 Ethiopia, 110, 208
 Ethiopian People's Revolutionary Democratic Front (EPRDF), 113, 136, 213, 215
 People's Movement for the Liberation of Angola (MPLA), 215
 Rwandan Patriotic Front (RPF), 82, 83
 and survival strategies, 205
Constitutional reform, 171
Cooperation definition, 22
Corruption
 Angola, 174
 Ethiopia, 71
Cost-benefit calculations
 Angola, 149

Cost-benefit calculations (*cont.*)
  cooperation on governance reforms, 22, 23, 37, 38
  Ethiopia, 26
  and survival strategies, 23
Cotonou Agreement Article (8)
  Angola, 153, 166, 169
  Ethiopia, 104, 120
  Rwanda, 53, 62
Cotonou Agreement Article (96), 43

D
De Oliveira, Soares, 161, 162, 171, 173
Death penalty (Rwanda), 54, 63, 66
Decision-making process
  democratic quality, 158
  transparency, 25, 39, 55, 154
Democratic reform indicators, 105
Democratic Republic of the Congo (DRC)
  natural resources, 84
  rebel groups, 50, 70, 83, 85, 89
Derg regime, 15, 100, 107
Direct budget support, 41, 42
Direct investments, 42–43, 45, 129
Divisionism (Rwanda's laws), 66, 74
Doing Business report, 76
Dominant party systems
  African governments' responsiveness, 29–31, 47–48
  aid and other official flows, 41–42
  China as alternative support, 45–47
  cooperating with China, 44–45
  economic dependence on the EU, 43
  EU good governance strategies, 25
  interaction effects, 30–31
  overview, 5–8, 37–38
  political contestation, 33
  political survival, 32–33

Donor-recipient relations, 14, 23
Dos Santos, President of Angola
  demonstrations to step down, 170
  dominant position, 150, 156, 171
  funding deals with EU countries, 176
  international donor conference request to EU, 153, 160, 162
  loan deal with China, 180
  partnership with China, 181
  political survival, 16
  visit from Wen Jiabao, 161

E
Elections
  Angola (2008), 157, 170, 171, 174, 199
  Angola (2012), 170, 175, 199
  dominant party systems, 31, 32
  Ethiopia (1995), 108
  Ethiopia (2000), 108
  Ethiopia (2005), 109, 111, 126, 138, 202
  Ethiopia (2008), 126
  Ethiopia (2010), 119, 123, 126, 136, 141
  Ethiopia (2015), 143
  EU observers, 109, 116, 122, 127, 164, 169
  EU technical assistance, 39–40
  Rwanda (2003), 53, 57, 58, 199
  Rwanda (2008), 67, 91, 203
  Rwanda (2010), 69, 73, 74, 91, 203
  survival strategies and structural factors, 100–101
Ethiopia
  Addis Ababa, 109, 112–113, 128
  aid as share of GNI, 110, 127, 128
  aid, loans and official flows from China, 130, 137, 142, 210
  aid policy dialogues, 120–121

INDEX 255

ceasing to engage with the EU, 116–117
China as a cooperative partner, 130
China model, 134
China's support during election crisis, 117
Chinese investment stocks, 128
corruption, 108
cost-benefit calculations, 201
counterfactual conjectures, 142
democratic institutions programme, 122
Derg regime, 15, 100, 107
economic dependence on the EU, 110–112, 127–129, 205–208
EIDHR projects, 123
election crisis, 114–118, 138–139, 197, 204, 207, 210
elections (1995), 108
elections (2000), 108
elections (2005), 109, 111, 112, 138, 202
elections (2008), 126
elections (2010), 119, 123, 128, 136, 141
elections (2015), 143
EU good governance strategies, 102–103, 110, 115, 118, 195, 196
EU governance aid, 102
EU statements and démarches, 103
exports, 111, 129
general budget support–EU, 110, 117
geographical position of importance, 212
government effectiveness and EU strategies, 118
government's public support, 124
government's responsiveness, 104–106, 115, 120–124, 139–141

Growth and Transformation Plan, 133
growth rate figures, 125
human rights record, 106
infrastructure projects, 113, 124, 138
investment by emerging economies, 134
Memorandum of Understanding with CCP, 136
net ODA as a share of GNI in Ethiopia, 111
party-to-party relations, 136–137, 213
positive conditionality and governance aid, 105–106, 121–124
public protests, 143
ranking in the WGI, 108
social services, 124
survival strategies, 106–110, 124–127, 200, 208
war with Eritrea, 101, 106, 107, 110
Ethiopian Bar Association, 126
Ethiopian Electric Power Corporation, 132
Ethiopian Investment Agency (EIA), 182
Ethiopian Ministry of Finance, 134
Ethiopian Ministry of Foreign Affairs, 122
Ethiopian parastatal companies, 132
Ethiopian People's Revolutionary Democratic Front (EPRDF), 125, 128
  access to public service conditional on membership, 140
  Communist Party of China (CCP), 113, 136, 213
  dissatisfaction with its political record, 116

Ethiopian People's (*cont.*)
  dominance in rural areas, 124
  dominance of, 15–16, 116
  overthrow of Derg regime, 100
  party structures, 124
  relationship with state, 106, 107, 110
EPRDF, *see* Ethiopian People's Revolutionary Democratic Front
Ethiopian Road Authority, 132
EU election observer mission
  Angola, 164, 169
  Ethiopia, 109, 116, 122, 127
  Rwanda, 56
EU good governance strategies, 37
  Angola, 151, 152, 164–166, 169, 194, 196
  approaches, 195
  China's engagement, 10–14
  conflictive strategy, 197
  confrontation and rewards, 28
  content and instruments, 23
  cooperative strategy, 165–166, 197
  cooperative-conflictive strategy, 28, 83, 197
  cooperative-rewarding strategy, 28, 64, 69, 83, 196
  dominant party systems, 37
  Ethiopia, 102, 115, 118, 121, 194, 204
  EU instruments to support governance reforms, 196
  EU's cooperative or confrontational strategy, 27–29
  explaining African governments' responsiveness, 47–48
  external actor, 27–29
  negative effects and unintended side-effects, 14
  and political survival, 31, 201
  positive conditionality, 121
  positive instruments, 8
  promoting good governance, 102–103, 118, 151–152
  public statements on Angola, 152, 166
  Rwanda, 51–54, 63–65, 195, 196, 203, 204
EU good governance strategies- *cooperative-critical* strategy
  Angola, 152–153, 155
  Ethiopia, 103, 114, 118, 123, 138
  overview, 28, 194
  Rwanda, 53–54, 56, 90
EU good governance strategies- *democratic government*
  Angola, 155, 164, 166, 169
  Ethiopia, 106, 115, 123, 128, 137
  overview, 26, 194
  Rwanda, 51–52, 63–64, 69
EU good governance strategies- *effective governance*
  Angola, 166, 169
  Ethiopia, 110, 127, 139
  overview, 26, 164–165, 195
European Development Fund (EDF), 103, 119
  Angola, 152, 165
  Ethiopia, 103
  Rwanda, 53, 55, 83
European Instrument for Democracy and Human Rights (EIDHR)
  Angola, 152, 164, 165, 176–179, 181–183
  Ethiopia, 103, 123
  Rwanda, 53, 64
Europeanisation (external), 10, 27, 127
European Union (EU)
  agenda-setting power, 23
  cooperation package, 208
  development aid provision, 23
  economic dependence on, 43, 205
  engagement and regime stability/instability, 204

instruments to support governance
  reforms, 196
statements and démarches, 54, 103
windows of opportunity–missed, 204
Export commodities
  African countries, 42
  Angola, 176–183
  China's importance, 133
  coffee, 60, 76, 129
  Ethiopia, 111, 129, 134
  oil, 160, 163, 176, 181
  Rwanda, 63, 76, 77, 206, 212
  sesame seed exports, 133
  sugar, 134
  See also Natural resources

F
Federal Ethics and Anti-corruption
  Commission (FEAC), 108
Food aid, 42
*Forces démocratiques de libération du
  Rwanda* (FDLR), 57, 70
Foreign aid, 8
Foreign direct investments (FDI), 45, 76
Forum on China–Africa Cooperation
  (FOCAC), 78, 112, 211
Fukuyama, Francis, 1

G
Gacaca system, 54, 73
Gallup polls, 70, 124, 170, 174
Génocidaire, 54
Genocide ideology commission, 66
Genocide ideology laws, 74
Genocide in Rwanda, 51, 59
Ginsburg, T., 34
Global Witness, 160
Good governance, 10, 11, 25, 26
Good governance support, 26

Governance incentive tranche
  Angola, 168, 170
  Ethiopia, 119, 121
  new instrument, 5
  Rwanda, 66
Governance reforms
  cost-benefit calculations, 22, 26, 37, 38
  external actors, 27–29
Government effectiveness and control
  of corruption
  Angola, 172
  Ethiopia, 109
  Rwanda, 71
Great Lakes Media, 68
Growth and Transformation Plan, 133

H
Hadenius, A., 6
Health care, 71–73, 124
High Level Meetings, 75, 120
Housing-affordable (Angola), 173, 181
Human Rights Commission, 56, 105, 127
Human rights violations, 43, 152
Human Rights Watch, 128

I
IMF conditionality, 172, 188
Imihigo performance contracts, 71
Indian EXIM Bank, 81, 134
Industrial and Commercial Bank of
  China, 180
Ingabire, Victoire, 74
Input legitimacy, 26, 102, 106, 118
Input-oriented objectives, 26
Interahamwe rebels, 54
Intergovernmental channel, 26, 52, 152

J
Joint Way Forward, 166, 167, 169, 187, 207
Justice sector reform
  Angola, 155, 169
  Ethiopia, 106
  Rwanda, 66, 68, 73

K
Kagame, President of Rwanda
  aid effectiveness agenda, 75
  constitutional referendum, 56
  developmental state model, 81
  domestic opposition, 70
  elections 2003, 58
  international debates, 212
  and international governance indices, 67
  loan agreement with China, 85
  meetings with donors, 65
  political survival, 16, 87, 91
  presidential elections, 73, 74
  third term preparation, 90
Keohane, R. O., 22, 41
Kricheli, R., 6

L
Levitsky, S., 33, 35
Ligue Rwandaise pour la Promotion et la Defense des Droits de l'Homme (LIPRODHOR), 58

M
Magaloni, B., 6
Media control, 171
Meles, Prime Minister of Ethiopia
  aid effectiveness agenda, 110
  death of, 143
  development lessons from China, 134
  EU election observer mission, 116
  political aid policy dialogues, 104, 115
  political survival, 16
  Western pressure on, 106
Military House, 157
Military spending, 173
Millennium Development Goals (MDGs)
  Ethiopia, 101–102, 115
  Rwanda, 64, 72, 83
Moustafa, T., 34
MPLA, *see* People's Movement for the Liberation of Angola

N
National Assembly (Angola), 154
National Authorizing Officer (Rwanda), 67
National Commission for Unity and Reconciliation (NURC) (Rwanda), 56
National Electoral Board (Ethiopia), 114
National Front for the Liberation of Angola (FNLA), 161
National Institute for Statistics (Angola), 154
National Union for the Total Independence of Angola (UNITA), 156, 161, 174, 215
Natural resources
  Democratic Republic of the Congo (DRC), 84
  Ethiopia, 101
  revenues from, 36
  See also Export commodities
NGOs (international)
  critical of Angola, 160
  critical of Ethiopian government, 203
  critical of Rwandan government, 70

Non-state actors
  capacities of, 27
  Rwanda, 52, 68, 83
Nye, J. S, 41

O
OECD aid statistics, 63, 118
OECD Development Assistance Committee, 5
Office for National Reconstruction (GRN), 157, 162, 171
Official development assistance (ODA)
  Angola, 159
  Ethiopia, 111, 112
  Rwanda, 60
Oil seed trade, 133
Ombudsman's office
  Ethiopia, 105
  Rwanda, 58
Output legitimacy, 25, 102, 141, 143, 207
Output-oriented objectives, 26

P
PAANE programme (Angola), 165
Pamuk, Y., 26
Paris Club creditors, 160
Paris Declaration (2005), 167
Parti Democratique pour le Renouveau (PDR), 57
Party-run companies, 15
People's Movement for the Liberation of Angola (MPLA)
  Communist Party of China (CCP), 215
  companies owned by, 171
  defections to opposition party, 170
  dissatisfaction with its political record, 199, 202
  military victory, 15, 156
  party membership, 171

Petrobras, 183
Political liberalisation and governance reforms, 30
Political regimes in Africa, 7
Political relations
  annual bilateral visits EPRDF-CCP, 136
  annual bilateral visits MPLA–CCP, 185
  annual bilateral visits RPF-CCP, 82
Political repression and public goods provision, 199
Political spaces
  Ethiopia, 108, 116, 124, 127, 140
  limiting, 53
  opening and closing, 35–36, 40
  Rwanda, 82, 87, 91, 203
Political survival
  Angola, 156, 170, 198
  arenas of contestation, 33–34, 57–59, 73–74, 108, 126, 158
  China as alternative partner, 45–47, 212
  domestic logic, 11, 17
  domestic opposition, 56, 70–73, 156
  effectiveness of government institutions, 70–73
  Ethiopia, 106, 124, 200, 208
  EU good governance strategies, 32
  political spaces, 35–36, 40
  regime stability, 69–70
  Rwanda, 50–51, 56–59, 68–74, 199, 208
  state institutions, 124–126, 156–158, 172, 198
  structural and situational factors, 36–37
Portugal relations with Angola, 160
Poverty reduction strategy paper (PRSP), 121, 125, 168
  Angola, 168
  Ethiopia, 121, 125

Proclamation on Charities and Societies (CSO law) (Ethiopia), 120, 123, 126
Protection of Basic Services (PBS) programme (Ethiopia), 121, 123, 128
Public Expenditures and Financial Accountability (PEFA) (Rwanda), 71
Public financial management, 104
  Angola, 155
  Ethiopia, 104
  Rwanda, 67
Public goods provision
  Angola, 173
  Ethiopia, 101, 143, 200, 202
  and political repression, 199
  Rwanda, 49, 76, 199, 202
Public Service Capacity Administration Programme (PSCAP) (Ethiopia), 105, 108, 115, 122, 142

R
Regime stability, 32, 69, 204
Republican Democratic Movement (MDR), 57, 73, 87
RPF, *see* Rwandan Patriotic Front
Rwanda
  aid policy dialogues, 55, 66
  China-economic role, 62, 78
  China's policy change towards, 85
  Chinese aid projects, 62, 78–80
  Chinese development aid, 212
  Chinese economic cooperation, 86
  constitutional referendum, 56, 87
  corruption, 72
  cost-benefit calculations, 201
  counterfactual conjectures, 90–91
  direct budgetary support, 75, 195, 206
  domestic opposition, 56, 70

  economic dependence on the EU, 59–61, 74–77, 84, 205, 208
  economic growth, 58
  elections (2003), 53, 58, 87, 199
  elections (2008), 67, 91, 203
  elections (2010), 69, 90, 203
  EU good governance strategies, 63, 87, 195, 203
  EU governance aid, 52, 68
  EU statements and démarches, 54
  exports, 60, 77, 206, 212
  genocide, 51
  government's responsiveness, 54–56, 87–89, 206
  official development assistance (ODA), 61
  peoples' confidence in government, 70
  positive conditionality, 55, 66
  presidential elections, 73
  rebel groups in DRC, 83, 85, 89
  survival strategies, 50–51, 56–59, 69–71, 199, 208
  taxes, 75
  UN Security Council, 85
Rwandan defence forces, 78
Rwandan Institute for Statistics, 67
Rwandan Patriotic Front (RPF)
  Communist Party of China (CCP), 82
  companies owned by, 50
  domestic opposition, 58
  gacaca system, 73
  political dominance, 15
Rwanda Revenue Authority, 71

S
Sarkozy, President of France, 177
Savimbi, Jonas, 156
Scharpf, F. W., 25
Selassie, Haile, 100

Sesame seed exports, 133
Sinopec, 182
Social services
  Ethiopia, 124
  Rwanda, 72
Sonangol
  domestic infrastructure responsibilities, 171
  efficiency and negotiating skills, 151
  financial transparency issues, 174
  government oil revenues, 15
  joint venture with Sinopec, 182
Stahn, A., 26
Survival strategies, *see* Political survival

T
Tadesse, M., 108
Taxes, 41–42, 75, 172
Technical assistance, 40, 46, 184
Teorell, J., 6
Textile company, 81
Tigrayan People's Liberation Front (TPLF), 100, 101, 106, 107, 139, 202
TPLF, *see* Tigrayan People's Liberation Front
Trade taxes, 42–43
Transnational channel
  Angola, 152, 164
  Ethiopia, 103, 106, 118
  Rwanda, 52
Transparency International, 174
Tutsi refugees, 50

U
UNITA, *see* National Union for the Total Independence of Angola
United Ethiopian Democratic Forces, 114
United Nations Development Programme (UNDP), 122
UN Security Council, 85

V
Vicente, Manuel, 156

W
Way, L. A., 33
Wen Jiabao (Prime Minister-China), 161
World Development Indicators, 76, 129
Worldwide Governance Indicators, 71

X
Xi, Jinping (President of China), 181

Y
Young, J., 108

Z
Zhang Bolun, 182
Zhong, Weiyun, 213

The manufacturer's authorised representative in the EU is Springer Nature Customer Service Centre GmbH, Europaplatz 3, 69115 Heidelberg, Germany. If you have any concerns regarding our products, please contact ProductSafety@springernature.com

Printed and bound by CPI Group (UK) Ltd, Croydon, CR0 4YY

23/03/2026

02076735-0008